MARTIN LUTHER KING, JR.
AND THE CIVIL RIGHTS MOVEMENT

Edited by David J. Garrow

A CARLSON PUBLISHING SERIES

The Highlander Folk School

A HISTORY OF ITS MAJOR PROGRAMS, 1932-1961

Aimee Isgrig Horton

PREFACE BY DAVID J. GARROW

CARLSON
Publishing Inc

BROOKLYN, NEW YORK, 1989

Library of Congress Cataloging-in Publication Data

Horton, Aimee Isgrig
    The Highlander Folk School : a history of its major programs,
    1932-1961 / Aimee Isgrig Horton.
        p. cm. —(Martin Luther King, Jr. and the civil rights
    movement ; 13)
        Originally presented as the author's thesis (doctoral-Univ. of
    Chicago, 1971)
        Bibliography: p.
        Includes index.
        1. Highlander Folk School (Monteagle, Tenn.)—History. 2. Adult
    education—Tennessee—History. 3. Labor and laboring classes–
    –Education—Tennessee—History. I. Title. II. Series.
    LC5301.M65H67 1989   374'.976879—dc20   89-7130
    ISBN 0-926019-13-9 (alk. paper)

Typographic design: Julian Waters

Typeface: Bitstream ITC Galliard

The index to this book was created using NL Cindex, a scholarly indexing program
from the Newberry Library.

For a complete listing of the volumes in this series, please see the back of this book.

Printed on acid-free, 250-year-life paper.

Manufactured in the United States of America.

Contents

Series Editor's Preface

Aimee Horton's careful and detailed history of the Highlander Folk School is a major contribution to twentieth-century southern history, for Highlander, as much as any other indigenous southern institution of the mid-century period, played a crucial role in a succession of significant southern social change movements, from organized labor to black civil rights.

Horton's study, first written in 1971, was a valuable precursor to the subsequent flowering of scholarly interest in Highlander, a flowering reflected by a number of useful books, particularly Frank Adams' *Unearthing Seeds of Fire: The Idea of Highlander* (John F. Blair, 1975), Carl Tjerandsen's *Education for Citizenship* (Emil Schwartzhaupt Foundation, 1980, pages 139-232), and John M. Glen's *Highlander: No Ordinary School, 1932-1962* (University Press of Kentucky, 1988). Horton's important volume merited publication well prior to 1989 and I am very pleased that Carlson Publishing's series of books on *Martin Luther King, Jr., and the Civil Rights Movement* can now bring Horton's work to the wider audience that it has long deserved.

Highlander's important role in assisting the southern black freedom struggle during its formative years in the 1950s and early 1960s is nicely highlighted in chapters twelve through fourteen of Horton's study. Participation in a multi-day Highlander workshop in the summer of 1955 had a crucial influence on Mrs. Rosa Parks five months before her refusal to surrender her seat on a segregated bus sparked the Montgomery Bus Boycott, and Highlander's Citizenship Schools program, initiated by long-time South Carolina educator and black activist Mrs. Septima Clark, made a major contribution to the grass roots strength of the southern civil rights movement both before and after it was transferred from Highlander's auspices to those of the Southern Christian Leadership Conference. Additionally,

Highlander in the early 1960s repeatedly served as a site for discussion and reflection on the part of the young college activists of the southern movement who made up the cutting edge of the black struggle in the South.

Aimee Horton's work traces not only Highlander's crucial civil rights contributions but also its earlier and oftentimes less-heralded efforts to sponsor and assist progressive southern unionism during the 1930s and 1940s. Her detailed history of Highlander's development and its program initiatives is extremely valuable both to students in her own field of adult education and equally, if not more so, to students of twentieth-century southern liberalism. Highlander's consistent emphasis on the long-term value of local organizing and indigenous community empowerment through grassroots educational initiatives has not only proven repeatedly successful in the past, but continues onward even now through the efforts of the present-day Highlander. Aimee Horton's valuable volume has already been of much value to students of Highlander's history, and now can be of expanded use to those interested in the ongoing lessons that can be learned from Highlander's important and instructive heritage.

David J. Garrow

Preface 1989

W hen I came to Highlander on a visit to the Tennessee mountain School in the winter of 1961, I was Director of the Illinois Commission on Human Relations in Chicago. The Commission, a largely ceremonial body that met periodically to hear staff progress reports on combating discrimination, had just received a disturbing report: students at Southern Illinois University were being refused service in local barbershops and other establishments in spite of a State public accommodations law in existence since the 1890s.

In contrast, at Highlander, leaders of the Student Nonviolent Coordinating Committee and adults from other movement organizations who had come together for a "New Alliances in the South" Workshop, were alive with news of what they were doing to open up facilities and what they planned to do to increase black voter registration.

That was in February. In April, 1961, I came back to stay as wife of Myles Horton, Highlander's founder. "To stay," as it turned out, was to be for only a six-month period. In the fall, the Highlander Folk School in Monteagle, Tennessee was closed and its property confiscated in an unprecedented action by the State courts. During these last six months, I served primarily as report writer and fund raiser among northern friends and supporters of the School, along with being an observer of its movement-related residential workshops and field activities. Among the residential programs was the so-called Citizenship School Program. It was designed to prepare volunteers from Deep South civil rights groups to teach the unschooled and disenfranchised in their communities to read and write and understand their State constitution in order to pass voter registration tests, to become "first-class citizens." Somehow, the development of literacy/voter education teachers took place in a one-week workshop. Somehow, a former beautician and Highlander student from Charleston, South Carolina, who had taught the first Citizenship School class on nearby John's Island was the educational director of the workshop. Somehow, most of the workshop participants—farmers, domestic workers, housewives, students—managed, when they returned home, to set up Citizenship School classes. And, somehow, in three months time, they produced numbers of students able to qualify as registered voters.

During this period and beyond, as one with a relatively traditional university background in adult education, I was primarily a learner. This dissertation represents the culmination of what I learned about the educational programs of the controversial southern School that John Dewey described as "one of the most important social-educational projects in America" and segregationist leaders of the Georgia Commission on Education labeled "the Communist Training School."

The kinds of research problems encountered when I undertook this first comprehensive study of the Highlander Folk School in the mid-sixties are not those generally encountered by one engaged in academic research. Beginning in 1958 and until the School's charter was revoked and its property confiscated in 1961, it was under mounting attacks by highly-placed government leaders and others in Arkansas, Georgia, Tennessee, and elsewhere, determined to put an end to the School and its program in support of the growing southwide civil rights movement. These determined attacks by Southern segregationists prompted the School to disperse its records for safekeeping. This dispersal both complicated the research process and reinforced my commitment to carry out this study of the small residential adult education institution whose programs so threatened the old "status crow" South, as one of the movement leaders expressed it.

The first major relocation of Highlander's historical materials occurred in 1959, after a summer workshop for church and community civil rights leaders was suddenly brought to a close when county law enforcement officials raided the premises charged with finding evidence to close the School. Shortly thereafter, many of the School's papers, including those related to civil rights programs and participants were shipped to California, to the home of a long-time board and early staff member. In 1960-1961, as legal efforts to close the School moved from the lower court to the Tennessee Supreme Court, it was the books and papers in Highlander's library which were at peril. In anticipation of the revocation of the School's charter and the confiscation of its property, former student and faculty friends signed out "on indefinite loan" many valuable books and resource materials on Southern history in Highlander's library.

Finally, in October, 1961, when word was received that the United States Supreme Court would not hear the Highlander Folk School's appeal, staff and family members, together with personal belongings and the remaining Highlander records, departed the mountain acres and the residential School to move by car and truck to urban, industrial Knoxville. There, in a rented, aging mansion, more recently a student rooming house, they opened a new school with a newly-obtained charter to be called the Highlander Research and Education Center. And, there, in a dark, third floor attic, miscellaneous School records were hastily deposited.

To retrieve and organize these many, widely dispersed materials, to interview key Highlander staff related to each major program and, finally, to write a dissertation, I applied for and received an American Association of University Women Fellowship. In awarding me the fellowship, the AAUW itself encountered an unexpected problem. A number of its more conservative Southern members angrily protested the award to support a study of the Highlander Folk School. To its great credit, the national leadership of the AAUW stood by the award and, in so doing, lost a number of members.

Credit is due many persons, both staff and students, who helped this learner understand the social movement-related programs of the Highlander Folk School. Credit is due those at the University of Chicago who guided the dissertation process. Cyril O. Houle, Professor, Department of Education, who recognized the uniqueness of the institution in American adult education, and John Hope Franklin, John Matthews Manly Distinguished Service Professor, Department of History, who viewed the institution, as I sought to do, in the context of recent Southern history. Above all, credit is due Myles Horton, the creator of the institution, who patiently and even with humor answered my endless questions, often raised in the midst of crisis situations.

But this preface cannot be concluded in the past tense, just as this study is not conclusive, but rather part of an on-going process. The Highlander Research and Education Center, chartered in 1961, continues as "Highlander" with the same commitment to relating its resources to people struggling to achieve social change. Located, again, in a mountain area near New Market, Tennessee, it is working with hard-pressed groups in Appalachia on economic and environmental problems and, in recent years, with their counterparts in Latin America.

And, as editor David Garrow noted in his Preface, historical research on the Highlander Folk School and the Highlander Research and Education

Center continues. The Highlander records are now readily accessible to researchers. Under an April, 1971, contract with the State Historical Society of Wisconsin, records of both institutions are now housed in a growing collection within the Historical Society's twentieth century Social Action Collections.[1]

Aimee Isgrig Horton
March, 1989

The Highlander
Folk School

ONE

Introduction

During the almost thirty year history of the Highlander Folk School, the independent residential adult education institution developed four major programs related to groups of people in the South confronted with problems and involved in movements for democratic social change. From the establishment of the Tennessee school in 1932 until its closing in 1961,[1] it evolved new programs, in turn, for its unemployed and impoverished neighbors in Cumberland Mountain communities during the Great Depression; for the new leaders in the southwide industrial union movement during its critical period; for groups of small farmers in Tennessee, Alabama and Virginia when the National Farmers Union sought to build a Southern organization; and for adult and student leadership in the emerging civil rights movement, as blacks in rural and urban communities across the South determined that the time had come to desegregate schools, to enjoy free use of public facilities and to gain their other rights as full citizens.

In relation to the industrial union movement of the thirties and early forties and the civil rights movement of the fifties and early sixties—two contemporary social movements which had great impact on the South—Highlander was in the forefront with adult education programs which anticipated and sought to encourage the process of change.[2]

Some of the School's efforts were premature or short-lived. Its early community and county programs to teach unemployed workers and their families how to build their own unions and self-help organizations were undertaken without a solid economic base in the region to support them. Later, for a brief time, Highlander initiated an educational program to develop leadership for a projected movement among small farmers and organized labor which failed to emerge. Yet even these programs were of significance. The community and county programs represented a sustained and, in some ways, successful effort to relate adult education to mountain people in one of the poorest areas in the United States. The organizing and educational program among small farmers, black and white, represented a limited revival of the Farmers Union in the South, dormant since early in the century.

3

Purposes of the Study

The central purposes of this historical study of the Highlander Folk School, 1932-1961, are to obtain through critical analysis of data related to the successive programs: (1) Knowledge about the institution and its major programs developed in support of black and white southerners involved in movements for social change; and (2) Insights into the processes of program development as pragmatically evolved over the thirty year period as the School related to groups rarely reached by adult education. Knowledge of the several social movement-related programs should prove of interest both to students of recent Southern history and of the history of the American adult education movement. What is revealed about the School's processes of program development should be of value to adult educators seeking to relate to minority and other poor communities and groups.

Questions Which Guided the Investigation

When I set out to examine the data regarding the development of each of the Highlander Folk School's major programs, I sought to apply a systematically conceived series of questions based on an accepted framework for analysis of curriculum decision-making.[3] The questions as such were not inappropriate: Who were the students? What purposes did the program seek to achieve? What kinds of educational activities were provided to attain these purposes? How were activities selected and organized? How was it determined that the purposes were attained? At what point did the School turn to the development of a new major program with a new group of students?

However, unlike traditional institutions, Highlander's program decision-making was not an educator-defined, sequential process. Its decisions, instead, grew out of the School's interaction with groups of people confronted with crisis and struggling through movement organizations to achieve economic and social change. Their movement-building efforts, in turn, were impacted upon by external events and changes in the social environment. Thus, although founder Myles Horton and his supporters had projected "a Southern Mountain School for the training of labor leaders in Southern industrial areas,"[4] the program focus of the Highlander Folk School in the earliest period was the depressed, little mountain community of Summerfield in which the new institution was located. With a barely-stirring labor movement in the fall of 1932, there was no immediate potential for a southwide, movement-related workers' education program.

As unrest among labor in the South grew from sporadic local strikes in the early 30's to a regional movement in the later 30's and 40's, the pragmatic leadership of the Highlander Folk School responded to labor's needs. The School changed from a community-serving institution with a small worker's education program to a southwide center for workers' education with a limited community program.

With the emergence of the civil rights movement in the 1950's, Highlander was able to develop vital, new, movement-related programs. Here again, the School's decision-making was governed by events and by the goals of movement participants. In 1953, the first School Desegregation Workshop in the South was convened at Highlander, bringing together black and white community leaders and educators eager to develop strategies for change in anticipation of the 1954 Supreme Court decision outlawing public school segregation. When a participant in Highlander's 1955 School Desegregation Workshop, Mrs. Rosa Parks, returned home and inspired the Montgomery Bus Boycott, movement leaders proposed a broadly-defined, new program for the following year. Thus, the agenda for the 1956 workshop, with Mrs. Parks as a key resource person, included: Passive Resistance, Registration and Voting, Transportation, Housing, Action through Churches and School Integration.

Sources of Data

Because this investigation focuses on the educational programs developed by the Highlander Folk School and the processes of program development employed, the chief sources of data, especially of primary source material, were the considerable quantity and variety of records of the Highlander Folk School, including annual reports, minutes of staff and Executive Council meetings, wire and tape recordings of workshops and workshop planning and evaluation sessions, School newspapers containing articles by staff and students and collections of stories by resident students, correspondence between the School and its students over the years and several documentary films, notably, *The People of the Cumberlands*, made in 1938, based on the School's early workers' education program.

A major source of primary data involved many interviews, formal and informal, with the School's educational director, Myles Horton. There were also interviews with staff members associated with each of the major programs and with a limited number of students who participated in the several programs.

In addition, beginning in the winter of 1961 and until the closing of the School, this investigator was a participant-observer of workshops related to the civil rights movement and, specifically, workshops related to the Citizenship School Program and the new student movement.

Three Highlander staff members published books which related, in part, to their roles and the programs which they helped to develop. These proved useful.[5]

Another group of primary sources were those Tennessee and other Southern newspapers, ranging from editorially friendly to moderate to hostile (with most in the last category), which carried news, feature stories and editorials about the School throughout its history. There were also national-circulation newspapers, notably *The New York Times*, whose coverage was occasional. Other useful sources were the national and regional labor and farm press, and in the later period, the major black newspapers.

Secondary Sources

A limited amount of data regarding the School and its programs during various periods was obtained from the literature of education. Most of the material consists of brief references within larger works on community education,[6] on workers' education[7] and on residential education.[8] With few exceptions, these are secondary sources.

There is one historical study of the Highlander Folk School in the early years.[10] It treats the educational program rather superficially, but is a useful study of the institution in relation to the Southern labor movement as viewed by the Tennessee press and labor leaders of the period.

In selecting from among the quantities of material on the South related to the several groups of people and social movements with which this study is concerned, two criteria of selection were employed. Those sources consulted were: (1) books and articles by recognized authorities which have provided background information, and (2) books and articles which represent the kinds of contemporary sources which the Highlander Folk school staff drew upon as background for program decisions.

Evaluation of Sources of Data

This investigator has drawn primarily upon the various records of the Highlander Folk School for data regarding the School's several programs and its processes of program development. Although there were many who were angry, vocal and even violent critics of the movement-related School, and although the Tennessee press and the Southern press offer ample documentation of their views and actions, these critics represented anti-labor and segregationist groups who were not inclined to focus their attacks in any rational way on the School's educational program. There were doubtless educators who were hostile critics of the unorthodox institution. Unfortunately, they have not put their views in writing or otherwise made them available.

There is one basic criticism of the data available from the School's many kinds of records, all of which have been made freely available. Data are sparse on programs, such as the early community cooperatives, and the Farmer's Union program which either failed or failed to be fully developed.

One other kind of question needs to be discussed: the capacity of this investigator to be "objective' as the wife of Myles Horton. In general, it is assumed that no one engaged in historical research, just as no one engaged in teaching, approaches the task value free. Value judgments are involved in the selection of a subject for study as well as in the interpretation of data. In relation to the present study, as has been indicated, most of the data on the Highlander Folk School programs, 1932-1960, was obtained from the School's many records. In examining this data, the opportunity to gain first-hand knowledge of its movement-related programs contributed significantly to understanding both the programs themselves and the educational processes involved.

Contributions of the Present Study

Almost twenty years ago, I wrote with cautious optimism regarding this dissertation, ". . . this study of the Highlander Folk School should prove of interest to students of recent Southern history. . . . Its interactions at formative moments with both the industrial union movement and the civil rights movement are especially worthy of attention." In the intervening years, the historical significance of the relatively little known institution has begun to be recognized. Its role in support of recent movements for social change, especially the civil rights movement, has been further documented by scholars and by thoughtful journalists[11] and a documentary filmmaker.[12]

In terms of its potential contribution to adult educators, I was more optimistic. "The present investigation, by undertaking to describe and analyze the evolving processes of program development and to make explicit, wherever possible, assumptions and values involved in decision-making, should contribute to clarifying this approach and to suggest . . . some operating principles." In fact, the study has yet to be used by more than a small number of adult educators except as the history of a unique and uniquely American institution. It may be especially worthy of attention today when educators and many others are uncomfortably aware of the nation's social-educational failures as reflected in the high drop-out rate among minorities, widespread adult illiteracy and the so-called "permanent underclass."

Aimee Isgrig Horton
March, 1989

PART ONE

The Founding
of an
Institution

TWO

The Shaping
of a
Radical Educator[1]

Little in the religious, individualist, Tennessee hill country family background of Myles Horton would have suggested that he would be, at twenty-eight, a Socialist, an advocate of radical industrial unionism or the founder of an unorthodox workers' education school dedicated to utilizing education "as one of the instruments for bringing about a new social order."[2]

His family, descendants of Scotch-Irish pioneers who had come to Tennessee shortly before the Revolutionary War to an area known as the Watauga Settlement, believed deeply in education. His parents, Elsie Falls Horton and Perry Horton, had served as grade school teachers in their youth with little more than a grade school education themselves. But their belief in education which they had communicated to their four children—Myles born in 1905; his brothers born in 1907 and 1910 and his sister, born in 1915—was the traditional American belief that with education an individual could better himself, could lead a more satisfying and remunerative life. Responding to this belief, all of the children completed high school. Thereafter, the younger brothers left the South and travelled West in search of a better livelihood and the sister married a high school classmate, son of a hosiery mill owner.

His family was concerned about those in a poor area who were poorer than themselves—the Negroes who lived in a segregated, across-the-tracks area in the poor section of town, who washed the clothes and planted the crops of white families, who took the menial jobs and accepted their mean status without overt questioning. They were concerned about poor whites who lived in a nearby segregated mill town and worked long hours for low wages, depressed in body and spirit. But their concern stemmed from a sense of Christian responsibility for giving what they could in time of need of their own meager stores of food, clothing or advice.

They were independent and outspoken but their independence and outspokenness was the product of an individualist frontier tradition. It took the form, in the case of Perry Horton and Mordecai Pinkney Horton, father and grandfather of Myles Horton, of voting Republican in a predominantly Democratic South. It took the form, too, in Perry Horton's case, of being against labor unions because they were an intrusion on that independence.

The family were active members of the Cumberland Presbyterian Church, a mountain branch of the Presbyterian Church, which was rational rather than revivalist and placed emphasis on good works in this world rather than salvation in the next. But neither they nor their local church presumed to examine the nature of society or the basic social problems growing out of the organization of that society.

The public school education available to children growing up in small towns of Tennessee in the first decades of the century, such as Savannah where Myles Horton began school or Humbolt where he attended high school, was a poor copy of public school education elsewhere in the country; falling far short of contemporary standards, for example, in teacher preparation, books and equipment and length of the school year.[3] In addition to being deficient, as sociologist Howard Odum noted a decade later, what was offered was frequently lacking in relevance to the lives of the learners, to the needs and problems of the region.

For an independent and inquiring young mind, therefore, the most stimulating opportunities for education were experiential. And as the oldest son in a family of small means and large hopes for its children, where the father's highest earnings were as a country court clerk in the years 1910-1918, followed by hard-pressed years as a small farmer and share cropper, many of those educative experiences for Myles Horton were work experiences. Working in a grocery store after school, he learned something about the social structure of the small southern community—about the Negro sharecropper families whose crops were owned by the landowner until their bills were paid and who were systematically overcharged for inferior goods; about the white business and church leaders who paid the bills for Negro women and their lighter-skinned children. Working in a local box factory in the summer, he learned something about the spoils system in southern industry where several hundred "grateful workers" were paid two dollars per day for producing thousands of wooden boxes which were sold to farmers for twice what they cost to make. And the cost, in turn, as he recalled many years later in a talk to worker-students,[4] was passed along to poor families in town who paid for the boxes filled with potatoes.

College Years, 1924-1928

In the years 1924-1928, the future radical southern educator and proponent of a new social order attended a rather undistinguished Presbyterian college, Cumberland University in Lebanon, Tennessee, where he had been awarded a scholarship. There he majored in literature and read the English classics from Chaucer to Shakespeare to the nineteenth century romantic poets as well as some of the classics emanating out of New England. Like other southern students of literature in the twenties, as historian Vann Woodward has noted, he was led to believe that "there was nothing issuing from his native region in the way of arts and letters that was worth his notice."[5] Nor did his readings of the period include the writings of radical social critics or educators. His most radical intellectual inspiration was derived from Shelley's *Prometheus Unbound* or John Stuart Mill's essay *On Liberty*.

As in his grammar and high school years, he recognized later, his most important stimuli to growth and development in his college years, his most vital insights and understandings, were acquired experientially in work and social situations, sometimes in social crisis situations. These learning situations began to occur almost as soon as he had arrived at Cumberland University when his cherished individual rights were infringed upon. "They didn't haze me in college," he recalled many years later. "I organized the freshmen and we weren't hazed . . . I refused to join a fraternity. They said you had to join, so I wouldn't join."[6]

He encountered other kinds of infringements on his rights and the rights of others which proved to be significant learning experiences. As president of the student YMCA, he attended a religious conference on the campus of Southern YMCA College in the relatively cosmopolitan city of Nashville. There, for the first time, his narrow, restricted world was socially integrated. For the first time he had the opportunity to meet students from India and China and to interact as equals with Negro students. He quickly discovered, however, that beyond the confines of the setting of the conference the barriers to social interaction remained. There was no restaurant where he could take an attractive Chinese girl whom he met. And there was no

13

place—not even the public library—where he and a Negro conference participant could relax and exchange ideas when the conference adjourned.[7]

His immediate reaction was one of personal resentment at "being limited in my desire for expression . . . then," he recalled, "I got to questioning it intellectually, ethically and morally." Generalizing on his experience he came to a conclusion that would have been worthy of his pioneer-stock, Republican father but was to have radical consequences, because he took it as the basis for action as an individual and, later, as the head of an independent adult education institution. "I made it more or less an operating principle," he explained simply, "that nobody should have their rights interfered with as long as they are attending to their own business."[8]

His concern for rights took him very soon beyond the world of Cumberland University and state YMCA conferences. When the president of the Southern States Industrial Council, John Edgerton, asserted in a speech before the Cumberland student body that working people were "wrong" to attempt to do things for themselves through unions and that he and other factory owners should decide what was good for people," Myles Horton's recently defined "operating principle," his insistence on basic rights for himself and others, was again challenged.

"I knew," he observed, "that people, my own relatives, my own family should have something to say about their lives." As a result, along with beginning to read about unions, he acted. After hearing Edgerton, he recalled, "I went down as president of the college YMCA and talked to his workers and told them that they as human beings had some rights and I thought they ought to exercise them."[9] Following this spirited appeal, Horton was warned to "stay away." After returning a second time, he was told by college authorities that he could not go back again. Although his foray produced no historic changes in the relationship of the president of the Southern Industrial Council to his workers, the future head of a southern workers' education school began to perceive some of the problems involved in achieving change.

In his Cumberland University years, too, he spent three summers getting acquainted with mountain people and their problems while organizing children's Bible schools for the Presbyterian Church (U.S.A.). During the last of these summers, in a little community called Ozone, he began to hold unconventional evening sessions with adults along with the conventional religious education program for children. This interaction with mountain people was to prove instrumental in shaping his thinking as a future radical educator.

Although the Bible school program itself was neither challenging nor creative, the four-county East Tennessee mountain area to which the young summer worker was assigned proved rich in terms of history and the individuals whom he encountered. Thus, he came upon the town of Rugby in Morgan County, site of a short-lived utopian colony in the late nineteenth century. Its believers left behind a well-stocked public library, some handsome hand-hewn homes and a chapel which stirred Horton's . . . imagination—if not the imaginations of their neighbors in the southern highlands.

In the farming community of Allardt in Fentress County, he came to know Joe Kelley Stockton and his wife, Kate Bradford Stockton, sturdy descendants of the signers of the Declaration of Independence, who were known not so much for their livestock or crop lands as for their lively interest in books and ideas and their espousal of Socialism. In the years which followed the Stocktons were to prove steadfast friends and supporters of Horton and his radical educational institution. Horton, in turn, was to support and encourage Mrs. Stockton in her radical effort to become the first woman and the first Socialist to be governor of Tennessee.[10]

By the summer of 1927, when he decided on his own initiative to embark on a program involving adults in neighboring Cumberland County, he was well known in the area through his Bible school classes for the children and his participation in the church and social life of the various communities. In the process he had become increasingly aware of the problems which confronted people of the region: the persistent, familiar problems of living and making a living in impoverished mountain communities if they chose to remain; the less familiar problems of working in mill or factory towns if they decided to leave.

His notion in offering the program, as he explained many years later, was a simple one. "I invited the older people to come in for discussions of whatever they wanted to discuss." What amazed and encouraged him was both their eagerness to come, travelling by foot from miles around to talk about their problems, and his capacity, without being an authority, to function usefully as a sort of "educational leader." Of their problems and his role as it emerged, he recalled

> I remember they wanted to know about farm problems. They wanted to know about getting jobs in textile mills. They wanted to know about testing wells for typhoid. We discussed these things. To my amazement my inability to

15

answer questions didn't bother them... That was probably the biggest discovery I ever made. You don't have to know the answers. You raise the questions, sharpen the questions, get people to discussing them. And we found that in that group of mountain people a lot of the answers were available if they pooled their knowledge.[11]

The "community meetings" as they were called were very soon so crowded that the novice adult educator was suspected by some in the rural program of the Presbyterian Church of having misrepresented his attendance figures. "Nobody," it was asserted, "ever got that many people to a meeting in the mountains."[12] Along with group discussions of problems, experts such as a health official or a county agent were invited to participate when their special knowledge was needed. The meetings were social as well as problem-oriented. There was a wealth of ballads and dances, called "singing games,'" Myles Horton wrote sometime later to a prospective donor for his proposed "Southern Mountain School." "There were also many wonderful stories . . . . which had been handed down from generation to generation."[13]

By the end of the summer, participants in the community meetings were urging their youthful "educational leader" to remain. In addition, a well-to-do woman, living at Ozone, who had been hearing accounts of the lively social-educational meetings and the unprecedented interest which they had generated, offered her home as the setting for such a program.[14] Deeply identified with the mountain people who had come to be his friends and excited by the possibilities which his experimental summer venture suggested, he began to imagine some sort of future educational role for himself in the southern mountains. His thinking, however, about just what he should do, and how was unclear. At the same time, he was filled with the need and desire to continue his own education before defining his role. To his potential donor in Ozone, therefore, he explained that be "had just discovered this thing and . . . wanted to think through it."[15] And to his friends in Cumberland County he promised that he would "come back someday" when he had "something to offer."[16]

Quest for Self-education, 1928-1929

During the year following graduation from Cumberland University, while working as Student YMCA Secretary for the State of Tennessee, Myles Horton continued to pursue his own education through an energetic program of reading, observing, questioning and challenging. Although both his reading and his experiencing were diverse, much of his self-development program was related, in one way or another, to understanding society and learning about ways of changing it.

In his desire to understand existing conditions and how to change them, Horton was an eager student of southern history. He began in a modest way to collect books and records of Tennessee history, including the history of the Watauga Settlement and his independent forbear, Joshua Horton, who was said to have obtained the first landgrant in the Wilderness in 1775. Of Joshua Horton and the little group of settlers whose "Watauga Constitution" was the first to be written and adopted by independent white Americans, Horton readily admitted, "I am proud of it . . . I think it is a good background."[17] He took an enthusiastic interest, too, in the history of the anti-slavery counties in East Tennessee whose citizen soldiers (which, again, included his father's family) fought on the Union side in the Civil War.[18]

And it was at this time that he began reading about another strong minded and independent group of southerners, the Southern Populists. In their boldly-conceived movement of the 1890s to better their own depressed status as small farmers, he took note, they also concerned themselves (for a time at least) with the rights of Negroes, the most depressed group in the rural South.

He was also reading about mountain people, their history and folk culture and the problems confronting them in mill villages. Of this latter concern, he explained, "An interest in the mountains naturally led to a study of the neighboring cotton mill villages where many of the folks from the mountains were being lured."[19]

Although he had been keenly interested in doing some sort of "educational work," as he expressed it, and took every opportunity afforded by his statewide YMCA job to visit and learn about the educational programs of high schools and colleges, the future founder of the Highlander Folk School read, apparently, few articles and no books in the field of education. Of his visits to Tennessee schools where he looked for examples of community and problem-centered education, he recalled, "At the time I was unfamiliar with educational institutions and I thought that the kind of program I had in mind was so natural and acceptable that it would be a part of any educational set-up in rural areas, especially a church-related high school or college."[20]

Instead, he observed, as a careful student of the people and institutions of the southern highlands had observed a decade earlier, the failure of the schools "whether church or independent, to make connection with the life of the people of the community and region . . . ."[21]

The reading in this period of self-education which probably most influenced his thinking as an educator was in the field of philosophy—the philosophy of pragmatism as set forth by William James and John Dewey. From his reading of James he derived, as he recalled years later, "a lot of useful ideas," significant among them that "you can change things . . . by your own actions."[22] This optimistic American notion—"the belief that the individual might through self-help, energy and hope overcome nearly all, if not all, obstacles," as historian Merle Curti has noted, "gave sustenance to the financiers, advertisers and successful men of action."[23] It was also strongly appealing to the socially minded young YMCA secretary who was hoping, by some educational means, to help mountain people change and improve their lives.

From Dewey (as well as from James), the would-be educator acquired a pragmatist's definition of truth which was to provide him with a basis for assessing the worth of his new and often unsure educational ideas. "If ideas, meaning, conceptions, notions, theories, systems are instrumental to an active re-organization of the given environment," he noted down from Dewey's *Reconstruction in Philosophy*, "they are reliable sound, valid, good, true."[24]

In his reading and thinking about religion during this period as well as in his actions as Student YMCA Secretary, Horton was becoming increasingly a critic of the tradition-bound role of the church. He gave evidence of a capacity for independence and non-conformity which was in the spirit of his anti-slavery ancestors and Populist heroes. Without asking anyone, the new YMCA Secretary for Tennessee held interracial meetings all over the state—meetings for high school as well as college groups, meetings in public places where there had never been interracial groups before as well as in the quiet confines of a campus. "They were as glad to have me resign as I was to resign after a year",[25] he admitted later.

In his statewide interracial meetings as in his earlier experimental adult education program near Ozone, Myles Horton was warmly supported by a Congregational minister with a church in Cumberland County, Rev. Abram Nightingale of Crossville. While working with the Presbyterian Bible school program and later with the YMCA, he frequently stayed with Mr. Nightingale. "He always had open house to people who would come and go—including tramps," Horton recalled. "We got to be good friends." It was his friend Mr. Nightingale, too, who first introduced him to a penetrating volume by Harry F. Ward, *Our Economic Morality*, and urged him to study with Ward and others at Union Theological Seminary. Knowing young Horton's inner struggles to decide what he was going to do and how, Nightingale advised, "They won't give you any answers to your problems but you need background. You just don't know enough."[26]

Union Theological Seminary, 1929-1930

The self-educated and non-conformist Tennessean came to New York City and to Union Theological Seminary in the fall of 1929 at the beginning of the decade of the Great Depression. There, along with encountering a stimulating group of Biblical scholars and social gospel theologians, he encountered Christian, Marxian and Fabian Socialism, the progressive education movement, the industrial union movement and a number of distinguished advocates of the new social order. In his search for educational models, he also began learning about and visiting workers education institutions and settlement houses.

Radical theologians at Union were prominent among the spokesmen for social change long before the chaotic last months of 1929. Before the Great War, the social gospel theologians such as Walter Rauschenbusch had called for basic changes, for an alliance of progressive forces in the church with the labor movement to achieve "the ideal of a fraternal organization of society." In *Christianity and the Social Crisis*, he had also hailed Socialism as "the ultimate and logical outcome of the labor movement."[27] The writings of Rauschenbusch and other theologians of the social gospel called forth an immediate response in Horton who at the personal level had already been questioning the low wages paid workers, the social barriers between races and the lack of relevance of the Bible school-type educational program to the problems of the mountain poor.

Reinhold Niebuhr was one of the younger and more outspoken advocates of a new social order on the Union faculty whom Horton came to know. Niebuhr, who himself in this period was seeking to formulate and give practical expression to his ideas and ideals took a warm and sympathetic interest in the aspiring southerner and his ideas for developing some sort of educational program to help mountain people deal with their problems. As co-editor of *The World Tomorrow*, "A Journal looking toward a social order based on the religion of Jesus," Niebuhr was writing ardent editorials hailing

Socialist gains and calling for "a new political alignment based on the realities of American life."[29] He was also lamenting the "good people in the world of education and religion who imagine they are creating a new and better world through intellectual discipline and religious inspiration" and pointing out that in modern society, "significant power derives from the ownership of property."[30]

Horton's growing interest in Socialism and his espousal, for a time, of the Socialist Party dates from this period. He came to know Socialist Party leader Norman Thomas, who was the founder and contributing editor to *The World Tomorrow*, as well as other notable seekers for "a social order based on the religion of Jesus."[31] He also became immersed in the study of early Christian Socialists[32] and the Fabian Socialists as well as the writings of Karl Marx. The appeal of all of them, he observed later, was an ethical one. "They talk about a society that brings the greatest happiness to the greatest number," he explained, and "a society where there is no exploitation that grows out of ownership of the means of earning a living."[33]

A major advocate of radical political and economic as well as educational change in this period was Professor John Dewey of neighboring Columbia University. "Dewey permeated the whole atmosphere at this time",[34] Horton recalled. With Niebuhr, Thomas and other radical educators and theologians, Dewey founded the League for Independent Political Action "'to educate the American public to fundamental economic realities and a new political order so that the spirit of democracy may have a rebirth."[35] At the same time, Dewey and a growing group of followers in the Progressive Education movement were articulating the kinds of ideas about the social role of education which the independent young Tennessean was attempting to conceptualize out of his own experience. In a copy of Dewey's *Democracy and Education* acquired while at Union, Horton underlined a definition of the aim of Progressive Education which later found its way into a early statement about the aim of the Highlander Folk School. "It is the aim of Progressive Education," Dewey emphasized, "to take part in correcting unfair privilege and unfair deprivation, not to perpetuate them."[36] To do this, he advocated a problem-centered approach to curriculum not unlike the approach which Horton happened upon. "It must," Dewey urged, "take account of the . . . needs of the existing community life; it must select with the intention of improving the life we live in common."[37]

Among Professor Dewey's Columbia University colleagues and followers in the Progressive Education movement whom Horton came to know and value in this period were George Counts and Edward Lindeman. Like Dewey, both men advocated fundamental changes in the society and in education. Counts called upon the schools to be honestly partisan, to teach children "a vision of what America might become in an industrial age." The vision, as he defined it, was "a coordinated and socialized economy managed in the interests of the people."[38]

Lindeman, whose writings had considerable meaning for Horton, declared that European adult education, related to "functional organizations" such as cooperatives and trade unions represented the most "vital adult education of our time. Of American adult education he predicted that it will become "an agency for progress if its short-time goal of self-improvement can be made compatible with a long-time experimental but resolute policy of changing the social order."[39]

In both Counts and Lindeman, Horton found educators with whom he could communicate. Recalling especially his meeting with Lindeman, he observed, ". . . up to that time I had never had any contact with educators who did not work within the structure of formal education."[40]

Although he had begun reading about unions soon after his encounter with the head of the Council of Southern Industries while a student at Cumberland University, Horton's first experience with the industrial union movement, North and South, and his espousal of the movement occurred during his year in New York. His interactions with radical theologians progressive educators and Socialist leaders who were advocates of a new social order reinforced his own reading and thinking. His intellectual identification with the labor movement became an emotional commitment when he came in firsthand contact with sweat shops in the New York garment trade and participated in an International Ladies' Garment Workers Union strike. That commitment grew more intense when, in the winter of 1929, he travelled to the scene of a prolonged and bitter textile strike in Marion, North Carolina.

The 1929 strike in Marion, described as "the first genuinely serious labor revolt the South had ever known,"[41] had a profound effect on Horton and on other sympathetic eye-witnesses. It revealed not only the intolerable conditions which caused the once-docile mill workers to spontaneously strike, and the violence and recrimination to which those who dared to strike were subjected, but the new brave spirit of hope and unity which was awakened. "It was the first time many of the workers had thought of themselves as anything but 'mill hands',"[42] wrote one labor observer, Tom Tippett, whose account of the strikes was dedicated "To the southern mill workers and the labor movement that they will one day build."

Tippett, a teacher at Brookwood Labor College in Katonah, New York, bitterly lamented the "indifference and tragic impotence" of the American Federation of Labor in its handling of the strikes which were finally and totally crushed. Based on the experience, however, he predicted confidently

A labor renascence is at hand. The American Federation of Labor can take it or leave it alone, but down underneath the southern unrest is a germ with a will to live that neither mobs, nor massacres, nor prisons can extinguish.[43]

And, based on this and other experiences at the scene of strikes, Myles Horton, in the spring of 1932, proposed to found a "Southern Mountains School"[44] to train local leadership for a barely-stirring southern labor movement.

Along with gaining first-hand knowledge of the labor movement and participating in strikes by the Garment Workers in New York and the Textile Workers in North Carolina, the would-be-educator theology student visited Brookwood Labor College, hoping to discover a model for his southern mountains educational project. Brookwood, a resident labor college, was founded in 1921 by A. J. Muste and a group of progressive trade unionists and educators (including Dewey) who, as Muste explained, "were interested in developing a labor education movement in this country that will be modeled after the movement in Great Britain."[45] Although he encountered a congenial group of faculty and students, among them Tippett, the academically oriented, British-inspired labor program at Brookwood seemed to have little relevance for the region or the people with whom he planned to work and little in common with the informal problem-oriented educational approach that he had found so promising in his community meetings at Oxone. Thus, although Brookwood reading lists, labor plays and outlines of labor history were later used by the Highlander Folk School, its future founder departed without an institutional model.

In New York City, where he worked part-time with a Boys' Club in Hell's Kitchen while attending Union, he became acquainted with Greenwich House and Henry Street Settlement House and their dynamic directors, Mary Simkovitch and Lillian Wald. These centers had the vitality, the informality, the relationship to the people of their surrounding neighborhoods which strongly appealed to Horton, but again, they did not seem relevant models for a rural southern mountain region. It was in this period of seeking models that he met a descendant of one of the founders of the Oneida Colony, a utopian colony in Oneida, New York. From her and from what he had learned and read about Rugby and other similar ventures, he concluded that they were too detached from life around them, too caught up in their own internal affairs to have any significant social impact.

Out of all his intellectual and social experiencing, Horton did not arrive at a "solution" to his ponderings regarding an educational program related to mountain people. But he acquired some rather definite ideas as to the political, social and economic problems of the ailing industrial society and the need for a new social order. At the same time he had become increasingly convinced of the potential role of the labor movement and of education in bringing a new order into being. In the process, he had gathered a small but important group of friends and future supporters for his southern mountains project. Thus, when he founded the Highlander Folk School in 1932, the school's Advisory Committee included Reinhold Niebuhr, Norman Thomas and George Counts and among its early contributors was John Dewey.

The University of Chicago, 1930-1931

When Myles Horton decided to study at Union Theological Seminary, he did not intend to become a minister. When in the spring of 1930, at the and of a year at Union, he decided to study sociology at the University of Chicago, he did not intend to become a sociologist. Instead, he was still trying to formulate his problem-centered educational program. "Almost by accident," he explained, "I found sociological surveys and sociological ideas illuminating and it was for this reason that I ended up at Chicago . . . ."[46] There he took courses both in the sociology department and at Chicago Theological Seminary and continued to interact with socialists and labor groups and to seek out creative individuals and institutions with something to teach him about how to develop his own educational program.

Among the notable group of sociologists with whom Horton studied in 1930-1931, Professor Robert Park was to have the most significant impact on his thinking as a radical educator. From Professor Park, Horton indicated, "I learned . . . that the only way to fully understand a situation was to become involved, but if that was impossible, to take a first-hand look at what was going on." Through Professor Park, too, he became acquainted with "the concept of conflict as a basis for social analysis."[47]

His interest in the conflict concept, in turn, led him to the writings of an earlier sociologist, Lester F. Ward, whose *Dynamic Sociology*[48] gave him an understanding of how conflict and crisis could be used to better society by presenting problems which must be solved. Park's concept of conflict as a basis for social analysis and Ward's ideas regarding its social stimulus value were to provide the future radical educator with a basis for analyzing situations and initiating educational programs which he would use throughout the history of the Highlander Folk School.

His study of sociology and especially some of Park's lectures and writings gave him, as well, an understanding of social movements as part of the forming and re-forming processes of society "beginning with social unrest, leading to mass movements and ending in the formation or modification of institutions."[49] This understanding of the sequential development of movements was to be of underlying importance as he developed educational programs related to a projected southern labor movement and, later, a projected civil rights movement. When, some years later he was asked to indicate sources in the field of education which had been useful to him in developing the early program of the Highlander Folk School, he replied, "My approach . . . was more from the point of view of a sociologist."[50]

Along with his quest for usable knowledge, Horton continued his education through social involvement in Chicago. He and some of his fellow members of the Socialist Club, for example, volunteered their help in organizing unions of the poor and unorganized—beginning with elevator operators at the University. Although they did not accomplish their goal, they did learn about the conservatism of the local American Federation leadership which rejected the students' offer because it did not wish to come into conflict with the University and because the dues-paying potential of the proposed union members was questionable.

Among the socially innovative persons whom Horton came to know during his year in Chicago, certainly the most innovative, the most remarkable, was Jane Addams, founder of Hull House. Of his talks with Miss Addams in the course of a number of visits there, he recalled

> She was extremely helpful in discussing the very rough ideas I had . . . In fact, she said that what I was trying to do was start a rural settlement house.[51]

Her analysis, he felt, was fairly accurate although, as he explained later, "I always thought in terms of an *educational* program which would use some of the techniques of settlement houses . . . ."[52]

From a Danish-born Lutheran minister, Rev. Aage Moller, Horton acquired his initial interest in folk schools. It was Moller who convinced him to go to Denmark and see the schools for himself after the many books which he read left him with basic questions regarding their educational approach.

All available accounts of these unique adult schools and the enthusiastic appraisals of progressive American educators convinced him that they had "something to offer." Edward Lindeman, after a visit to Denmark in the early twenties where he noted of the Danish economy that there was "neither wealth nor poverty" and of the farmers in the folk high schools that they were "studying for the purpose of making life more interesting," declared unequivocally, "One finds an educational ferment such as motivates no other people in the modern world."[53] John C. Campbell, in his definitive study of southern mountain people concluded, "The folk schools with their extension systems might be adapted readily to meet the changing and varied needs of this land." He admitted "The difficulties of finding persons possessing the proper spirit and personality to conduct the folk schools" but he stated confidently, "Such workers can be found and can be trained."[54]

Horton read with interest the story of how the folk schools originated, beginning in the mind of a "radical minister," Bishop N.S.F. Gruntvig, who, after the defeat of Denmark in the Napoleonic wars, "pondered over the problem of how to awaken the people" and decided that "what was necessary was a free school for adults."[55] He read the history of the various schools and responded readily to the notion that they were developed "not by the government but by the voluntary work and sacrifice of the people themselves" and were, therefore, "freer in form and more closely connected with the life of the people than would have otherwise been the case."[56] Yet descriptions of the educational program with "informal lectures and song" as the "main method" failed to explain the much acclaimed vitality of the institutions and their impact on the lives of rural people. ". . . the results they achieved," he was sure, "could not have been achieved by the methods they described."[57]

Denmark, 1931-1932

There were valid reasons in the summer of 1931 why the partially trained student of theology and sociology, with no funds and a considerable sense of responsibility for doing something to help in a deepening social and economic crisis affecting the nation and the South should not have gone to Denmark. Professor Park offered him an assistantship with the opportunity to complete his doctorate in sociology. The head of the American Missionary Association offered him the principalship of a church supported secondary school in Tennessee, Pleasant Hill Academy.[58] Only Reinhold Niebuhr, to whom Horton had communicated his growing interest in folk schools and in the possibility of adapting the folk school idea to the southern mountains, supported him in his contemplated trip. Although Niebuhr himself believed that his determined and independent former student could achieve his radical social change goals within the framework of a rural church, he wrote in response to a letter

> you say that the people of the mountains integrate their social and religious life around a personality, and I imagine it wouldn't take so long for them to find out just what kind of religion is on tap in your particular church. But on the whole you will have a freer hand if you organize a folk school. I think a visit to Denmark for study would be splendid.[59]

By the end of the summer, Horton had managed to work his way to Europe, eager to discover, at last, the kind of educational program, the kind of institution which might awaken depressed southern mountain people as it has awakened the depressed Danes. Instead, he discovered primarily himself. While looking at Denmark's relatively sound, planned economy, its strong trade union movement, its flourishing farmers' cooperatives,[60] he was reenforced in his beliefs regarding the need for a new and more democratic social order in America. Looking at Denmark's once radical folk schools, his thinking was crystallized regarding his own role as a radical educator relating to quite different people under quite different circumstances.

In attempting to clarify his future role, while in Denmark, he set down a rambling analysis of America's and the South's needs based on his reading, thinking and experiencing during his years in the Tennessee mountains, in New York and in Chicago. He stressed the need for "economic as well as political democracy" which for him as for the radical educators and theologians who had helped to shape his thinking meant some form of

Socialism.[61] It meant, too, a strong American labor movement which he predicted was "the basis on which Socialism would ultimately be built."[62]

Turning to what his role as a radical educator should be, he asked himself, "Was not my interest in the mountains only sentimental after all? Would not my efforts have a greater social value elsewhere?"[63] After examining various alternatives (including working in industrial areas "where the opportunity for immediate results was best") he came to the decision that he should do what he had wanted to do: return to the South, to "the backward mountain sections at least one hundred years behind the most advanced parts of the country" and there help to develop much-needed local labor leadership. Projecting a continued influx into the South of New England industrialists for whom, he observed "mountaineers furnish a reserve from which cheap labor can be drawn for many years" and projecting, too, continuing labor unrest as had erupted in the Marion textile strike, Horton concluded that he could best contribute to a new social order by allying his educational efforts with the anticipated southern labor movement. "Intellectuals," he wrote, "need movements to make their efforts count."[64]

The young Tennessean, pondering his role as a radical labor educator in the depressed southern mountains, while he struggled to learn Danish and find something relevant in the many folk schools which he visited, had at least one basic value in common with his Watauga settler ancestors and his Republican grandfather. His notion of the social function of education would have been foreign to their individualist natures. So, too, would his religious-ethical values which, again, placed emphasis on social morality. His concern for the poor which took the form of aspiring to help them assume leadership of a mass movement to basically change society would have seemed perhaps most foreign of all. But his independence, his determination to trust in his own ideas, to create the kind of institution and define the kind of program which he felt were needed, would have been not only understood, but commended. Years later, this descendent of pioneer settlers and anti-slavery southern Republicans wrote

> . . . the School was started so we could have a place to teach what we believed in.
> Perhaps a good part of my own personal activities grow out of my desire to be unlimited. I resent anything that hinders the fullest development of my personality or the personalities of anyone else, or any barriers that hinder the fullest development of people anywhere.[65]

THREE

The Shaping
of a
Radical Institution

The fall and winter of 1931-1932 which Myles Horton spent in Denmark continued to be a learning, a germination period. But only a small part of the learning was derived from his observation of the folk schools. The months in Denmark, instead, provided an opportunity to re-think and gain perspective on the institution-without-a-model which he was to found in the fall of 1932. The fall and winter of 1932-1933 was also a learning period. During the early months after the founding of the Highlander Folk School, Horton and those associated with him in the venture were learning from their first, tentative interactions with the people of the community in which the School was located and with the little group of resident students which they slowly managed to gather.

Although much about Denmark was inspiring to a young American seeker after a new social order, he was disappointed, in some ways, with the schools themselves. Their once vital spirit had become "rather vague," he observed. "They are looking backward trying to conjure up enemies long vanquished." The folk high school movement had been built around the idea of the 'living word,' the spoken word, dealing with subjects of deep concern to teacher and students. "But fighting the ghosts of their grandparents' enemies does not call forth the 'living word,'" he lamented.[1]

What he did admire was the strong sense of purpose which had characterized the early folk school movement. "The idea of an emotionally charged and moral mission," he wrote to another American student of folk schools, "seems to me. . . to explain the success of the early schools."[2]

But only in a few of the more recently developed folk schools for workers was he able to find something of this old purpose and spirit reinterpreted to meet new needs. Of the workers' schools, he observed

> Here the purpose is clear. The battle is between capitalism and socialism. Workers are being prepared to live in a new society which they are to help make... One feels that the "living word" is being heard.[3]

As he traveled about Denmark visiting, observing, meeting students and teachers and occasionally giving lectures on the United States at the folk schools, Horton's thoughts regarding his radical southern mountain folk school began to take some sort of shape. Piecemeal notes describe the kind of setting which he hoped to find for the school—"If possible, on a farm . . . where the scenery is beautiful, where there is opportunity for being alone, where there is timber for extra buildings, where food could be raised and trees planted."[4]

They describe, too, his various ideas regarding the community and movement related program which he was trying to conceptualize. "Community work would he carried on . . . under my direction," he wrote, "which will insist [sic] the support of neighbors in the school." Such work, he indicated, might include a cooperative providing "a place where people could do productive work." At another point he noted, "School and community life should be built around get-togethers such as singing, dancing, discussions, dinners, etc." Beyond the immediate contribution to school and community life, Horton suggested, the community program would be an educative experience for residential students who "could learn not only what to do at home but have a chance to study social forces at work."[5]

He found it more difficult to imagine the kind of program which might be developed to prepare students for participation in the future southern labor movement. Of the students (whom he referred to as "fellow workers") he wrote, ". . . they will he picked for their ability and the direction of their interests . . . We shall consult and share plans, working together when possible. The program, he indicated, would be "flexible" and an effort would be made "to help all do what they wish most to do . . . At the same time," he noted, "An effort will be made to keep them in the ranks of labor, but intelligently so." To this end and to help establish a vital relationship between the school and the labor movement he proposed, "I can . . . go to strike situations and take students with me, thus helping labor and education at the same time." Looking further ahead, he predicted hopefully, "the students who will go into industry will make it possible for me to have a direct contact with [local] labor movements."[6]

In another set of notes made on Christmas night in Denmark in 1931, he added to his ideas regarding the kind of institution, the kinds of learners and learning activities which he visualized. The school, he wrote, would be for "young men and women," some from the mountains, others from factories and, he added specifically, "Negroes should be among the students." They would come, he indicated, "for a minimum of three months," would live "in close personal contact with teachers" and out of their "living, working and studying together" would come an understanding of "how to take their place intelligently in the changing world."[7]

Learning, as he imagined it, would occur in a variety of ways, utilizing a few of "the usual educational techniques" but emphasizing various kinds of experiential learning. This learning would grow out of the "life lived together," out of "song and music" as well as working and studying together. It would grow out of interaction with people "from the whole mountainside" and with visitors who would share their several talents and viewpoints. Among those who would be encouraged to visit would be "artists of all kinds" and, Horton wrote, "Such a school should be a stopping place for traveling [sic] liberals and a meeting place for southern radicals." The educational program, he emphasized, as he had in earlier notes, should include opportunities to help students "broaden their outlooks" and "acquire definite information" by "observing, taking part in and analyzing situations of interest."[8]

The collection of notes which Horton amassed during his Danish travels contained a number of imaginative ideas, some of which were to prove educationally sound and useful. But they were ideas, not a blueprint for an institution. It was on this same Christmas night in 1931 that Horton made the decision to cease his note taking, as he had ceased his quest for an educational model, and get on with the creation of his radical institution. Years later he recalled vividly that decision which marked the end of his stay in Denmark and the beginning of the Highlander Folk School:

All at once I said to myself... all you do is get a place and move in. You're there. The situation is there. You start this and let it grow. You have your idea. You know your goal. It will build its own structure and take its own form... find the place, the people, the situation. Use your ideas as your lodestone and move into the thing and start.[9]

Six months later, through the good offices of the minister who had first urged him to study at Union Theological Seminary, he was given the use of a substantial house and forty acres of mountain farm land for his experimental school. The house and land, located in a rural community on the Cumberland Plateau some fifty miles from Chattanooga, belonged to Dr. Lilian Johnson, prominent Tennessee educator, who was about to retire and wanted her property used for a "good cause."[10]

The funds needed for basic supplies and equipment for the modest new venture—furniture, books and food—were raised, in large part, through the efforts of Reinhold Niebuhr and a little group of radical theologians and educators from Union Theological Seminary and Columbia University, The University of Chicago and the South. The initial fund-raising letter, signed by Dr. Niebuhr in May 1932, did not attempt to describe all the various kinds of social and educational activities and functions contemplated for the unique institution. Instead, the letter stated, "Our project is the organization of a Southern Mountain School for the training of labor leaders in Southern Industrial Areas."[11]

The Community: A Place to Begin with Workers and their Problems

Although Myles Horton and his supporters had projected a southwide center "for the training of labor leaders," the major focus of the Highlander Folk School program in the earliest period was the impoverished little mountain community of Summerfield where the new institution was located. The community represented a place to begin in November 1932, when there was one resident student. It represented an opportunity to learn and experiment in workers' education in a community made up almost entirely of working-class people while looking toward the development of a southern industrial union movement. And it represented, to Horton, the fulfilling of a deeply felt social responsibility to relate the School to the actual conditions and problems of community life.[12]

As a sociologist by training and a pragmatist by conviction, the founder of the Highlander Folk School, in the company of one other young Southerner and would-be radical educator, Don West,[13] spent the first months in Summerfield not teaching but learning from the community. An early account begins:

For two or three months we just lived, put in a late garden, cut a little wood and tried to get acquainted. We didn't say much about the school. When people asked us about it, we explained the best we could and went on about our work.[14]

Out of this experience came a good deal of knowledge about the community and its problems and the beginning of a relationship to the School's neighbors.

The Depression Comes to a Depressed People

In determining to base its educational program on people's problems, the Highlander Folk School was located in a most appropriate community. Estes Kefauver, in fact, as a concerned Tennessee congressman, once called Grundy County, where Summerfield was located, "the problem county." Their problems were those of a much-studied region—problems of wasted and neglected resources, human and material, as described in voluminous detail by a major student of the South, Howard Odum, in *Southern Regions of the United States*,[15] and in a brief report to President Roosevelt on *The Economic Conditions of the South*.[16] The most terse summary of all was made by the President himself when he described the South in the midst of a national depression as "the nation's No. 1 economic problem."[17]

Their problems were those of a once prosperous county whose two industries—coal and lumber—had begun to collapse some decades before the depression. It was an irreparable collapse, and as these resources were exploited in classic nineteenth century style, there was left behind only mined-out coal fields, cut-over timberland and unemployed and underemployed workers. A county school teacher and resident of Summerfield put the results of the economic situation most succinctly: "Grundy County, since its mines and forests have been depleted, has been populated chiefly by poor people."[18]

There were almost no alternatives to the disappearing jobs in the coal and timber industries. A handful of persons in the entire county had work with the one hotel and a contractor. In the summer, a few women were able to earn a small amount doing laundry for tourists in the nearby town of Monteagle. Otherwise, some 500 families managed to live by farming. But the soil on the mountain plateau was thin and sandy. Even resourceful early

33

settlers, Horton learned, had failed to make a success of it.[19] And the farm skills and tools of the unemployed miners and timber workers were poor as well as their land. In spite of these conditions, the number of farm families almost doubled with the depression[20] and the return of kinfolk who had escaped to the city and then were forced back to the mountain. These were tiny subsistence farms undertaken in desperation, and many of the families soon found themselves deeply in debt and in need of relief.[21] Perhaps the extent of the human crisis situation is most clearly to be seen in the numbers of people who were on relief. Not only did the county have by far the highest relief rate in Tennessee, but it was one of the eleven counties in the United States with the highest proportion of its population in that destitute condition![22] "Seventy-two per cent of the entire population of Grundy County was on the relief roll, at one time or another, between November, 1933 and February, 1935," a State study disclosed.[23]

With these problems, inevitably, were the accompanying problems of poor diet, health, hygiene and housing characteristic of poverty-stricken areas, especially in the South and in Southern Appalachia. Government and regional studies of the period collected by the Highlander Folk School represent grim catalogues of the kinds of problems to be found in the surrounding community and county.[24]

The desperate economic situation spelled out in human terms meant that a great deal of ingenuity was required just to live. Typical of those among the seventy-odd families in Summerfield who were poor and struggling but not defeated was a sixty year old Methodist lay preacher, his wife, their sons and their sons' families. "Uncle Billy" Thomas was the most skilled woodworker in the area. He and his two sons managed to earn a yearly income of slightly over $100 from the sale of their hand-turned chairs at seventy-five cents apiece and from the peanuts and potatoes which they could grow on five acres of land. Another of Uncle Billy's sons worked first in coal, then in timber, and finally, exchanged his year around labor for the rental of a small cabin, a garden plot and occasional produce to feed his wife and four children.[25]

Of the poorest families in this poor community, the founder of the Highlander Folk School noted, "Supplying food, clothing and shelter has sapped them of any interest in cultural things."[26] Such families, at the lowest level of existence, knew not only suffering and hardship but hunger to the point of starvation. One of these bitter examples, a crippled, unemployed railroad worker, his wife and four children, lived in the stall of a barn because "the wood ran out" to finish their one room cabin. Several other children had not survived the harsh existence. Their year old child was found to be starving. Their ten year old child had never attended school. Their sometime income was fifty cents a week which the mother earned when she was able to do laundry for a family in the town two miles away.[27]

What emerged clearly for community student Myles Horton as he observed his neighbors' determined struggle to survive, was the separateness of each family's struggle. In spite of the fact that the community, like other Southern mountain communities, was extremely homogeneous—white, working class, descendants of pioneers, with the same economic interests and the same problems, "there was little unity and practically no native leadership."[28] The families' common background and history included also bitter memories of feuds and strikes. Their common problems of joblessness resulted in intense competition between family and family for the few jobs available. The tradition of individualism which served their forbearers well as isolated mountain families in a pioneer period where "each family in its hollow lived its own life,"[29] persisted as a dominant trait among Summerfield families in an industrial period when their lives and livelihoods were bound together with the whole sagging economy of the county, the region and the nation.

Community social and church-going patterns tended to perpetuate the separateness of families and little groups of families. Many families kept largely to themselves and their relatives. Of the three small churches, two were fundamentalist sects whose narrow, judgmental preachments did not make for a greater sense of humanity or community. Not even the once-valued heritage of Southern mountain music, dance and folklore brought the families of Summerfield together. Songs were still sung in some of their homes, tales were still remembered by the older people of the community, but the occasions for sharing them were few, and square-dancing, when the Highlander Folk School was founded, had been banned as irreligious.[30]

Nor was there any community program of recreation or educational activities for the adults in Summerfield. One of the church leaders encouraged social evenings and Sunday afternoon games for young people. There were monthly or by-monthly adult Sunday Schools. But these were for small segments of the community. Otherwise, people were left to their own devices.[31]

Above all, as Myles Horton noted, except for the local elementary school, there was not another community institution in Summerfield in 1932. And the only community-involving activity, he observed, was cooperative grave digging.

In spite of the vastness and complexity of the problems converging on the little community of Summerfield, Myles Horton was not without hope for its future. Its people with their stubborn vitality and determination to survive represented, as Odum described the people of the South, "the living, striving, creative wealth of the region."[32] There was great strength and vitality in the closeness of their family living. The children in these mountain families shared in every aspect of life—and death. In the daily housework and chores and in caring for the smaller children, at church revival meetings, the county fair and buryings, everyone was included.[33] There was a vitality in their humor which had long carried them through the crises of their hard-fought existence. Even in the most dire of circumstances, they seemed to be able to laugh.[34] Religion, too, although the rural ministers were inclined to emphasize the thou-shalt-not aspects, was a source of strength for many. Among these were the independent believers who "never doubted the truths of the Bible," but "did not frequent the churches."[35] And among these, too, were the radical believers such as a book-reading member of an old Summerfield family, the Marlowes, who when asked what he liked to read replied readily, "books on Socialism and the Bible."[36]

There was hardiness, too, in a folk culture which was not dead but only dormant when the Highlander Folk School came into the community. Elements of it persisted, not only in homes and family groups, but in the local school where mountain "singing games" and stories were part of the children's experience as they had been an important part of the experience of their teacher, May Justus, herself a child of the mountains.[37] And there were still singers in the community who persisted in singing mountain songs and fiddlers who persisted in fiddling mountain tunes.

There was even in that independent, individualist mountain community the memory, on the part of some, of being organized, of standing together for their rights. The father of "Uncle Billy" Thomas, he recalled, had belonged to the Farmers' Alliance (which later became the Farmers' Union) before the turn of the century.[38] The fathers and grandfathers of some of the depressed citizens of Summerfield and Grundy County in 1892 had the proud distinction as "free miners" of opening the stockades and freeing convict labor in the mines.[39] This was but the first of many embattled efforts in which these mountain miners, first as members of the Knights of Labor and, later, beginning in 1898, as members of the United Mineworkers, fought to protect their jobs and their rights.[40] It was not, in fact, until 1926, after several prolonged strikes, the last one ending after more than two years, that the miners and their union went down in defeat.[41] Since that time, there had been no new leadership developed, no new industries, but the potential for leadership had been demonstrated.

Thus, when Myles Horton stated that the newly-established Highlander Folk School was guided by a belief in the possibility of "a genuine democracy" achieved through the participation of "the masses" in "their own economic and political organizations,"[42] there was some basis for that faith in the community, in spite of the obvious lack of organization or leadership. And when he asserted, further, "We hold that the new society must be built upon the best elements of our present social order",[43] his confidence in the heritage of the people of Summerfield was not without foundation.

While becoming educated himself about Summerfield, Myles Horton gave a good deal of thought to the question of how the educative process could best be facilitated in the community. He was convinced, as a student of sociology as well as of Hart and Dewey, that education was a function not primarily of formal learning activities, but of the total social environment. His convictions were borne out as he analyzed the discouraging efforts made by the local elementary school over a period of years to improve community living by improving the education of its children. In 1925, Dr. Lilian Johnson, subsequent donor and life-long friend of the Highlander Folk School,[44] brought two highly qualified teachers[45] with an understanding of mountain children into the substandard little Summerfield school. In spite of their dedication and high hopes, he noted, they watched "a discouraging proportion of these children being swallowed up by the indifferent life of the community."[46]

He was aware, too, of the frequently unsuccessful efforts made by Dr. Johnson herself over a sustained period. Coming to live in Summerfield in 1915, after successful careers as a college teacher, President of Western College for Women in Ohio and aide to President Wilson's Commission for the Study of Agricultural Cooperatives in Europe, she was determined to make her home a community center for the depressed mountain community where children could come for games and social gatherings and their parents could attend meetings and hear speakers. She had hoped, in fact, that the building might be owned by community members paying five dollars a share.

But, as she recalled later, "they were not ready for that." They were not ready, as it turned out, to accept a number of her far-seeing ideas. She faced years of suspicion and resentment on the part of her independent mountain neighbors who looked at the highly educated outsider and asked, "Why has she come?"

Ultimately, she won the gratitude and respect of many for her contributions to improving agriculture and education. She started a county fair, secured a Smith-Hughes agricultural teacher and served on the county school board as well as bringing able young teachers into the county. And the teachers, with her encouragement and support, not only enriched the experiences of the children by bringing them poetry and literature, arts and crafts, but offered night classes in their home to teach reading and writing to the adults of Summerfield.[47]

Yet for all the individual children who caught a glimpse of beauty in literature or in their own handiwork, and the few who went on to high school and even to college with Dr. Johnson's help, for all the individual adults who for the first time were able to form letters and read words, and the individual farmers who increased production on their meager acreage, the basic community environment was unchanged. The deep-seated social and economic problems, the inter-family tensions, the lack of common purpose or leadership in the community remained. And, in 1930, when the weary philanthropist-educator talked of turning the job of community betterment over to someone else, the persisting problems had been intensified by the depression.[48]

Thus in projecting what he called "the folk school idea" in the Summerfield community (and later over the South), Myles Horton thought in terms of educative environments, two of which seemed to him crucial. One was the community itself, not as a "chance environment",[49] but "as a consciously experienced set of conditions and surroundings" where by examining "conflict situations" and crises thrust upon them, people could come to understand "the real nature of our society . . . in all its ugliness."[50]

The other crucial environment, as Horton analyzed it, was the one which he and others hoped to achieve, "the new society." This environment, he believed, could be represented by the School itself as a democratically conceived, cooperatively administered center for the community and Southwide workers' education where resident students, community members and staff would think and work together on community and larger problems and share social and cultural activities as well as manual labor and chores.[51]

In setting forth his ideas on the two educative environments in some early notes, written, as they often were, to clarify his own and staff thinking, Horton stated that the School must "try to give the students an understanding of the world in which we live (a class divided society) and an idea of the world we would like to have." He did not, however, he stated explicitly, conceive of the School as an ideal community within the community. "The tie-up with the conflict situations and participation in community life," he emphasized, would keep the School "from being a detached colony or Utopian venture."[52]

Early Social and Educational Activities

In attempting to communicate to friends and potential contributors something of what was occurring in the interactive environments of the experimental School and the depressed mountain community in the fall and winter of 1932-1933, Myles Horton concluded that it "cannot be described." He indicated that even coming for a visit would not be enough. You would "have to come a number of times, or stay with us for a while . . . ."[53]

Some who observed the institution in this early period or learned of its activities might have called it, as Jane Addams had, "a rural settlement house. "In some ways, the new school certainly performed the functions of a mountain settlement." Beginning with its first evening, called a "Community Meeting," attended by some fifty parents, grandparents, children and young people who sang and talked and played games, the School became a center for weekly social-recreational gatherings for Summerfield families.[54] And in spite of the disapproval of the more conservative church members, increasing numbers of families took part in the Community Nights, as they came to be called. During the first months, these evenings consisted almost entirely of informal and spontaneous entertainment. As a staff member later described it, "If someone happened in with a guitar or fiddle, we would have a treat of popular old songs and mountain ballads." Otherwise, there would be social games and singing. "Hymns and revolutionary songs were equally popular," it was observed. Later, one of the women suggested that they establish a committee to plan the weekly program. This marked a beginning of active community participation in creating the new environment.[55]

Building on the old environment, there were also Sunday evening religious meetings where, along with hymn singing, there were lectures and discussions on the Bible and Christianity. But unlike the local churches or more

39

traditional religious meetings, the emphasis was on the here-and now—the ugliness of the depression and their depressed standard of living. Topics embarked upon by the radical young co-educator and preacher, Don West, included "Jesus and American Conditions," both of great interest to religious and poverty-stricken mountaineers.[56]

Other activities came about simply because someone from the School or the community identified a need to he filled. No one was trained in group work, but Don West's sister, who came to help at the School at his urgent request, took the job of organizing a girls' club in Summerfield while helping to manage the household and working in the office. And still other activities were offered because some staff interest or talent found a response in the community. Thus, because two of the early staff members combined training in music[57] with their other skills and abilities, some twenty Summerfield children who would never have imagined the opportunity were able to take piano lessons and perform for their proud families.[58] And, when a young man skilled in wrought iron work came to the School for a time, there was a community class in that specialized craft.[59]

The several accounts of how the first classes were initiated—and even what classes were initiated—are not always in agreement. However, the process was generally begun informally, sometimes almost accidentally. The psychology class, the first to get underway some two weeks after the community-resident school opened its doors, had its beginnings with the wife of a neighboring farmer "remarking about her unruly child" which, in turn, led to a lengthy conversation involving the farmer, his wife, a resident student and Horton. The next evening, this account of the casually interactive approach to adult education programming concludes, "The discussion was continued at the School and at the request of the neighbors and students, a class in Psychology for Adults was announced."[60] During the first month three other classes came into being, a class in Cultural Geography grew out of an evening of European travel pictures as chaired by Horton and West; a Social and Economic Problems class had its starting point with the discussion of a "community conflict" (never further identified), and a Social Literature class began with the reading of mountain poetry by poet Don West.

In February 1933, another community-resident class, Religion and Social Change, was begun. The teacher was Reverend John Thompson, fellow Southerner and classmate of Horton's at the Union Theological Seminary, who served for several months as a visiting Highlander staff member.

Although the Tennessee press was describing the new institution as a "Socialist School," Thompson viewed it as basically Christian in its role and purpose.

Of the community-resident evening classes developed during the first five-month resident term, attended by twenty to twenty-four neighbors, eighteen and over, together with the resident students, all but the class on Religion and Social Change were discontinued before the term ended. Thompson's class was continued at the request of the community. One reason for terminating the classes, it was explained, was that "most people were having to work late getting in a crop and were too tired to come out at night."[61] The record also indicates that following an Influenza epidemic, in January, "Class attendance was very slow in building up again" and "one class was unable to start at all."[62] Added to these reasons, it would seem that, given their zeal and their recent academic conditioning, the youthful teachers moved considerably beyond the perceived problems and interests of their mountain neighbors. Notes on the Psychology for Adults class taught by Horton indicate that it included "a brief survey of the nervous system" along with discussions of "How to think straight" which was the particular subject the group voted to concentrate upon.[63] Apparently Horton did attempt to relate and apply his proposed systematic process of thinking, of problem-solving, to personal and community experience. However, his teaching notes suggest that the sources which he used and the principles of analysis which he introduced were too abstract to be meaningful to his unsophisticated adult students.

As the number of resident students increased from one in the fall of 1932 to eight by the spring of 1933, their willing and flexible talents were added to the School's community staff. Dorothy Thompson, John Thompson's sister, who came to Highlander originally as a resident student and secretary, served as school-community librarian, giving some rudimentary order to the increasing number of books being donated to the School.[64] Others of these early students who were deeply concerned with workers' problems and the building of a labor movement locally and in the South, spent part of their time (as one student, son of a coal miner was described in a letter) "carrying on a vigorous crusade for a new social order" by holding meetings in numerous neighboring communities.[65]

The School was also becoming a center for a variety of political, religious and other gatherings "a meeting place for Southern radicals," as Horton had imagined it while travelling in Denmark. For example, the Fellowship of

Southern Churchmen, a group of primarily young Southern ministers attempting to give social voice to their religious concerns met at Monteagle with Highlander staff members as prominent participants.[66] And what was described as the first annual Socialist Summer School in the South" was convened at the Highlander Folk School in June 1933, with fifteen students in attendance.[67]

The developing School environment, too, was attracting a wide variety of visitors, writers, ministers, musicians, labor and political leaders, students, educators, government officials, social reformers. A note on one of the annual reports indicates "scarcely a day passed without at least one visitor."[68] Some of these came for a brief view of the unorthodox institution; some came as speakers; some as staff members for varying periods of time. Thus, the educational institution which was evolving in Summerfield in the winter and spring of 1932-1933 was unique.

Although Highlander's co-founder asserted that the School and its various social-educational activities "cannot be described," two of its major programs—its community program and its workers' education program—were in the embryonic stages of development. One of the difficulties in describing these early programs was their interrelatedness. Not only did the community and resident group share the same setting and staff, but they participated in many of the same community and movement-related activities. And, in fact, after the first year, even their membership overlapped, with some of the community members becoming resident students. Although the program continued, to some extent, to be interrelated until the end of the thirties, a community and later a countywide educational program related to the mountain poor was developed in the years 1933-1939. This program will be examined in Part II. At the same time, Highlander's workers' education program which was barely getting underway in the first year developed, during the next decade, into residential and extension programs related to the southern industrial union movement. These programs will he examined in Part III.

PART TWO

Crisis Education
for the
Mountain Poor

FOUR

A Community Program
for the
Mountain Poor

The Highlander Folk School which was to develop community and county programs for impoverished mountain workers and their families in the years 1933-1939[1] had begun, in the first year, to take shape as an institution. However exploratory the early educational efforts, Horton and West, functioning as the School's teachers, its administrators and the holders of its common property, evolved an internal structure which was to be on-going. In October 1934 the teaching staff, grown to five, obtained a State Charter of Incorporation for the Highlander Folk School.[2] In it, the teacher-incorporators, Myles Horton, Elizabeth Hawes, James Dombrowski, Rupert Hampton and Malcolm Chisholm, were named the first Board of Directors of the not-for-profit adult education institution. Thereafter, until 1940, the School's governing body consisted solely of its teachers.

Although all within the governing body shared responsibility for decisions affecting the School as they did for teaching, the allocation of major areas of responsibility to individuals according to their talents and interests began very early. Thus, Horton assumed responsibility for directing the educational program—a role which was formalized in 1934 when the staff named him Educational Director.[3] At the same time, the staff named Dombrowski, southern-born, Columbia University educated historian and Christian radical who came to the school in 1933, administrative head of the School with the title of Secretary. (He continued to carry this responsibility until he left the Highlander staff in 1942. Thereafter, Horton assumed the role whenever there was no one else on the staff qualified and willing to accept it.)

Early and continuing sources of funds were also identified in the first year. Primarily for the purpose of attracting interest in and support for the new institution, a group of nationally-known theologians, educators and others sympathetic to the School's new social order goals was asked to serve on a Highlander Folk School Advisory Committee. Members of the Committee were: Reinhold Niebuhr, Sherwood Eddy, Norman Thomas, George S. Counts, Joseph K. Hart, Arthur L. Swift, W. W. Alexander and Carl G. Taylor. Most of the $1,435.30[4] received by the School in the first year came from persons of similar backgrounds and persuasions, some forty in all.[5] And most of these continued to contribute to the School.

The careful way in which Highlander's co-founders husbanded the first meager funds—with no salaries and with the work of the School shared by students and teachers—was to become a part of institutional policy. As its income, in the form of contributions from organizations and individuals and tuition, increased to more than $6,000 in 1933-1934 and to four times that amount in the next decade,[6] the teaching staff continued to receive only living expenses and to participate with students in the work of the School.[7] In this way, it was not only possible to utilize more of the funds for the expanding educational program, but, as Horton explained, the School was able "to demonstrate how much can be done in educating for the new social order without much money.[8]

In terms of a permanent physical setting, the future of the Highlander Folk School was unclear in its first year and for several years thereafter. Not until 1935, when she felt assured that the "experiment" had proved itself, did Dr. Johnson decide to deed her mountain home and property to the School.[9] For a brief time, in the uncertain interim time, plans were made and work begun on the construction of a residential center at Allardt in Fentress County, Tennessee, where the School had been given some land.[10] As it turned out, Dr. Johnson's original frame house, somewhat enlarged, together with additional cabins for staff and students, and the original land, with an increase in acreage from forty to 200 acres, were to continue to serve as the physical setting for the Highlander Folk School.

The Bugwood Strike: The Beginning of Crisis-related Community Education

Highlander had begun to play a part in the lives of many families in the community in its first winter. Here, they could talk over their survival problems in community classes or discussions around the fire when they dropped by to visit or borrow a book. Here, they could also look beyond their immediate problems as they gathered for social evenings of music and square dancing , for "speakings" and for meetings with "people of the world," as a child in the community once described the School's visitors.

Yet for the aspiring staff members of the Highlander Folk School, relating education, as they did, to the building of a new social order, the School's community role was not yet a vital one. As Myles Horton expressed it

> There was a gap between our classes and the natural learning process which is life itself . . . It soon became apparent that basic emotional forces must he utilized if society is to be radically changed.[11]

There were two kinds of pre-conditions, the School believed, to developing an educational program which could basically influence community life. First, there was the relationship between the school and the community. The school and its teachers, it was emphasized, needed to be "a natural part of community life."[12] This relationship had been created consciously, day-by-day, since the School's co-founders had made their unobtrusive entry into Summerfield.

The other necessary pre-condition had to originate within the community: some generally perceived crisis situation which could rouse people to want to do something. As Myles Horton explained it

> You can only develop leadership capacities of people when they are involved in something, people in motion. Then you can get your educational ideas across.[13]

This crisis condition was supplied in the summer of 1933 by the "Bugwood" Strike—so named for the local split timber sold for distillation purposes. There had been discussions at the School for some time about the need for more income, the need for organizing. But the strike arid Highlander's educational support of it represented the first putting into practice of what Horton referred to as "purposive education."[14] The community program was to include, henceforth, not only discussion of subjects of concern and social and recreational activities, but direct participation in achieving an improved (if not a new) local social order.

The immediate circumstances of the strike were not numerous or complex. The Tennessee Products Company of Nashville contracted through a local agent to purchase 300 cords of timber per day. They hired the men at seventy-five cents per cord. This meant, the strikers calculated, that they were being paid seventy-five cents for working a ten-hour day.[15] And they recalled, "The timber is worse now than when we cut it for a dollar and a half . ."[16]

The strike was started by Henry Thomas, son of lay preacher Uncle Billy Thomas, in July 1933. Of himself and other men in the Summerfield Community of Grundy County, woodcutters of the cut-over land which they called "Bugwood," unable to subsist on the wages paid them, he exclaimed:

It takes a sharp ax, a strong hack, and a weak mind to cut Bugwood at seventy-five cents a day. Let's strike![17]

What followed is carefully chronicled in Highlander reports and correspondence. Excerpts from notes kept by resident student-community worker Dorothy Thompson reveal the day-by-day events and the School's role in them.[18] It is apparent that, from the first, the strike leaders turned to the Highlander Folk School to obtain counsel, to discuss with the staff, "What do we do now?" (It should he noted that these leaders, Henry Thomas and Bill Marlowe, along with other strikers and their families, had been enthusiastic participants in the School's classes and community program during the preceding months.) The early meetings of the strikers and their sympathizers held at the Highlander Folk School were latent with emotion. The slow-to-anger mountain people were, meeting by meeting, beginning to grow in their sense of common indignation. The School offered what was vitally necessary: an environment in which people felt free to speak out. The notes describe one such meeting, held on the school lawn, just about the time the moon was rising, which showed duly hardened lines in the men's faces, sunken cheeks from undernourishment, and ragged clothes. As the discussion proceeded, "A number of them got up and spoke about how hard they had to work and how little they got out of it."[19]

It was, however, when the strikers and their community supporters "were on fire to organize" that the School's role changed from a supportive to an active one.[20] For in the strikers' and strike sympathizers' desire to stand together, the School saw the possibility for encouraging a more broadly-based community organization, so lacking in Summerfield.

What emerged after lengthy public meetings, small group discussions and meetings of the so-called "Constitutional Committee," made up of community and strike representatives together with Myles Horton and Dorothy Thompson, was a unique kind of community organization, the Cumberland Mountain Workers' League.[21] Its purposes, as set down in the League's Constitution: "1) to prevent wholesale destruction of our forests;

and 2) to better the condition of the community by raising wages of members of this organization"[22] were not only diverse, but inconsistent. As the Secretary of the League explained later, "Our purpose was a little mixed up because we didn't want to cut the trees at all; but on the other hand, there wasn't any other kind of work to do."[23] Nevertheless, for Summerfield and the Highlander Folk School, the Constitution represented a major achievement the first community effort to set forth some agreed-upon goals.

Myles Horton, in a field report for a little Southern workers' education bulletin, announced hopefully, "Highlander Folk School is using the Monteagle Bugwood Strike and the resulting organization the Cumberland Mountain Workers' League, as an educational instrument . . . co-operating in every way, from picketing to advising."[24]

In developing an educational program related to the Bugwood Strike and the new Cumberland Mountain Workers' League, the School made imaginative and frequent use of working committees. Beginning with the committee to frame the League's Constitution and the Strike Committee to plan protest strategy, these committees, of which Highlander teachers were active members, provided functional centers for introducing new learning experiences. Committee meetings, in a real sense, served as classes, but classes with urgent decisions as the subjects under discussion. When the League decided that its first responsibility lay in redressing the strikers' grievances and that an appeal should be made to the government, it was necessary to form a committee which would acquaint itself with the relevant laws and codes and the agencies set up to administer them. To do this, men and women, most of whom had not finished elementary school, had to put their requests for information in writing, had to pore over the technical letters and reports coming to them in reply, and, on the basis of these, recommend to the larger membership what appeal should be made, what action taken. Highlander members of the committee, mindful of their educational role, sought not to dominate but to raise questions and suggest sources of information which would assist the corporate decision-making.

Committee functioning, especially in this period, was cumbersome. The letters composed by committee members to agency officials were laborious efforts much discussed and criticized before a final draft was agreed upon. But the results were honest, forceful statements which could only have come from the distressed people themselves. Their desperation is clearly communicated for example, in the opening sentence of a letter addressed to the Secretary of Labor, Frances Perkins, in November 1933

Winter comes early up here on the mountain and the promises made by Mr. Hugh Johnson that all industries would be forced to pay a living wage couldn't be used for buying food and clothing.[25]

Along with learning to function together in thinking through and analyzing their grievances and in framing letters to government agencies, the League members learned, painfully, slowly, the problems involved, the persistence required in trying to obtain help from the Federal bureaucracy. At first, some thought that their letters would bring results by return mail. Reports and articles during this period describe graphically the anxious wood cutters gathered outside the post office to get the news from Washington.[26] As their days of waiting turned to weeks and months and the letters outlining their wage grievances were referred from the Labor Department to the Department of Agriculture to the administrators of the National Recovery Act, the strikers became embittered. Jobless and wageless, with families close to starvation, many expressed the desire "to take matters into our own hands."[27]

Instead, they were encouraged in Highlander-led discussions to examine the political as well as the economic realities of their situation. Out of these discussions, it was decided that the Cumberland Mountain Workers' League should take a delegation to Washington to present their case directly to the Secretary of Labor. A Press Committee was formed to put together letters and articles describing their prolonged grievances and their delegation's plans. Articles announcing "Woodcutters Take Troubles to Washington" and "New Deal Slow in Tennessee Hills" appeared in papers, especially labor papers in various parts of the country, in the *Chattanooga News*, the *Milwaukee Leader* and the *Bridgeport Herald*.[28]

At the same time, through informal talks with several strikers from nearby hosiery mills and mines attending the Highlander resident session, the delegation was asked to describe the plight of some 2,000 of their fellow strikers as well. Thus, instead of reacting out of frustration as individuals, the League members were learning to act as an organization after step-by-step strategy planning and the gathering of wider support.

The trip itself produced no tangible results. When the delegation from the Cumberland Mountain Workers' League, including Highlander staff members and woodcutters, arrived at Secretary Perkins' office on November 23, 1933, a day well-remembered in local history, they were told that she was in conference. When they offered to wait, it was explained that "she could not be expected to give her attention to every delegation . . . who came to Washington." Even when they indicated their willingness to stay over for two or three days "if our money held out," they were told that the Secretary could not see them. They did note afterwards with some satisfaction that when they stopped at the NRA building, "Everybody knew about us," and then added sadly, "but no one knew what to do."[29]

Added to the disappointment of the unsuccessful delegation to Washington, the Tennessee Products Company announced summarily that it was cancelling all community contracts for the cutting of wood. Thus the strike which had begun with such bold optimism ended essentially in a lock-out.

But the spirit of solidarity engendered by the strike and the confidence in their ability to cope with basic problems, growing out of forming their own "people's organization," could not be discouraged by these set-backs. At the same meeting of the Cumberland Mountain Workers' League, members heard the report of their delegation and of the cancellation of local woodcutting contracts and turned their thoughts to the future. Having had many informal "classes" as a part of their committee work they now requested that Highlander classes "be conducted in conjunction with their regular League meetings."[30] They began to discuss, too, the idea of some sort of community self-help venture. Their spirit was perhaps best captured in a letter written by the League's secretary to President Roosevelt some months later

> Don't get the idea that we have been sitting around waiting. We lost all faith in the NRA doing anything soon after our trip to Washington . . . we decided to do something for ourselves.[31]

In retrospect, the strike continued to have great significance in the mind of the man who started it and in the mind of the School's founder and educational director. Thirty years later, Henry Thomas, an almost blind old man sitting on his cabin porch in Summerfield, recalled the depression, the strike and the early days of the School. "People were in pretty bad shape," he commented, recalling the period when his family had barely enough to eat. He mentioned the speakers whom he heard and met, the singing, the ways in which his entire family were involved in the School. Of the Bugwood Strike and the subsequent meetings and classes held at Highlander he said, "The most important thing that people ever learned from Highlander was what we learned then: how we could help ourselves." He went on to enumerate some of the things that they had learned, "How to handle our daily problems, to do by organizing, by showing our power and our strength. . . . "[32] And Myles Horton, looking back to the organization of the community around the Bugwood Strike, stated

> This was the first opportunity involving the recognized needs of the people around which we could develop a vital community education program. A similar use of crisis situations on a Southwide-scale provided the basis for the development of subsequent educational programs with farmer and labor organizations and civil rights groups.[33]

From Crisis to Cooperatives: The Community Learns to Help Itself

In December of 1933, just one month after the Cumberland Mountain Workers' League had faced the facts of the unresolved strike, community members decided on the organization of a cooperative as "the only sensible line to follow" in solving their "living problem." The Highlander educational director wrote to Dr. Lilian Johnson, "At present, there is a class going on in which the practical elements are being worked out."[34]

Although cooperative enterprise in the United States was growing sufficiently in the twenties and thirties to be referred to as a "movement",[35] it is doubtful whether the movement would have come to Summerfield without the influence of the Highlander Folk School. Dr. Johnson had attempted to introduce the idea of cooperatives early in her efforts to educate her wary mountain neighbors. She had begun a credit union which she was convinced was needed. But her convictions were never widely shared, and she was finally left to pay back its small number of investors.[36]

In contrast, Myles Horton talked about cooperatives in relation to the Danish farmers' experience, but made no attempt to teach about them or urge them upon the community. It was, instead, the environment of the School with staff and students and community members coming to cooperative decisions about classes and community activities to be undertaken which gave Summerfield citizens their first understanding, experientially, of the cooperative idea. Later, in the summer of 1933, the School initiated a cooperative buying project whereby families who wished to do so joined with the school in buying basic food stuffs.

Most important for the community members, they had been learning to cooperate, to work together, in the Bugwood Strike and the Cumberland Mountain Workers' League. Thus, when the first cooperative enterprise was established in Summerfield, its leaders were the leaders of the League and they called it, appropriately, the Cumberland Mountain Cooperative. Once the decision had been made to embark on a community cooperative, the Highlander Folk School was needed as it had been when the striking wood-cutters decided to organize. It was needed in helping, technically, to put together a proposal for the Federal Emergency Relief Administration funds. And it was needed, above all, in teaching people the principles of organizing a cooperative and helping them to develop their own plans and procedures.

The comprehensive proposal of the Cumberland Mountain Cooperative as submitted to the FERA in January 1934 represented the collective dreams and efforts of emerging community leaders in consultation with Highlander staff and specialists from the Tennessee Valley Authority. It included the leasing of a farm to be cooperatively run; the establishment of a cooperative laundry which, it was indicated, would supply cash income to the women of the community and the securing of a small, cooperative industrial shop.[37]

In a letter to the administrator of the FERA, Harry C. Hopkins, endorsing the application, a TVA official emphasized the feasibility of the Cumberland Cooperative. It could, he stated, "make fifty families, most of them now on relief, entirely self-sustaining." He cited as a major asset the presence of "the teaching and training staff" of the Highlander Folk School.[38] As it turned out, Federal funds for the proposed budget of some $19,000 were not forthcoming to the inexperienced and, above all, politically insignificant Cumberland Mountain Cooperative.

But the Highlander classes on cooperatives carried on with high interest. A staff report observed, "There was more time spent on talking, discussing, arguing and planning the various cooperative ideas than can be shown on paper." Along with the staff presentations and animated group discussions and the bringing in of agricultural extension resource persons, the community students did a survey of their neighbors to assess their readiness to join the cooperative venture and their talents and resources for assisting it. The survey-makers verified the fact that the families were "all unemployed" and "all favorably [sic] to co-op plans." They also noted that the community skilled labor force included five carpenters, two stone masons, one mechanic, one cobbler and two practical nurses and that other resources included thirty-seven acres under cultivation and a livestock population of three horses and six cows.[39] In the process, they learned to make simple questionnaires and put together their findings. More important, they had an experience in thinking together cooperatively in preparation for working together.

Beyond this, a Highlander Folk School staff report expressed the optimistic hope that they were helping the men and women of Summerfield "to know what cooperatives mean to working people," not just as an end to themselves, "but as a step toward a new social order."[40] No doubt, some members of the Cumberland Mountain Cooperative saw the long-term possibilities of achieving a better society through cooperative enterprise, particularly those among its leaders who were also members of the recently-formed Socialist local in Summerfield. However, the majority of community members subscribing to the idea were, as the Secretary of the Workers' League put it, "tired of going hungry because of insufficient relief and no jobs."[41]

Determined to carry out some part of their broad plans without the Federal funds, women members of the Cumberland Mountain Cooperative, including women staff and students at Highlander, formed a new organization, the Highlander Folk Cooperative. It defined as its immediate objective a community canning project, and noted that the Highlander Folk School "wants to do all of its canning with us." But like the Cumberland Mountain Workers' League, the new organization projected a much broader purpose. It might undertake, the women agreed, "any kind of cooperative activity that will help the community and prove that better ways of living can be worked out."[42]

A number of meetings and many work hours later, the Highlander Folk Cooperative was able to report proudly that "eleven hundred cans of vegetables were canned." More than that, Summerfield had come alive with the cooperative activity. A report written in the midst of that activity best describes the community's involvement and high hopes

> The Cooperative Cannery is now in operation. Children, boys and girls, and men all helped, in the canning, in woodcutting, and hauling water; Elsie Pearl Horton is going to take care of the children while their mothers are at work . . . men and women in the community drop in from time to time, and many of them, whether or not they have joined the Cooperative, lend a hand.[43]

Looking ahead, the author of the report, a member of the Women's Managing Committee predicted

The Cooperative Cannery is going to realize its purpose of getting more canned goods into the homes against the hard winter and of proving that cooperative living is not only more beneficial, but more pleasant and easy than "each fellow for himself."[44]

The potential for cooperative enterprise and education which loomed bright and hopeful in Summerfield in the summer of 1934 was never realized or even fully explored. What was lacking was neither willingness nor imagination, but the requisite funds for any such major community undertaking. Inspired by their modest success, the Highlander Folk Cooperators, working with the Highlander Folk School staff, again applied for Federal funds. This time their proposal and budget were more soundly and specifically defined, based both on rethinking and on recent experience. This time, too, they were mindful of the need for broader support, and thus their applications to the FERA included the endorsement of a carefully selected advisory committee which included the Grundy County Superintendent of Schools, a prominent farmer and Justice of the Peace, the Postmaster of Tracy City (the county seat) and the Smith-Hughes teacher of agriculture in the county high school.[45] The School was able to further strengthen the application by gathering support for the self-help application from its friends around the country among labor, liberal clergy and educators.

Ironically, in March 1935, when the Federal Emergency Relief Administration finally announced a grant of $7,000 to the jubilant Highlander Folk Cooperative, the School was the cause for the funds being summarily withdrawn by the Tennessee Emergency Relief Administration. In its less than three years of existence, the very name, Highlander Folk School, had come to inflame Southern industrial leaders and their conservative allies in State government and the press. They were quick to protest a grant to the little group of Summerfield families whose cooperative bore a dangerously similar name. The cooperative was obviously associated with the "radical school" which, in turn, actively identified with strikers and emerging unions and dared to proclaim the desirability of a new social order.[46]

An article in the ultra-conservative Knoxville Journal quoted the angry President of the Southern States Industrial Council, John Edgerton, as saying

It would be interesting . . . for the taxpayers of Tennessee and of this Capitalistic nation to know just what the relationship is between this so-called Highland Folk Cooperative and the Highlander Folk School. . . .[47]

Edgerton, a major spokesman for the anti-union forces of the South, had long been able to boast before his organization and its counterpart, the National Association of Manufacturers, that in his section of the country labor unions had made little headway. The founding of the Highlander Folk School in the fall of 1932 had been an affront and its influence on a small but increasing number of organized working people in Tennessee and beyond, a threat. Added to these grievances, the educational director of this School teaching "un-American doctrines" had dared to invite the President of the Southern Industrial Council to speak at the Highlander Folk School and on the same program with a union leader! Still stinging from this "greatest insult ever known to the Anglo-Saxon South," as he expressed it in a letter to his fellow manufacturers,[48] Edgerton was pleased to lead the way in getting the grant revoked.

Moral indignation was added to this protest by evangelist Billy Sunday who, holding a revival in Chattanooga, preached a special sermon on the "Iniquities of Reds and Labor Organizers" and condemned the grant.[49] And far off in the North, another conservative voice, *The Chicago Tribune*, contained an accusing article about the allocation headlined "Relief Grant to Radical School Stirs Citizenry."[50]

What was surprising was not that this storm of protest could cause the Tennessee Emergency Relief Administration to use its discretionary powers in choosing not to give the Highlander Folk Cooperative a grant, but that so great a protest had occurred. Clearly, conservative forces in Tennessee, in the South and beyond were believers in the power of crisis and social movement-related education!

Although,with the help of the conservative southern press, the Highlander Folk School and its radical young leadership which called for a new social order were having an impact far beyond the Tennessee mountain area where the School was located, its efforts to help the people of Summerfield develop their own cooperative organizations as one step toward economic democracy were hardly a threat to the old order. Subsequent school efforts to help the community develop cooperatives not dependent on government funds, including a furniture-making cooperative and a consumers' cooperative store never materialized. In the case of the furniture cooperative, exploratory discussions were held with experienced mountain craftsman Uncle Billy Thomas who was willing to take on jobless young men of the community as apprentices in his shop. Under his leadership, it was agreed, they could acquire artistry and skills as they made chairs and other articles which "could be bartered to advantage" or "sold in the valley" or in Chattanooga "through the help of unions." Since Uncle Billy needed only twenty dollars to enlarge his shop, a sum quickly contributed by Dr. Johnson, the project seemed practical as well as desirable.[51] What was needed, in addition, were young men who wished to be apprentices and these, apparently, were never forthcoming.

There is no indication in program reports as to why the cooperative buying club initiated by the School and a small group of families did not grow into a consumers' store, as had been hoped. But given the poverty in the community and the meagerness of Highlander's resources as a residential community school, it is difficult to imagine how such a venture could have been undertaken without some sort of outside assistance—no matter how great the local enthusiasm for cooperatives. There also remained the question as to whether, once under way, the community would have been able to muster sufficient purchasing power to keep the store in operation.

What School and Community Learned from the Program

Viewed substantively, in terms of what the several early organizations achieved in relation to their goals, they could not be described as "successful." The woodcutters' strike produced the Cumberland Mountain Workers' League but no increase in their impossibly low wages and, in fact, they lost even these wages. The Highlander Folk Cooperative produced big hopes and 1100 cans of food.

Viewed as educative experiences, the organization of the Cumberland Mountain Workers' League and the several cooperative ventures were of value both to the inexperienced radical educators and the inexperienced community participants. The community and the School learned from the failures as well as the successes of the organizations. Thus it was learned, however painfully, that cooperatives which were dependent upon considerable government or other outside support were not sound ventures, at least in the depressed mountain area, in a period of national depression. It was learned, too, that any cooperative venture, no matter how objectively sound and practical, must relate to perceived community needs or interests.

Two cooperative ventures were subsequently undertaken which met these criteria and which, as a result, played a part in community life for a decade or more. One of these was a sewing cooperative among the women of the community who came to the School once a week to make quilts and other articles to be sold "wherever there is a market." This modest little producers' cooperative not only succeeded in finding a market for its handiwork over the years, but, as a staff member pointed out, it was "giving hardworking and shut-in women a chance to exchange ideas and information over colorful materials."[52]

The other and most successful cooperative venture—in terms of its social-educational contribution to participating parents and children and its involvement of total community support—was the Summerfield Nursery School.[53] For this Highlander-community developed institution, the School secured the services of an innovative young teacher, Claudia Lewis of the Bank Street School in New York, and community members provided whatever they could—milk, produce, fuel, equipment, quilts, and rag dolls, as well as their services to assist the day-by-day program.

The community learned, as well, that no matter how strong the local support of their organizations, they needed to be more broadly affiliated, they needed to be part of an organization or a movement larger and stronger than the Cumberland Mountain Workers' League or the Highlander Folk Cooperative. This need for broad affiliation had been apparent to the founder and friends of the proposed mountain school who had projected an institution which would develop local leadership for a southern labor movement. It began to be apparent to the Cumberland Mountain Workers League at the time of the unsuccessful Bugwood Strike. When they sought the support of the Tennessee Federation of Labor, its Secretary had replied, "I am not permitted to ask for the recognition of an independent organization," and added, if the men of your community desire to affiliate with the bona fide labor organization, I shall be glad to render any assistance I can."[54] Later, when the community lost its grant for the Highlander Folk Cooperative, that learning was underscored. Their opposition in the South and nation was well organized; their friends were not.

Of all the kinds of learning opportunities presented by the evolving community program, the most important for Horton, as an experimental educator, was the opportunity, for the first time, to apply the ideas he had gathered from sociologists Park and Ward to program development. These ideas which he tested out in Summerfield—that understanding can best be achieved through involvement in an actual situation and that conflict or crisis situations can be utilized to bring about social change—were to become operating principles as the school developed programs in relation to labor and political conflicts in Grundy County and, later, in relation to the southwide labor movement.

FIVE

A County Program
for the
Mountain Poor

The decision of the Highlander Folk School, toward the end of 1935, to move beyond its community program to a countywide program of union organizing and education among relief workers came about as a result of developments on the national as well as the local scene. Nationally, the pro-labor policies and programs of Franklin Roosevelt's New Deal government provided the larger environment in which such a union organizing program was possible. Locally, the extremely low wages paid relief workers, coupled with widely reported corruption and mismanagement in county relief administration and county government[1] brought about the unrest, the crisis situation which was the immediate basis for the program.

The coming of the New Deal marked a turning point for the depressed working people of a depressed nation. New relief work agencies were created to give employment to the unemployed. New labor legislation was enacted to protect the rights of workers, including relief workers, to organize and bargain collectively. In Grundy County, as in other counties over the South and nation, a local office of the Federal Works Progress Administration was opened where unemployed miners, woodcutters and others were hired to work on local road improvement and school building projects. But in Grundy County, relief workers were paid the lowest wages paid relief workers in this lowest of southern low wage areas—$19.20 per month![2] "This," a Highlander staff member wrote to a friend in the East, "is not the weekly wage, it constitutes the monthly wage." And she went on to describe men going without a meal on the job to leave the food for their families.[3]

Along with a core group of awakened men and women from Summerfield whose experience in the Cumberland Mountain Workers' League and the Cumberland Mountain Cooperative had won them to the potential of organizing, there were other ready participants for the program throughout the county: ex-miners whose fathers had learned to "do by organizing" as early members of the Knights of Labor and the United Mine Workers. It was with this background and these resources in mind that the Highlander Folk School began to make plans for a countywide workers' education program. The young son of an ex-coal miner who with his father was active in the county program, Lewie Vaughn, recalled in one oversimplified, but not inaccurate sentence how it began

> After President Roosevelt was elected and the NRA was set up, several of the workers, along with Dad and myself, with the help of the Highlander Folk School began organizing again, as most of our unions were torn to pieces.[4]

Education As a Part of Union Organizing

In developing county plans, the School clearly drew upon its recent experience in helping community members acquire new skills and understanding through the process of building local self-help organizations. In this case, it proposed to relate its educational efforts to the organizing of underpaid relief workers into locals affiliated with the International Hod Carriers, Building and Common Laborers Union, A.F. of L. Myles Horton explained candidly to the district organizer that Highlander was utilizing the organizing of Common Laborers' locals as a basis for carrying out an educational program in the county. Valuing Horton and his staff as co-workers and fellow members of organized labor, the union leader agreed to assist the program. Cooperation with the School and its workers education program is indicated not only by the special low dues rates and many letters of advice which the district organizer wrote to the Highlander staff and the inexperienced presidents of new locals, but his participation in weekend workers' institutes held at the Folk School as well as in county mass meetings dealing with "Discussion of vital matters pertaining to WPA workers and their families."[5] Highlander-trained local leaders such as Bill Marlowe, who had been a leader in the Bugwood Strike and subsequently was a Highlander resident student for an eight week workers' education term, worked with the staff in helping to organize the local unions. In the process, he and Vaughn's father and others received training as leaders and developers of other leaders.

At the same time, officers of the new locals with varying degrees of competence were learning how to bring their fellow workers into the organization and, having accomplished this, how, democratically to run a meeting and work on local problems. In turn, relief workers, as union members, were learning within the locals about the rights guaranteed them by their government employer and how, together, they could go about securing them. In organizing a union, the problems and, therefore, the learning process of the county field worker began with helping a potential leader convene an exploratory meeting. There is considerable correspondence, for example, with one such anxious but interested local leader about where to hold the meeting—whether it would be "unwise to meet at the Court House," whether the men "might feel afraid that the WPA administrator will get the news and take action against them."[6] When he finally felt sufficiently supported and strengthened to convene a meeting, the first important step for both the field worker and his protege had been taken.

In another instance, setting a meeting date presented problems. Again there is a sheaf of correspondence between a local convener and a patient organizer. Letters indicate that careful plans were made to meet with WPA workers on a given date in a given community and then cancelled twice without warning, first as the local representative explained later, "because they didn't get the notice until it was to [sic] late" and later because by waiting until payday, "they might have their dollars to join our organization.[7]

Education within local unions

Once a union was organized, the Highlander teaching staff devoted considerable time to attending early local meetings—two to four per week, School reports indicate. The setting and the democratic processes utilized at these meetings tended to he quite primitive. A librarian who served as a workers' literature teacher, Berthe Daniel, wrote graphically of meetings held "out on the mountain where we gather in an old shack." She described the relief workers who arrived early, before dark, and "squat about in small groups—such as the miners are used to" conducting their union business. "Someone goes out for a lamp when dusk gathers," she explained, "and they continue. In the circle of the light's rays . . . they bring forth their grievances."[8]

Although the setting for these meetings remained primitive, there is considerable evidence in the records of meetings of increasing sophistication in the new members' understanding of unions and of using union machinery.

Notes on the earliest meetings indicate grave concern with the question of whether, as WPA workers, they might be accused of organizing against the government. This question was only resolved when copies of official memos from the WPA office in Washington were secured by Highlander and circulated through local leaders stating that "this administration holds that workers have the right to organize."[9]

As members of a local union moved in their agenda of problems from the right to organize to their individual and collective grievances, they learned, with a Highlander staff member as guide, orderly procedures for dealing with them. With increasing skill, they learned how to hear and discuss complaints, to appoint committees from the membership to study them and how (with the aid of appropriate directives and background supplied by Highlander) to define and establish those grievances before bringing them to the County WPA administrator for action.

In discussing and analyzing their most basic grievance—their lower-than-subsistence wage scale—and in studying government directives, they came to understand the reason for that low wage scale. Grundy County was classified as an agricultural area, putting it in the lowest possible wage category. The leaders, in turn, held a joint meeting of the Executive Committees of the several locals and, aided by Highlander staff and reference materials, put together an array of data to prove that the county should be reclassified as industrial, thereby automatically raising the wages for common labor.[10]

As in the past, a committee was formed to write a letter to the government on behalf of the locals, this time to WPA Administrator Hopkins.[11] Having grown in their understanding of political as well as grievance processes, they did not merely send the letter and wait. Instead, the leaders approached their Congressman, Sam D. McReynolds, who suggested that they back their request for reclassification with a countywide petition. In chronicling the increasingly skillful tactics of their relief worker students a Highlander report notes that the union petition "was signed by practically every businessman and office holder in the county."[12]

By such carefully planned appeals, the Common Laborers' locals of Grundy County, in their first year of existence, gained the attention and respect of WPA administrators at both the county and regional levels.[13] They gained, too, however, the enmity of the anti-union, anti-Highlander State WPA Administrator, Colonel Harry S. Berry, who expressed publicly on many occasions his hatred for the School as "a communistic organization" which he asserted was "feeding muscovite hops to the relief clients of Grundy County"[14]

In spite of Colonel Berry and their inability to obtain reclassification of the county and the wage scale, the WPA locals continued to grow in membership and respect. They were able, in some cases, to obtain wage increases. An article in the School newspaper, the *Highlander Fling*, announced in its September 1936 issue, "The Palmer Local with the help of the United Mine Workers in that end of the county, in a week's peaceful strike, recently won an increase from fifteen to twenty-three cents" for semi-skilled work.[15]

Along with these gains, Highlander's developing program of residential workers' education had begun to inspire members of locals to broaden their organizational objectives. They moved in their concerns beyond their own pressing daily needs to a concern for "organizing the teachers to work for higher educational standards in the county." And, stimulated by a Highlander-arranged visit to a cooperative store operated by an Alabama textile workers' local, the Grundy County locals raised $600 among their members "toward a fund to start a cooperative store."[16]

Interaction of Relief Workers and Resident Students

In helping the WPA workers within the framework of their local unions to broaden their social objectives and perspective on the labor movement, the Highlander Folk School provided a variety of opportunities for interaction of county union members and their families with students and staff of Highlander's small but growing residential workers education program. (The experience, of course, was also important for the resident students who gained first-hand knowledge and insights through relating to local workers, their problems and organizations.)

One intensive kind of interaction occurred when members of community and county organizations attended resident sessions with students from other parts of Tennessee and the South and, occasionally, from other parts of the country and other countries. Thus, for example, among the resident students in the Highlander Folk School Winter Term for 1935 were an Arkansas college graduate with a degree in music who was seeking to find her role in the movement;[17] a member of a Clothing Workers' local from Knoxville, Tennessee;[18] a young textile worker from Atlanta and a transport worker from Finland, active in unions and cooperatives in his county, along with four men and women from the community who had taken leading roles in the Cumberland Mountain Workers' League and the several cooperative ventures as well as in the new local unions.[19]

At the same time, many meetings and conferences were held at the School in which community and county as well as the resident students participated. They participated, for example, in a Build the Union Week in 1935 which brought a national labor education figure, Mark Starr of the International Ladies Garment Workers' Union, to Highlander, as well as representatives of southern workers' education, the southern labor movement and the Tennessee Valley Authority.[20] The staff also conducted evening classes involving community students. Of local attendance at "speakings" and classes, one account of a resident session indicates

> When we have visiting speakers at the school, usually twice or more each week, the community makes up a large portion of the audience. Few live in the neighborhood who haven't at one time or another attended speakings as well as classes.[21]

And on a wider, more informal basis, community and county families continued to participate with resident students in the weekly square dance, music and social evening, still called a Community Night.[22]

Along with these several kinds of interaction taking place at the School itself, interaction between resident students and members of Grundy County locals occurred out in the county. As part of their field training as union leaders and workers' education teachers, all of the resident students took part in countywide WPA workers' union rallies and mass meetings and in weekly union meetings and other activities of the new locals.[23] They attended first as observers who returned to their Highlander classes to evaluate what they had observed. Later, in conjunction with such classes as Labor Problems, Public Speaking, Labor Drama and Labor Journalism, they contributed their newly-acquired skills by leading discussions, giving talks, putting on plays and skits and helping the WPA locals get out news sheets related to union plans and protest demonstrations.

And, moving far beyond the School and the county in their shared learning experiences, Highlander arranged for its resident and county students to visit and participate in strike situations, to view and learn first hand about the regional development projects of the Tennessee Valley Authority, to meet with students in other workers' education centers such as the Southern Summer School for Workers in North Carolina and to observe some of the most promising new unions in action—for example, the Huntsville, Alabama, union which had developed a members' consumer cooperative.[24] Highlander made it possible, too, for representatives of both groups to participate in State and Southern labor conferences. Here, at such meetings as the All-Southern WPA and Relief Workers' Conference in Chattanooga in March 1936,[25] they not only met union and relief worker delegates with problems akin to their own, but they got a sense of the excitement and potential power of the awakening southern labor movement. It was all part of the crisis-related program which began three years before when a group of Summerfield woodcutters laid down their axes and refused to cut "Bugwood."

Labor's Political Conference of Grundy County

In his earliest broad projection of an educational program for the Southern Mountains School, Myles Horton had been convinced that in order to have a genuine democracy, people needed to learn to develop their own political as well as economic organizations. Full recognition of the need in Grundy County was slow to develop. The crisis was a prolonged and bitter one. Leaders of local WPA unions, so hopeful in their first year of operation, were more and more frustrated in their efforts to settle members' grievances. Non-union men were given preference in jobs. Many union men were laid off. State policies became increasingly punitive toward the out-spoken Highlander-educated local unions. They had learned, too well for the conservative State authorities, their collective rights. Myles Horton, describing the situation in the winter and spring of 1937 wrote:

> Knots of gloomy men watched the gains of more than a year of hard work and sacrifice slipping through their fingers. Word that the union was done for spread through the county. Membership dropped.[26]

In desperation, the WPA unions called a countywide strike. Others joined them, determined to stand together against the continuing anti-union policies of State administrators. But at the end of long months of protesting, there were increasing numbers of jobless union members and hungry, disheartened families. It was only, as a Highlander staff member expressed it, when "politics had entered the picture" that the strikers got results. It was only when a county union committee, in consultation with the Highlander Folk School, threatened an organized vote against Congressman Sam McReynolds, coming up for re-election, that Washington officials began to heed local complaints. And it was only then that Tennessee officials agreed to adhere to national regulations and re-hire the union relief workers.

Shortly thereafter, in April 1938, a new organization came into being: Labor's Political Conference of Grundy County. Its members included not only the four WPA Common Laborers' Unions but locals of the United Mineworkers, Bakery Workers and the American Federation of Teachers, made up of Highlander staff members—ten local unions in all. In forming the Political Conference, Myles Horton indicated, the ground work had been carefully laid.[27] Before any action was taken in the county, representatives of the several local unions, along with a group of Highlander Folk School teachers and resident students, attended the founding of the first such political organization in the state in nearby Hamilton County, an urban labor stronghold. Returning to their locals, the Conference idea was discussed and approved by the several locals. Thus, when the meeting to set up the conference was convened, some 250 union members were present and committed to act. At the meeting, they approved a constitution based on the organization in Hamilton County; they heard from statewide and regional union leaders who stressed the significance of their new endeavors, and they made plans to select a labor slate of candidates for the coming county elections.

At the organizing meeting, it was agreed that all candidates would be "invited to appear before local organizations" and the Conference, and "given ample opportunity to present their views before a labor slate was finally approved."[28] The political education program which Highlander, working with Conference leaders, developed included a series of carefully planned rallies throughout the county. Sponsored by local unions, the rallies featured southwide labor leaders who gave broad perspective to the Grundy County contests. In small mining towns such as Coalmont, people were given the opportunity to hear Roy Lawrence, Director of the CIO's Southern organizing campaign for the hosiery and textile industries. Lawrence, who enlisted the talents of much of the Highlander staff in the campaign,[29] appreciated the relationship of the School's local union education efforts to the larger movement.

Along with the rallies, a mimeographed county labor paper, *The WPA Worker*, appeared for a time. Prepared by local union leaders with the editorial assistance of Highlander resident students and staff, its purposes were to urge "all organized WPA workers in the county . . . to go to the polls and support the candidates of the Labor's Political Conference" and to encourage other workers to join the WPA locals—preferably before the election. The paper also attempted to educate readers to national developments in WPA policy and program and to acquaint them with some of the reasons for the considerable wage differential in the North and South.[30]

Response to labor's candidates grew as more and more people over the county were reached by the rallies and news sheets and by the devoted efforts of members of the WPA locals. "The union campaign fund of $20.00," a Highlander staff account observed, "was augmented by scores of voluntary campaigners who tramped through the county for weeks prior to the primary."[31] As incumbent politicians and the interests who had selected them became alarmed, labor candidates were branded as "reds." As elections grew closer, there were frequent reports of poll taxes being paid off and, when the day arrived, of voters being bought off with whisky.

The results of Highlander's and local labor's first political education campaign were close but successful. Labor's Political Conference of Grundy County elected a Sheriff, three Road Commissioners, a County Court Clerk and a Superintendent of Schools. The Highlander Report for 1938 includes a section entitled "Political Activities" in which it announced

All the unions united for the first time in a joint campaign. The liberal element of the county was appealed to and the Conference was successful in electing to office a complete progressive slate. Considering that the Conference had only short four weeks in which to work, and that it had the vigorous opposition of coal interests that dominated this county for fifty years, this record is truly remarkable.[32]

Not long after the victory, a writer visiting in the region, impressed with the way in which local unions had used the ballot to upset the dominant interests, observed, "Something is to be said for the idea that the way to effective political action in the South starts with the counties."[33] If a closer analysis had been made, the author might well have suggested instead that the way to more effective political action in the South might start with workers education in the counties.

Stay-In of WPA Strikers and Their Families: Education in a Protest Situation

Probably Highlander's most dramatic and imaginative use of a crisis as the basis for the local workers' education program occurred within the "stay-in" of jobless WPA workers and their families who moved into Grundy County WPA office on February 10, 1939, and refused to leave until they were promised work. As one of the county participants who was a Highlander student recalled the action

> About five hundred men, women and children moved into the WPA office at Tracy City crying, "We want our jobs back and we are staying until we get 'em," and stay they did, day and night. Ten days and ten nights we held possession of the building.[34]

The stay-in protest came after renewed punitive action against union members and union-backed county officials by the State WPA Administrator. When he could not force the resignation of several labor-backed local officials against union opposition, he summarily closed down all county works projects, leaving some 700 WPA workers with neither jobs nor relief.[35]

Historically, there were precedents for the stay-in of county WPA workers in the widespread sit-down strikes which were called by unions in a number of industries across the nation beginning in 1937. However, the Grundy County protest was unique in its involvement of whole families and in its democratically planned and administered daily program of educational as well as strike activities. With the help of staff and students of the Highlander Folk School winter resident term, the stay-in itself was a kind of spirited, short-lived residential session, in spite of its setting. Along with daily discussions and speakers on "What we are fighting for," featuring Southwide and local leaders and Highlander participants, there were evening recreational programs of games and skits, music furnished by mountain fiddle and guitar and group singing with a favorite song being "We Shall Not Be Moved." The group had its own mimeographed newspaper, *We the People*,[36] put together daily at the School office; its bulletin board announcing the latest developments and its several special committees: a Press Committee, a Relief Committee, a Negotiating Committee. There was even a self-appointed body to keep order: three union deputy sheriffs selected from among the demonstrators.

Judging by accounts in the daily news sheet, morale of the workers and their families was high. One such account opened with characteristic cheerfulness, "WPA office of Tracy City running full-time, day and night—twenty-four hour service—meals served—everyone having a good time . . ."[37] However, the success of the stay-in, Highlander and protest leaders knew, depended not only on high morale and a stimulating educational program to give the strikers a larger sense of purpose, but upon tangible public support. Food, fuel and equipment were needed and funds to transport workers and their families from all sections of the county. With Highlander's assistance, the protesters were able to present an effective appeal to their fellow citizens in the county and to unions and friends of labor in the North and South. In the county, they held meetings and rallies, staged a jobless parade and distributed their outspoken little newspaper. Not only did they obtain the support of other union members, but of some local merchants who donated food, money, a stove and even a tent which served as an emergency soup kitchen. In Tennessee and other parts of the country, Pictures and news releases portraying the stay-in and the issues behind it were carried by the labor press and the general press. In addition, an appeal letter was sent out to hundreds of friends of the School, describing the mass stay-in of jobless WPA workers coming in from all over the county in spite of rain and cold. The letter emphasized, unless the "unions win their fight, all their struggle and sacrifice . . . will be lost."[38]

As a result of the public education efforts and the "preaching, singing and parading, one of the participants recounted with enthusiasm, "We have won the sympathy of all the people and an impartial investigation from Washington and a promise of work cards."[39] On February 16, 1939, a WPA administrator flew in from Washington to investigate. Not only did he instruct all officials concerned that the discrimination against unions had to end, but, as a local leader proudly noted, he complimented union officials on the strength of their organization.[40]

In practical effect, however, the stay-in victory was an empty one. As Union President Dillard King observed several weeks later, "A few more work cards have come out—most of the union leaders receiving theirs—but those who need them most—those with large families are still out of work."[41]

Where Education Was Not Enough: The Lack of an Economic Base

Prior to the stay-in, the State WPA Administrator was the enemy, against whom the unemployed workers and their families had been roused. During the disappointing weeks of waiting after the successful demonstration, the workers, led by members of a Highlander class for WPA union members,[42] began to face up to the more complex enemy: the basic economic problems plaguing the county. The WPA had helped. It had served as a stop gap during what the Federal Government had looked upon as an emergency period. It had furnished temporary employment at meager wages to desperate men and women. But it was becoming apparent to the worker-students that this source of jobs was diminishing in the county as in the nation. The continuing lack of opportunity had to be faced. It had to be faced because as *Work*, a national newspaper for WPA workers and the unemployed put it, "There is nothing but WPA in Grundy County."[43]

The basic economic problems had been apparent to the Highlander Folk School before it embarked on the program of workers' education in the county, utilizing the WPA unions as a vehicle. The staff was convinced that the divided, hard-pressed mountain people had to learn how to work together collectively within community organizations and local unions in order to cope with immediate problems and to relate to the new southern industrial union movement. Through participation in the larger movement, with the collective political as well as economic power which this implied, mountain problems might be given a significant voice. With this organizational experience, the workers and their families who left the area would be better able to assume more effective roles elsewhere.

In deciding what should be done about the county's problems, discussion moved quickly from the WPA class to a public meeting. Under the leadership of Dolph Vaughn, Highlander-trained Business Agent for the county unions, "a committee from the class went all around the county" urging that a meeting be held and inviting delegates from the Common Laborers' Union, the Workers' Alliance, the United Mine Workers and the American Federation of Teachers to bring their ideas.[44] The meeting which was convened at the County Court House on February 26, 1939, as described by a participant from the School, "turned into a general meeting of the citizens of Grundy County" with merchants, farmers, WPA workers, miners, coal company and local officials in attendance. [45] Present also at the invitation of the School and the unions were special resource persons, the

Commissioner of Public Welfare for Tennessee and representatives of other State agencies.

Out of this meeting came many descriptions of the county's problems, many tributes to the hardiness of its citizens and the establishment of a committee to arrange for immediate relief and consider a long-term program for the county. Those elected to the committee included the educational director of Highlander and several of the WPA union leaders trained by the School along with representatives of farm, business and other interests. Out of this meeting, too, came a frequently stated recognition of the need for thinking together for a solution beyond the WPA. As an ex-miner, member of the Workers' Alliance put it, "I have always been a working man, but I've only worked one day this year. We need WPA work, but that barely keeps you alive," and then he added with emphasis, "It is time something is done . . ."[46]

This recognition was never followed by State, Federal or other action commensurate to the task, although there were other meetings held, including a meeting to discuss recommendations for action based on an American Public Welfare study of Grundy County problems.[47]

With the collapse, in 1939, of WPA projects in the county (and elsewhere) and the inevitable falling away of members of the Common Laborers and other relief workers' union, Highlander's workers' education program was neither relevant nor feasible. At the same time, the CIO's southern organizing drive of the late thirties had produced a growing industrial union movement and, in turn, a growing need for trained local leadership to which Highlander sought enthusiastically to respond.

Thereafter, the School's role in the community and county was a marginal one. Except for those individuals, such as Lewie Vaughn, who participated in resident workers education terms, it served largely social and recreational needs, along with sponsoring a few cooperative activities.[48] But Highlander had ceased to try to bring a new social order to Grundy County. It was concentrating those efforts on its southwide labor movement-related program.

Evaluating the effects of the program

Highlander's countywide organizing and educational efforts among underpaid and voiceless relief workers and their families might well be described as a largely effective educational program which failed to solve the underlying problems of the "problem county." It achieved the broad objective of teaching people how to act together in crisis and protest situations and how to build their own unions and other organizations. In the process, local leadership was developed and the county, Myles Horton observed hopefully at the time, was well on the way to becoming solidly organized. (Some 1,000 WPA workers and miners—more than one tenth the local population, it was estimated—were union members.)[49]

The organizations, in turn, in spite of their inexperience and the kinds of bureaucratic and anti-labor forces with which they had to contend, managed to deal with some of their immediate problems. Joint action of the four Hod Carriers and Common Laborers locals, backed by other unions in area, resulted, for a time at least, in "improved working conditions and a slight increase in wages"[50] for its WPA worker members. Labor's Political Conference of Grundy County, after a brief but intensive political education campaign, achieved an unprecedented victory with its entire slate of labor candidates elected to office. The dramatic stay-in protest by jobless WPA workers and their families won them support not only in the county, but in Washington.

Beyond these results, much of what was learned about program development through the county workers' education program was to be of value to Highlander in developing its subsequent movement programs. Thus, conflict and crisis and the heightened need and desire to learn growing out of them were to provide, again and again, the emphasis and focus for the School's residential and extension programs related to the labor and civil rights movements. Problems of organizing and learning to work together within organizations were to continue to be used as the basis for developing vital educational activities within programs for members of new CIO unions and the Southern Farmers Union, and, as in the Grundy County program, the "classroom" was very often a union meeting, a rally or a strike situation.

In addition, the Grundy County program demonstrated that the staff as well as students could be developed in the course of a developing program. Just as relief worker-students had been stimulated to learn in the context of dealing with their problems and assuming new leadership roles, so staff members (and resident students) who worked with them learned in the context of assuming new workers education roles. Since only one of the early staff members came to Highlander with any special background or training in workers' education and her background was the academically-oriented program of Brookwood,[51] all of the School's early teachers in real sense had to be developed in the field! As the mountain school became a truly southwide educational center, it continued to use this field method of staff development. In explaining what he believed to be the long-term value of the early programs to teach mountain people how to build their own cooperatives and unions, Myles Horton referred to those organizations as "the schools in which they are being trained for the new society." He might well have noted that the community and county programs were the schools in which the Highlander Folk School educational director and staff were being trained for their roles in the new industrial union movement and movements yet-to-emerge.

PART THREE

Education for Leadership in the Southern Industrial Union Movement

PREFACE

Between 1932 and 1947, unrest among labor in the South grew from sporadic local strikes by largely unorganized workers to a southern industrial union movement. The pragmatic Highlander Folk School in these years grew from a community-serving institution with a small workers' education program to a southwide center for workers' education. An examination of its various programs and services throughout the period reveals five phases, five major responses by the School to the changing educational needs and opportunities presented by the developing labor movement. In the years 1932 to 1934, the earliest phase, Highlander initiated a small, rather vaguely-defined residential workers' education program to prepare would-be local leadership for a role in the anticipated southern labor movement. Little groups of worker-students came to live and study at the School for longer or shorter periods of time, interacting with staff as a community of learners, participating in the community program and making occasional strike-supporting field visits to nearby mining and mill towns.

During the second phase, 1935 to 1937, in the wake of rising labor unrest and requests for help from hard-pressed local leadership and, later, from the leadership of the first southern organizing drive of the Congress of Industrial Organizations (CIO), the School moved its program increasingly into the field. In the third phase, 1938 to 1942, Highlander's primary emphasis shifted from extension services to intensive residential terms to strengthen and develop local leadership for newly-organized unions over the South. This emphasis on the training of small groups of leaders at Highlander had to be curtailed in the wartime fourth phase of the School's programming for labor, 1940 to 1944. In response to the rapid expansion of southern defense-related industry and southern industrial unions in these years, its resources were devoted, more and more, to developing large-scale extension programs to meet immediate needs for membership orientation and officer training. In the fifth and final major phase of developing programs in interaction with southern labor, 1944 to 1947, Highlander related its resources in a more specialized way to the organizationally-defined needs of an increasingly institutionalized labor movement. Thus, in lieu of general residential workers' education terms, it offered terms developed with and for individual industrial unions and with and for the Southern CIO. The programs and services as developed during these successive phases will be described and analyzed in the five chapters which follow.

SIX

Preparation for the Union Movement: Early Resident Sessions

Highlander Becomes a Southern Workers' School

The transformation of the Highlander Folk School from primarily a mountain community school to primarily a center for workers' education in the South, and more specifically, a center for educating local leadership for industrial unions, may be assessed in terms of the deployment of staff and other resources as well as in terms of the numbers and kinds of students served. Although none of the five to seven college-educated members of its teaching staff were drawn from the labor movement, they were increasingly movement-involved and, increasingly, labor leaders were invited to be special teachers for Highlander resident sessions. During most of 1937, most of the staff devoted full-time to activities related to the CIO southern organizing drive. And, in the ten year period beginning in 1937, the School estimated that 90 per cent of its income and staff were devoted to educational programs for CIO-affiliated unions.[1]

Highlander's small but growing body of resident students came, more and more, from local unions. In 1932-1937, its resident terms were made up of diverse groups of from seven to twenty-three "workers with hand and brain," including unemployed mountain relief workers—a total of some 100 in the period. After 1937, its resident terms consisted of eighteen to forty-seven primarily industrial worker students—some 800 in the decade ending in 1947. Similarly, the School's extension program which reached eighty-five striking workers in nearby communities in the first year reached as many as 1,300 union members per year in southern industrial areas in the forties.[2]

In 1940, the Highlander Folk School formed an Executive Council which included a majority of regional labor leaders who, henceforth, participated with the staff in formulating programs and policies.[3] In spite of its close, longtime relationship to the southern labor movement, the School remained financially and ideologically an independent institution. For two years, in 1944 and 1945, some 50 per cent of the School's financial support came from CIO unions.[4] Yet, overall, only about 10 per cent of Highlander's income came from unions in the decade 1937-1947.[5] Nor did the School allow its broad social-educational goals to be influenced by the labor organizations with which it worked. When, in the post-war years, there was pressure on Highlander from cautiously conservative CIO leadership to modify its radically democratic Statement of Purpose and to cease working with certain left-leaning unions it elected instead to cease being primarily a workers' education center and to begin to relate its resources to new and more inclusive groups.

The Emerging Resident Program, 1932-1933

In examining the piecemeal records of the kinds of educational experiences which were offered and those which "occurred" during the first and second resident sessions, one finds that they included, on the one hand, broad, academically-conceived courses and, on the other, direct involvement in School and community problems and nearby strike situations.

The academic activities of the small and changing group of resident students[6]—some eight in all—who participated in the first five-month workers' education term were highly flexible and individualized. The activities were flexible, in large part, because of Horton's commitment to developing the educational program out of interaction with the students. They were also flexible because there was no well-defined labor movement to which the School and its little group of worker-students could relate.

Along with being encouraged to have "their own particular lines" and being "supplied with books with which to pursue them," a report indicates that they participated in what was referred to as "an informal seminar on 'History of Social Change' and in some discussion of 'Social Survey Technique' for those," it was added, "who are interested."[7] They also attended the several community evening classes in Psychology, Cultural Geography, Social and Economic Problems and Social Literature that evolved in the first months which, although they were initiated in response to local interests and concerns, often moved beyond them.

Judging by descriptions of the students and the learning in which they were engaged, they were intensively involved in quite diverse ways in criticizing the old order and planning for a new one. On one occasion, for example, when the School was visited by a group of Chattanooga business men, ministers and journalists, the students read and discussed their papers on such subjects as "Technocracy and Socialism" and "Socialism and Christianity". One youth, it was noted by a newsman, "was particularly opposed to present organized religion and engaged in warm debate with the ministers." A young woman student, a former hosiery mill worker, the same newsmen noted, "hopes to change the attitudes of Christians, she said, and will preach if given the chance."[8]

This committed little group of resident students not only expressed their several views on the need for social change to Highlander visitors. According to articles and letters to the editor appearing in the local press, Walker Martin, the first resident student and one of his two teachers, Don West, spoke at a series of well-attended meetings at county school houses on such socially-challenging subjects as "Conditions in America Today," "Denmark—with not one millionaire and not one pauper!" and "America as she might be." Several results ensued. The meetings gave both student and teacher an opportunity to share their outspoken views with a wider audience of mountain neighbors. The speakers called forth an angry public reprisal from the head of the Grundy County School Board who announced that the Board would prohibit any further use of county school buildings by the Highlander Folk School whose representatives had engaged in "political teachings."[9] They also inspired warm support on the part of some of the audience members. In a letter to the editor, one enthusiastic admirer of Don West and his message urged that "the Board . . . open the school doors again to our young friend and teacher who is devoting his life to lifting the poor laboring people . . . If nothing else," she offered, "he may hold the meetings in our homes."[10]

Learning From Social Conflict—the Wilder Strike

There is no recorded assessment of the educational value placed on the conflict between the conservative school board and the teacher and student proponents of a new social order. The School placed considerable value, however, on the firsthand study by students and teachers of a coal miners' strike in Wilder, Tennessee. ". . . the School," Horton wrote in one of his early notes to clarify his own educational thinking, "could best help the students . . . by introducing them to conflict situations where the real nature of our society is projected in all of its ugliness."[11] The Wilder strike provided a clear-cut example of such a conflict. The Fentress Coal Company had refused to negotiate with the Mine Workers' local and demanded that the miners accept a 20 per cent cut in their already low wages. "Even while employed," the *Mine Workers Journal* noted, the miners were "forced to solicit aid from farmers and other charitably inclined persons to feed their families." When the miners decided to go out on strike, the coal company retaliated by hiring non-union workers, described as "thugs and gunmen."[12]

It was with the idea of helping students to learn from this conflict that Horton, on Thanksgiving Day, 1932, made an exploratory visit to the Wilder strike scene. There, he ate a striker's meager meal with the local union leader and his family, talked with members of the striking local and observed the behavior of some of the rifle-carrying soldiers, sent in to protect law, order and property, who, miners complained, were drinking and endangering the lives of their families. As the teacher-analyst of the industrial conflict situation was departing with his carefully-noted observations, he became, instead, a participant in the situation. In his words, contained in a widely-publicized letter to the newspapers throughout Tennessee

> I was out of the strike area and on my way home when I was overtaken and returned to state police headquarters. I was charged . . . with "coming here and getting information and going back and teaching it."[13]

This was the beginning of a new reality-oriented phase of the Highlander Folk School's evolving program to develop leadership for the projected southern industrial union movement. It was a phase which was as involving and possibly as educational for the teachers as for the resident students. Along with vaguely projected student papers on "Socialism and Religion" were papers on "Analysis of the Wilder Situation" which included not only broad, impassioned statements about the "misery, hunger and suffering" of the miners, but interview data gathered by the staff and students on the actual wages and wage cuts received by specific miners and the itemized company deductions from those wages for coal, lights, doctor, bath house and school dues, which left them in debt to the company at the end of a work period.[14]

Beyond studying conditions on the strike scene, staff and students became involved in a number of strike supporting activities. Files of the period contain letters of appeal for funds to help the miners' families, clippings from the labor press[15] describing a miners' mass meeting with Norman Thomas as the speaker[16] and lists of projects, including the development of a cooperative garden to be developed at Wilder.

Out of their various efforts, wide-spread interest was awakened in the strike and the welfare of miners' families. Support came from a variety of liberal political, church and other groups. Important for the history of the Highlander Folk School as a workers' education center in the South, the School's involvement with the striking Mine Workers marked the beginning of the identification of southern unions with the little-known school. Staff and students also formed a close relationship to the strikers and their families in the mining camp. Out of this relationship grew an interest in the School itself and what it was teaching and, as a result, three of the resident students for the School's second winter term were members of striking miners' families from Wilder.

Learning from Cooperative Living

Believing that it was a "simpler task" to help students understand the problems of the existing social order than to "gain an idea of a new social order in which workers have control," the School sought to provide in the day-to-day life of the residential community, an experience, in Horton's words, "of learning to live out our ideas of a workers' society."[17] The ideals which they sought "to live out" included staff and students sharing the work of the School, maintaining the farmhouse which served as the resident-community center and growing their own food on the forty acres loaned them by Dr. Lilian Johnson. It also included their sharing "equally in the opportunities the school offered" as well as in determining how the modest budget, averaging, it was calculated, $130 per month, would be spent.[18]

The financing of this microcosm of the New Social Order, described by one Tennessee newspaper as "a tiny Socialist republic",[19] was achieved by contributions from individuals and groups interested in the School's work. In addition, contributions were made by the students themselves "who brought what they had of money or farm products." One can assume that more farm products than funds were contributed by early students. One of them, for example, a former hosiery worker, gave canned fruits as her "tuition."[20]

Judging by early correspondence and records, students and teachers alike took pride in the fact that they were able to live and carry on an educational program by dint of their own labors and a small amount from contributors but with no dependence on or connection with outside political or other groups. Writing to a student of folk schools who asked about the Highlander Folk School's political or other affiliations, Horton emphasized, "All work is done by teachers and students and no one receives a salary. By growing our own food supply we have been able [to] operate independently of any organization. We feel that we can contribute more to the radical labor movement in this way."[21]

If the creation of a financially independent "workers' society" proved remarkably feasible, minutes of early staff meetings and recorded staff and student criticisms indicate that at the day-to-day level, a good deal of time was devoted to getting assigned chores carried out and to achieving and maintaining a balanced work-class-study-recreation schedule.[22]

There were also, inevitably, interpersonal tensions which, when they involved the early co-directors, Myles Horton and Don West, were profoundly disturbing to at least one of their earliest resident students who wrote a several-page critical analysis of their differences. No official staff minutes or other records of the School make mention of any of these internal differences but the model "workers' society" was a very small one to have two strong-willed, independent, young radical educators sharing the leadership role. It was not surprising, therefore, that an early report announced that on April 1, 1933, Don West left the Highlander Folk School "to work permanently in his native state" (Georgia) where "he plans to build a chain of workers' cooperative libraries, and to establish another school similar to this, in an effort 'to educate farmers and industrial workers for the cooperative commonwealth.' "[23]

There were other differences among the staff. Ardently zealous adherence to the social ideal seemed to characterize at least two of the young women who early joined the School staff. One of these, Dorothy Thompson, had a religious commitment to the work of the School, especially in the immediate impoverished mountain community. The other, Zilla Hawes, Vassar and Brookwood Labor College-educated daughter of a New England minister, had an equally zealous commitment to the cause of a radical southern labor movement. Each expressed keen disappointment when individuals, whether staff or students, fell short of the idealistic roles which they had defined for the School and for themselves. As Dorothy Thompson expressed it, "I feel very strongly that people working with the labor movement and for a new social order should set almost perfect standards for themselves personally."[24] Zilla Hawes was not so demanding, but seemed to serve as a gadfly to the staff, pointing out, "We may give lip service to our revolutionary ideal, yet even fail to make a start, in which case it were better not attempted."[25]

Fortunately, in their attempt to "live out" their ideals of a "workers' society," the striving, self-critical little group of staff and resident students were continually in interaction with the very real world of their mountain neighbors and therefore could not become, at least for any period of time, overly subjective. As Horton himself observed, "Grappling with vital problems growing out of our close connection with conflict situations and participation in community life kept our school from becoming a detached colony . . . "[26]

Along with their joint participation in evening classes, Community Nights and gatherings to hear and meet visiting clergy, educators, social reformers and others, they also met together in a sort of loose-knit "community council." Special meetings of staff, students and neighbors were called, a report indicates, "for enlisting the active cooperation of the entire community" or "when a controversial issue arose." At such meetings, "Parliamentary procedure was reduced to a minimum and everyone was encouraged to express opinions."[27]

In addition, some resident students and community members joined together in a Socialist Party local which one of the resident students helped to organize in the spring of 1933. Shortly thereafter, representatives of the local attended a so-called "Third Continental Congress in Washington, D.C." composed, it was said, of "all the important labor and farm organizations and unemployed Councils."[28] And, as a Tennessee newspaper also noted, members of the new local were among participants in the first Socialist Summer School in the South which was held in June at the Highlander Folk School.[29]

In July 1933 the strike of local woodcutters began. The School became involved in strike activities and in forming the Cumberland Mountain Workers' League. The would-be center for training local leadership for a southwide labor movement began to relate its resources directly to the development of workers' organizations. Not only did Highlander's involvement contribute to the building of cooperatives, relief workers, unions and other local organizations, but resident students were able to gain practical knowledge of how they were formed and the problems and potential represented by them.

As Myles Horton looked back on the first year of the School's pragmatically evolved workers' education program, he concluded, "Participation in industrial conflicts gave our resident students a taste of reality but even this was incomplete since the vital cultural forces in such situations could only be sensed and not felt." He proposed, therefore, that the School, in its future resident sessions, place greater emphasis on relating directly to community life and organizing around local problems. "No artificial curriculum," he stressed, "should be allowed to isolate the students from the vital social forces around them."[30]

The Academic Resident Term, Spring 1934

In spite of the determination of the educational director of the Highlander Folk School to avoid "an artificial curriculum", the second resident term, March-May 1934, represented an almost classic example of academically-oriented workers education. Although the Cumberland Mountain Workers' League had formed a Cumberland Mountain Cooperative and the School was engaged with local leaders in a lively community class to examine problems and develop plans for their cooperative enterprise, the resident courses continued to reflect the fact that the School was seeking to build a workers' education program in relation to a vaguely projected industrial union movement. The generalized courses reflected, too, the fact that those members of the educational staff, now grown to five, with some experience in working with unions, were not, for various reasons, serving as teachers. Zilla Hawes was developing her own understanding and skills as a union organizer by assuming responsibility for the Amalgamated Clothing Workers' southern organizing efforts in Knoxville, Tennessee. Myles Horton, who had been gaining his own strenuous firsthand education in labor organizing through developing an action-oriented workers' education program in the community and through participation in area strike situations, was forced, for health reasons, to take a two months rest.[31] As a result, Dorothy Thompson, with liberal arts-theology background (except for her recent community experience at Highlander) and Rupert Hampton, newly arrived from Union

Theological Seminary, where he was a graduate in church music, served as the instructors for the five courses offered. These were listed as: Industrial Problems, Public Speaking, English Grammar, Labor History, and Literature.

Fortunately for the vitality of the program, three of the students for the ten week workers' education term came from miners' families in the Wilder area and another was a textile worker from Knoxville. They brought with them, therefore, a firsthand kind of knowledge of southern industrial problems and recent labor history. However, there is little evidence in the teachers' precisely written "brief description of the courses" to indicate that they made significant use of their students' knowledge. The course on Industrial Problems, they explained, followed rather closely Tippet's *Your Job and Your Pay* as the main text and guide for the course. Ten sessions were held and notebooks were kept by the students in which they wrote answers to the questions in Tippet's book. There were also "outside readings" assigned, including Tugwell's *American Economic Life*. Apparently some effort was made through class discussion to relate books to the students. Apparently, too, some learning occurred, however late, on the part of inexperienced teachers who concluded with regard to the Industrial Problems course, "There should have been more time spent in the study of the Wilder strike, Marion strike, Brookside strike and possibly others."[32]

According to the two admittedly academically-oriented workers' education teachers, the literature course "was probably the least valuable of the group." Listing the classics in prose and poetry which they sought to encourage their worker-students to read, they observed, "Much of the material was too heavy for the students," and confessed, "It was a real effort for the students at the winter session to read, and they did not read heavily."[33]

The only course that would seem to have related directly to the students' experience and to their interactions with the surrounding mountain community was Public Speaking. Although it began as academically as the others with "fundamental principles," the speeches which students wrote and worked over were presented at local public meetings including a meeting of the Cumberland Mountain Workers' League "when all four students made speeches from the cross ties." Of such occasions, the teachers observed, "They all became quite a bit more at ease and when they were on fire with their subject found no difficulty in talking in public . . ." But true to their own academic standards, they added, "though the English remained very much according to custom."[34]

Student activities other than classes are mentioned only briefly in reports on the 1934 winter session. Actually, only one hour of class work was scheduled daily with "the remainder of the students' time . . . spent alone or with a tutor in preparation, taking part in community activities and two hours of manual labor."[35]

In assessing the significance of the second resident term to the little group of students, there are two indices of its value. One is the fact that three of the students, those from Wilder miners' families, returned for the summer school. The other is an article entitled, "As a Student Sees It," written by Evalyn Howard, one of the Wilder students, describing some of the meanings of the experience for her. Of the course work she mentions only one experience—"We have learned something about public speaking, enough to go out and get on a pile of cross ties and speak to the Bugwood Cutters who are members of the Cumberland Mountain Workers' League and enjoyed it." She makes more mention of other aspects of the School where "life is very simple and enjoyable," where "teachers and students together" do the housework and gardening and where on Community Nights "all the old and young people come in and play, read and talk." Beyond her valuing of the student-staff-community relationships, this early worker resident student, speaking for her fellow resident students, seems to have been highly motivated by her months at Highlander. Indicating that before coming, "We all felt like there was no choice," she concluded, "Now we feel like we have an aim in life. We are planning on going out and organize labor and try to change the system of things."[36]

A Resident Program Related to an Emerging Movement, Summer 1934

The Highlander Folk School workers' education resident program for the summer of 1934 represents significant development in the direction of greater integration of theoretical learning and practical experience and greater emphasis on the acquiring of skills directly relatable to the emerging southern labor movement. The changes in content and approach in the teaching of workers' education came about, in part, as a result of the staff's criticism of its book-oriented offerings of the previous winter session which had been received with only slight enthusiasm by the worker-students and had little relevance to the School's goal of workers' education leading to "class conscious action."

More important, changes in the School's resident program came about because of growing and militant activity on the labor front in which the Highlander staff was taking a direct part. The main impetus for this new activity was the year-old National Recovery Act and, specifically, Section 7A of that Act, which declared the right of workers "to organize and bargain collectively through representatives of their own choosing."[37] By the summer of 1934, a contemporary observer of the labor scene wrote, "The picket-line has become an established part of the American scene." And, looking beyond the immediate protests of mine, clothing, textile and other industrial workers, he predicted, "Out of the chaos of strike and picket line the new labor movement is being born."[38]

The story of the School's direct involvement in helping southern industrial workers to organize and achieve their rights had its beginnings with a modest entry in a 1933 field activities report by Zilla Hawes. Of her part-time role in the new movement she wrote, "Sent to Knoxville by Amalgamated Clothing Workers of America as organizer. On August 13, 1933, Shirtworkers Local 90 formed with 13 members."[39] Her efforts and those of the School were subsequently recognized in an historic publication of the ACWA, *Bread and Roses: The Story of the Rise of the Shirtworkers, 1933-1934*. Zilla Hawes, as organizer of the Union's first local in the South, and the Highlander Folk School, as its base of education and support, were listed is the Union's Honor Roll of organizers and organizations.[40]

Other unions attempting to take root in resistant Tennessee soil also sought the help of the Highlander Folk School and its staff. Zilla Hawes provided what she termed "unofficial leadership" in a strike called by the United Textile Workers against the Brookside Cotton Mill of Knoxville in November, 1933.[41] Additional members of the School staff participated in the strike and, during the prolonged protest effort, they established a circulating library in the local union hall. Later, when strikers who had been fired from their jobs for attempting to organize appealed to the National Cotton Textile Board, staff attended the hearings. They were present, too, for the adverse ruling by the Board, which declared that the strike had not been necessary. Along with labor, they denounced the decision in speeches and articles.[42]

During the winter and spring of 1934, Highlander continued to respond to the urgent invitations of recently organized and besieged locals asking for its support and educational services. School records indicate that in the case of striking Harriman hosiery workers, whose mill-owner bosses repeatedly rejected their request for union recognition, support moved beyond participation in strike rallies to confrontations with the law. An article in *The Fling* observes enthusiastically, "The strikers continue to show a fine spirit of militant American independence. By filling the jails to overflowing, they forced an anti-labor judge to modify an injunction."[43] A month later, School Secretary James Dombrowski, a frequent speaker on the strike scene, wrote to a friend of organized labor and the School, Dr. Reinhold Niebuhr, "They have a warrant out for Zilla's arrest in Harriman where we are continuing to help in a losing battle, but a grand struggle."[44]

During the winter and spring of 1934, the Highlander Folk School held weekly workers' education classes at the headquarters of the Shirtworkers in Knoxville for members of the local and other workers, organized and unorganized. The classes were under the direction of Zilla Hawes who, as she indicated in a letter to Local 90 members, was serving in the capacity of "your organizer" and "also a teacher at the Highlander Folk School."[45] These classes, including "History of the Working People in America," "How Religion Helps the Worker," and "Ourselves and Our World," were taught for a five-week period by James Dombrowski, Zilla Hawes and Myles Horton.[46]

Thus, by the summer resident term of 1934, Highlander teachers could bring to the task new and vital firsthand knowledge and experience which they had been acquiring through work with militant Tennessee labor groups in the forefront of the awakening local and larger movement. Added to this, more than half of the students recruited for the summer school were drawn from these groups. By offering "a few scholarships to workers who are out on strike",[47] the nineteen member student body included four students from the Wilder strike situation and three from Harriman, "straight from the firing line of a labor case of national significance," as well as three from the local community who had been involved in the less famous Bugwood strike and one from the Amalgamated Clothing Workers' organizing drive in Knoxville.

As a consequence, although Zilla Hawes, in her classes in Labor History, attempted, using pictorial charts and outlines, "to aid the students in visualizing the story of the working class from feudalism up to the present American scene," she also related that history to immediate situations known personally to the students and herself. In her words, "The teacher brought in her own experience organizing for the Amalgamated Clothing Workers . . . in Knoxville, and the experience of the Harriman strikers and Wilder students."[48] She managed, in fact, to relate the class even more closely to immediate local history by describing organizing and strike tactics in connection with a plan to organize employees of the local hotel at Monteagle and by discussing the organization of farmers with the assistance of a visiting delegation of farm-hands from nearby Sherwood, Tennessee, brought to Highlander by a former student, Dee Ferris.

Myles Horton, in his revised class in Psychology which began as it had previously with "a brief discussion of the nervous system and mental processes involved in thinking," moved on to examine "prejudices and other psychological handicaps that weaken the labor movement," and "to draw examples from labor situations familiar to the students." Like Zilla Hawes, Horton was able to relate to the students' experience because he had been working with many of them. He also sought to make use of their immediate residential experience by encouraging the class to discuss "problems growing out of group living at the school." Of these discussions, he noted, "conclusions arrived at were immediately put into practice."[49]

Judging by reports on other classes, a good part of what was taught in the summer of 1934 was "immediately put into practice." The class in Labor Journalism, for example, instead of concentrating on grammar and form, produced five issues of a militant little mimeographed paper, *The Fighting Eaglet*, described as "fifth cousin to the parent bird in Washington" but "not recognized in the *Eagle Social Register*."[50] The paper, with a student editor who was one of the strike heroes of Harriman, communicates the enthusiasm of worker-students alive to the developments and potential of the labor movement and their roles within it. A spirited column, "On the Firin' line," contained strike news. Cartoons poked fun at both big business and "Ma NRA." And an inspired worker-poet expressed their collective hopes for the movement in an epic poem exalting the "one long fight for liberty."[51] *The Eaglet*, it was hoped would furnish students with a model for producing mimeographed shop papers for their own local unions. At the same time, a number of student news articles were immediately picked up and published by the labor press and the paper itself was read by labor friends. A School report notes, "Bundles of *The Eaglet* were sent weekly to the local Hosiery union at Harriman, the Textile unions in Lenois City, a Socialist local at Wheat, the farmers' organization of Sherwood, the United Mine Workers locals at Wilder and Davidson and to the Norris Dam" as well as to "workers' education centers in the South."[52]

Like Labor Journalism, a course in Labor Drama emphasized learning which could readily be used. It included "writing of plays, building an outdoor stage, and the production of a one-act play," and sought to educate students to the potential of labor plays as a vehicle for educating their fellow workers at the same time that it taught them how to write and act in plays based on their own experience. Again, their dramatic efforts were immediately shared with a community audience and, it was noted, plans were being made by the Harriman students "to reproduce the play for their union and in neighboring communities."[53]

Only Public Speaking which had already departed from the textbook approach remained essentially unchanged. A statement about the course indicates, "Speeches to members of a local Workers' League delivered from cross-tie formed the basis of the class . . ."[54]

Two other activities were included in the education program in the summer of 1934. One, a Highlander-sponsored Workers Education Conference "for directors and teachers of labor summer schools in the South,"[55] gave students an opportunity to gain a broader perspective on the field and its potential contribution to the labor movement. The other, a so-called Labor Union Week, provided students with an opportunity to gain a broader perspective on the labor movement itself and to interact informally with leaders. Participants in the Labor Union Week, along with staff and resident students, included two strike leaders from Harriman, several members the Shirtworkers local from Knoxville and representatives of the Cumberland Mountain Workers League. Speakers and resource persons for this special session were described as organizers from the United Textile Workers and the American Federation of Hosiery Workers as well as representatives of other labor and radical groups." Their roles were to lead discussion and hold informal conferences with individual students on "organizing tactics, strike methods and problems of industrialization of unions."[56] Two of the speakers, J. H. Daves, a Negro professor of sociology from Knoxville College and Howard Kester, a southern white reformer, Secretary of the Conference on Economic and Social Justice, spoke on "the relation of Negro workers to the labor movement in the South" and "the need for cooperation between Negro and white workers within the unions."[57] The forward-looking views expressed were no doubt new to many as was the experience of having them put forth by a Negro professor.

The Workers' Council

The Summer of 1934 also marked the beginning of a formally constituted and elected Workers' Council, made up of students and staff members, each having one vote. The Council not only governed "the life and activities of the Summer School" from collecting songs and planning special programs to supervising teacher-student work schedules, but it voted on and implemented both labor organizing and community action projects. The later included supporting the Cumberland Mountain Workers' League, working with the community in its cooperative cannery and, "in response to the request of striking farm laborers in Sherwood," sending students "to organize the farmers, workers and unemployed."[58] If these responsibilities for internal governing and external action were not a demanding enough educational experience for the new body, a report by the Public Speaking teachers notes, "Some parliamentary law . . . was taught in connection with the weekly meeting of the Workers' Council."[59] In keeping with staff effort to integrate knowledge and experience, the same teacher who, a few months before, had sought to teach "basic principles" now introduced them where they were of immediate use and in a context which had relevance to future chairmen of union meetings.

Evaluation of the Program: Its Effect
on Students and Future Resident Terms

In the lengthy staff meetings devoted to assessing the summer resident term and planning for the following one, it is perhaps notable that little time was devoted to criticism of the educational program. Instead, the staff turned its attention to such problems as the establishment of more careful and systematic procedures for the selection of resident students. This presented a new kind of problem to the School. Having begun with one resident student two years before, the concern now was to screen and limit the student group. It was agreed that the minimum age should be twenty-one, except for community students, that it would be desirable to have more men than women and that students, whenever possible, should come as representatives of their unions.[60]

The first three resident terms as they evolved in the winter of 1932-1933, the winter-spring of 1934 and the summer of 1934 cannot readily be generalized about or summarized. From the length of the terms to the nature and content of the courses offered to the kinds of learning activities growing out of interaction with visiting speakers and staff, with the community and its organizations and with strikers on picket lines, each was distinct and different. It is perhaps the fact that each term was different—that the School's leadership demonstrated the capacity to learn from and respond to new groups of worker-students, to learn from and respond to changes in the larger social situation—which was significant.

Within these varied residential workers' education terms, one major common characteristic of the educational program is apparent. The program, with the greatest degree of effectiveness in the summer of 1934, combined broadly-defined courses which sought to enlarge the students' vision of the future southern labor movement with other learning activities which, it was hoped, would be of practical value to new local strike leaders and union organizers. This dual emphasis within the resident program continued to be characteristic of Highlander as a workers' education school, whether it related its resources to students drawn from dissident groups of mountaineers and miners or from the southern industrial union movement.

It was in its extension program and services, beginning with its early field services to striking workers and new unions—to be examined in the following chapter—that a primarily utilitarian emphasis can be discerned.

SEVEN

Helping to Build
the Movement:
From Picket Lines to
an Extension Program

In his pre-Highlander notes in which he sought to conceptualize his tactical "Southern Mountains School," Myles Horton thought in terms of a southwide center for residential workers' education which would, at the same time, serve as a social-educational center for the surrounding local community. Although he observed, "I can go to strike situations and take students with me, thus helping labor and education at the same time," he did not, apparently, project a field or extension program, but rather field visits related to the residential program. His pre-Highlander notes, of course, also emphasized that the institution would be an evolving one which would build its own structure and take its own form." Thus, beginning with the Wilder and Harriman strike situations in 1933 and 1934, the School and its resident students were to become more and more involved in movement related field activities. And, in 1935 and 1936 the emphasis on Highlander's workers' education program changed from a resident program with some movement-related activities to interactive resident and extension programs with a significant part of the students' learning experiences growing out of their participation in extension activities and a significant share of the School's resources being so deployed.

Increasing Labor Unrest, Increasing Field Activity, 1935

The change in Highlander's program emphasis in 1935 can he explained only partially in terms of the benefits which had begun to accrue from its early participation in organizing activities and strike situations. Clearly, in identifying potential worker-students, in developing a more relevant, more vital program and in beginning to gain a base of labor support, the School had benefitted considerably. The change, above all, was a response to the change in a struggling labor movement itself—a growing unrest among workers in southern mill towns and with that unrest, in Highlander's view, an opportunity to experiment with new kinds of movement-building education.

By the end of 1934, newly organized workers in southern textile mills, described as "one of the most sweated industries in the country," were embittered by their low wages and oppressive working conditions and the failure of both the New Deal government and their union, the United Textile Workers, to do something about those conditions. In their rising resentment against unresolved grievances and their fervor for unionism, southern delegates to the United Textile Workers convention in September 1934, convinced their fellow delegates to join them in a short-lived, ill-fated General Strike.[1] Defeat occurred in a matter of weeks. Writing of the unsuccessful strike in the *Highlander Fling*, Amalgamated organizer and School Advisory Committee member Franz Daniel attributed its loss to the "old and inadequate union leadership" of the AFL, "unprepared physically and mentally" and to the new members, "unaccustomed to discipline and strike activity." Like others associated with Highlander in the new movement however, Daniel was undeterred by the defeat. "No strike is ever lost," he asserted, "and least of all this one . . . The lessons of the first battle will not be forgotten—the war goes on!"[2]

And in the months ahead, the war did go on—with spirited battles fought in several southern textile towns not far from Highlander—in Rossville, Georgia, home of the Richmond Hosiery Mills, and across the border in Soddy and Daisy, Tennessee, where branch mills were located. Records of the battles are to be found in the terse headlines of articles in Georgia and Tennessee newspapers and in the labor press, all carefully preserved in Highlander's growing files on southern industrial strikes: "Richmond Mill

Union Rejects Cut in Wages," "Guardsmen Seize 60 in Crowd at Rossville Plant," "Soddy Strikers Sing Hymns, Hear Pastor Plead for Peace," "Union Pickets and 'Agitators' are Arrested," "Hosiery Union Member Killed, Another Hurt."[3] It was in response to these kinds of events that Highlander Folk School staff and students during the 1935 winter term made a number of trips to the strike scenes, armed with mimeographed song sheets, some unorthodox ideas of workers' education and a high sense of a movement in the making.

Of their activities in support of "the bitter Richmond strike," a report on the winter term indicates that "at the request of officials and members" of the American Federation of Hosiery Workers, staff and students presented "educational speeches," helped plan and carry out a demonstration of strikers and strike sympathizers and organized folk dancing and other recreational activities.[4]

In the course of their several days' service on the Rossville strike scene (and in subsequent such periods) the School was concerned with ensuring the educational value of the field program for resident students as well as strikers. Thus, "while living in strikers' homes," the report notes, "staff and students met each day to pool and analyze their experience."[5]

Such picket line workers' education was not without hazard. During the same winter term, participation in a union parade and rally in strike-torn Daisy, Tennessee, ended with the group being fired upon and one of the staff members getting shot. The initial description of the occasion in the School's day-by-day record of its developing extension activities was a fairly typical entry:

> Feb. 22 George Washington parade to Daisy mill. Highlander Folk School given credit for help by hosiery workers and leaders, but very little publicity, fortunately. Zilla Hawes made speech on Labor History to pickets.[6]

A later record of the day's events, in a diary kept by Hilda Hulbert, the School's librarian of six months and a Wellesley College graduate with a deep interest in women's trade union activities, gives quite a different view. "I'm sitting here," she begins, "in a chair by the fire in the home of a Daisy union worker about a half block from the mill. I have been here since 2, when they brought me back from the hospital." Of the shooting (which resulted in considerable publicity for the activist school in labor and anti-labor papers), her recollection was vivid but incomplete. She recalled that when striking workers and a group from Highlander marched into the mill yards "shots came out of the mill windows . . . I heard Myles saying, 'Don't shoot. A woman's been shot!'. . . They say they kept shooting, but I didn't hear it after I got mine",[7] she concluded.

Among the School's less publicized field activities initiated in the winter of 1935 was the organizing of three local study groups for the American Federation of Hosiery Workers, two in Tennessee and one in Georgia. Their immediate purpose was to give members of the embattled union an opportunity "to study and discuss causes of depression and labor problems." The longer term purpose, as a School report explained, was to provide "a training group for rank and file leaders, so that they might start groups in their own shops . . ."[8] In addition, through such activities, Highlander was able to identify promising local leader-resident students.[9]

In August and September, following the summer term of 1935, another extension program was initiated, a so-called Labor Chautauqua. Modeled, in a general way, on the labor chautauqua developed by Brookwood, Highlander's travelling workers' education program included "labor plays, puppet anti-war plays and group singing of labor songs" with staff and students serving as speakers, actors, puppeteers and song leaders. In its first season, the School noted, the group played before enthusiastic union audiences as far distant as the International Ladies Garment Workers Union in Atlanta.[10]

Expanding Extension Plans and Activities, 1936

The increasing eagerness and confidence with which the Highlander Folk School sought to relate directly to southern labor in its movement building struggles are clearly reflected in its projected program plans and policy statements for 1936. A School announcement for 1936, circulated among a growing group of labor friends and contacts, stresses the year-round involvement of Highlander's teachers in "the organizational and educational work of trade-unions and farmers' organizations" and the students' "actual experience in the field as part of their work." It states with considerable assurance that after Highlander students complete a resident term, they "return to The Labor Movement as active union members, officers, organizers, Central Labor Union delegates... teachers in labor schools, leaders in cooperatives." The same announcement sets forth as a new requirement for admission to Highlander "your organization's endorsement"; thus attempting to insure that students would, in fact, "return to the Labor Movement."[11]

A staff memorandum on "Program for 1936" outlines recommendations for a greatly expanded extension program "if feasible with one person in full time charge in the field." Among the activities to be continued and expanded were "promotion of study groups in increasing number and effectiveness, promotion of other schools and centers for workers' education" and "experimentation in the field of workers' dramatics" including specifically "more Labor Chautauquas." Among the new extension and extension-related projects recommended were "the supervision of an educational program for 6,000 organized textile workers in Huntsville, Alabama, in cooperation with the local organizer for the United Textile Workers," educational work in Chattanooga, especially with the American Federation of Hosiery Workers and "writing and publishing of material for southern workers, to be used in residence courses [and] in study groups."[12]

In part, no doubt, because those responsible for writing the program reports were overextended in carrying them out, Highlander reports on its resident and field programs for 1936 are rather sparse. And, in keeping with the School's direct involvement in the movement, the brief educational reports are interspersed with information about labor developments throughout the South. A one page statement on the summer program and fall plans, for example, begins with a description of "'runaway shops' being set up on every hand by companies seeking to evade the unions in the East." It describes also the "violence and terror" experienced by "workers who protest sweat shop conditions" and specifically the violence experienced by three summer students, hosiery workers from Rockwood, Tennessee, who "came out on strike and tried to organize a union for self-protection."[13]

This same report suggests some of the ways in which the School was seeking to carry out its ambitious extension plans. Of the recommendation to promote more workers' education centers and activities, the report indicates, "Seventy trade unionists from Georgia and Tennessee participated in a conference on workers' education at Highlander Folk School." Of the proposed expansion of the Labor Drama and Labor Chautauqua, mention is made of "the Highlander Players," "who were enthusiastically received by audiences in Knoxville, Norris and Atlanta." And of its services to the American Federation of Hosiery Workers for which it had proposed to do "educational work," the same report of June 1936 states simply, "The

Tri-state Council of Hosiery Workers will take over the school next weekend."[14]

Judging by an article in the School paper for September, entitled "Taking Education to the People," a Highlander staff member directed the singing for what was described as "the South's Greatest Labor Day Parade" led by President Green and was devoting six weeks to the development of a local workers education program in Knoxville in cooperation with a committee of representatives from the Hosiery Workers and the Amalgamated Clothing Workers there. The same article reports that Myles Horton had recently spent two weeks "teaching in the Southern Tenant Farmers Union School for organizers at the Delta Cooperative Farm" and that there were plans for a December Tenant Farmers School for organizers at an institution called the "New Era School."[15]

One other evidence of the Highlander Folk School's growing movement-related program in the summer and fall of 1936 was its picket line classes for some 500 striking Hosiery Workers at the Holston Mills in Knoxville as heralded in two labor publications, *The American Teacher*, publication of the American Federation of Teachers and the *Labor Advocate*, a Tennessee labor paper. Both describe picket-line classes, discussion groups and other activities and the Advocate added, "When the strike ended the workers asked that the classes be continued."[16]

A later and fuller report on early Highlander extension activities indicates that along with these picket line classes, believed to be the first in the South,[17] a picket-line dramatic group was organized "to tour the gates each morning with programs of skits and songs."[18]

The Effect of the Program on Highlander and its Resident Students

It would he impossible to assess the effects on striking workers—educational and morale-building—of each of the many and varied kinds of field activities and services which Highlander staff and resident students undertook in the years 1935-1936. It is possible, however, to identify two major cumulative effects of those activities: the development of a small but committed group of picket line-educated and tested resident students who left Highlander to assume active roles in the southern industrial union movement; and the establishment (in part through these students) of an increasingly close relationship between the School and the movement.

Some fifty workers' education students emerged from Highlander's interrelated resident and field program in 1935 and 1936 just as southern labor, encouraged by New Deal legislation and labor action elsewhere, was becoming a significant force. Files of correspondence with individual students over the years, along with School reports and articles from the daily and labor press, reveal that they contributed in a variety of ways to the building of the movement, locally and regionally. Their contributions ranged from those who returned home to pursue their same union activities with greater dedication to those who assumed major new roles. In the first group, for example, was a middle-aged member of a Clothing Workers' local in Atlanta who wrote back enthusiastically a few months after attending the 1936 winter term, "Came back to go right back on the picket line" and added, "still going to four classes a week."[19] Among those in the latter group was J.D. Bradford, a young mountaineer with an eighth grade education who came to Highlander in the summer of 1936 as president of what he called "a little union down there in the limeworks." Bradford went on to become an organizer of integrated Deep South locals and a vice president of the Lime, Cement and Gypsum Workers of America. He also managed to return to Highlander as a teacher of organizing tactics at a number of resident sessions.[20]

Out of these early resident groups came Zilphia Mae Johnson of Paris, Arkansas. When she arrived at the School in January 1935, Zilphia Johnson was a graduate of the College of the Ozarks and a concert pianist with an idealistic concern for working people of the South and their problems. Her concern for the South, her talents in music and drama and her ability to relate to people found a compelling focus in the workers' education and action programs of the Highlander Folk School. She also found a compelling personal focus. In the spring of 1935, she and Myles Horton were married at Highlander. (The minister who officiated, appropriately, was a local supporter of the School's strike-related activities in Soddy and Daisy, Tennessee.) Thereafter, until her death in 1956, she was a teacher and later an Executive Council member of the School, distinguished in workers' education, in the labor movement and among collectors of folk music.

More typical of the early resident students was (Miss) Walter Brady, active member of a Clothing Workers' local in Knoxville. After being selected by Highlander teacher-organizer Zilla Hawes to attend a resident term in the winter of 1935, she returned to the School in 1936 as secretary of her local to describe a new workers' education program which she had been instrumental in developing. Letters in the School's files indicate that she also worked with the Highlander staff as a behind-the-scenes advisor in the organizing of other Amalgamated Clothing Workers' locals in nearby communities.

Another student in this period, Matt Lynch, who had come to Highlander from Rossville, Georgia, where he had been a local leader among the striking hosiery workers, attempted to analyze the effect of the educational experience on himself and others already in the movement. Looking back, he recalled that he acquired a broader knowledge of labor history, some ability to lead discussions and talk before groups and, above all, "confidence." Of the little group of staff and students who held classes near picket lines and led rallies at armed mill gates, he emphasized, "People weren't afraid to speak out!"[21] Lynch himself went on to be a regional organizer for the Textile Workers' Organizing Committee and gained fame not only for his organizing skills, but also for his refusal to he intimidated when he was beaten up and kidnapped by "company militia."[22] As an alumnus who was vitally interested in workers' education, he subsequently became a member of the Highlander Folk School Executive Council along with other southwide labor leaders.

Highlander Joins the Textile Workers Organizing Drive, 1937

The year 1937 marks the culmination of the Highlander Folk School's increasingly field-centered workers' education program. It became, in that year, a field-based school offering its program and services primarily in mill villages and factory towns, on picket lines and in union halls. The intensive resident sessions which had, over several years, produced some promising leadership for the emerging labor movement, was set aside in the spring of 1937 in favor of an extensive program of organizing and education in direct support of a southwide campaign to organize the textile industry.

At the outset of the year, the School's program, as projected in staff minutes and described in the announcement of the summer term, was rather similar to that of the two previous years. Three months later, when the Congress of Industrial Organizations, through its newly-formed Textile Workers Organizing Committee (TWOC), announced an industry-wide campaign "for the education and enlistment of all textile workers into the union," the Highlander Folk School was quite ready to revise its total plans and offer its staff services to the southern campaign. In a brief note, made sometime during the days when the organizing drive had just been announced, educational director Myles Horton recorded his decision which would reshape the program for 1937: "Alex Cohn asked me to recommend twenty organizers." There is no indication as to how many organizers he recommended, but he added, "I offered my services."[23] In April, the entire Highlander staff was invited to attend the opening conference of the TWOC southern drive in Atlanta. By early May, the secretary and lone administrator of the School's affairs explained in a memorandum from the quiet Tennessee mountain top

> The present organizing drive of the TWOC is the biggest thing that has happened in the southern labor movement. Over 300,000 textile workers are to be reached. Results thus far have been most gratifying. Workers are flocking into the union. Manufacturers are signing agreements. The Highlander Folk School is placing all of its resources at the disposal of the committee.[24]

Highlander staff members responded immediately to the opportunity to participate in the organizing drive. They were keenly aware of the bitter recent history of textile workers' efforts to improve conditions in the mills in the South. Moreover, the drive represented the first major CIO organizing campaign in the South and the CIO represented, to the Highlander staff as to many hopeful observers, the future of industrial unionism in the South and the nation. They were convinced, as a Garment Workers official predicted following the stormy A.F. of L. convention where John L. Lewis and other industrial union leaders formed the CIO bloc

> An opposition was born at this convention that will ultimately change the character of the American labor movement. The opposition centers around the question of industrial unionism . . . The progressive ranks will grow during the next few years and as they grow, new issues will he brought into the struggle."[25]

Summer School for a New Clothing Workers Local, La Follette, Tennessee

The most ambitious, most publicized educational venture to be undertaken during Highlander's year in the field was an experimental five-week workers' education school held in La Follette, Tennessee, from May 29 through July 5. The idea for the summer school originated with Charles Handy, Highlander resident student in the winter of 1936 who, by the spring of

1937, had organized some 1,000 women and girls from two shirt factories into Local 95 of the Amalgamated Clothing Workers. "Organizer Handy," a report on the so-called Workers' Education Rally explained, "was anxious to have an educational program in La Follette to teach these new union members the elementary facts of the labor movement."[26] In agreeing to undertake the program for the La Follette Shirtworkers' local, the School hoped to achieve two immediate objectives: "First, to work intensively with the most able members of the union to develop latent capacities for leadership . . . through making these people responsible for the program" and second, "to reach as many of the membership as feasible in a much more informal program, hoping to build a greater emotional loyalty to the union and to enlarge their conception of the significance of the labor movement."[27] Underlying these objectives, the Highlander Folk School considered the La Follette School an opportunity to experiment with the techniques and especially with a new large scale approach to workers' education which might be applicable to other situations in the South. Acutely mindful that "the work of the CIO is bringing into the union thousands of workers with little or no previous experience in the labor movement," they were eager to develop a program which would reach these growing numbers "who must be taught the ABC of unionism."[28]

From its inception, the development of the La Follette program involved a close collaboration with union leadership, probably the closest in Highlander's early history. At the Atlanta conference opening the southern drive of the TWOC, a report indicates, "most of the staff of the Highlander Folk School met Jacob Potofsky and outlined the plans for the La Follette School." To which, it concluded, "Brother Potofsky gave his approval . . ." With the blessing of the President of the Amalgamated Clothing Workers, the School submitted a lengthy outline of the proposed program to J. B. S. Hardman, Educational Director for the Clothing Workers and a major spokesman for workers' education within the labor movement. Out of an exchange of correspondence between James Dombrowski of the Highlander staff and Hardman came a tentative program which, in turn, Zilphia Horton submitted to members of a special education committee of Local 95.[29] It included five major lecture-discussion topics on the history and workings of American trade unionism as recommended by Hardman: "Why Workers Need the Union"; "The Structure of the Union"; "The Clothing Industry and the History of the ACWA"; "Industrial Unionism: The AFL and the CIO"; and "Labor and the Law." Also included were two other broad topics,

"The Cooperative Movement" and "Labor's Fight against War and Fascism" which the Highlander staff apparently felt were desirable for the liberal education of its shirtworker-students. In the course of several planning meetings, the education committee somewhat modified and simplified the program. Instead of discussing the cooperative movement and the international fight against fascism, committee members decided on a topic of more immediate concern, Social Security. They also decided that weekly workers' education classes would be offered in La Follette and the neighboring community of Careyville rather than in five area communities as the Highlander Folk School staff had originally proposed.

The opening rally of the workers' education school-in-the-field was an impressive and well attended occasion with J. B. S. Hardman giving the principal speech and a city judge welcoming the Shirtworkers, Mine Workers and other assembled union members and their families in behalf of the mayor of La Follette. Also addressing the group were organizer Charles Handy and the chairman of the Local 95 education committee. Highlander staff members, making a pointed effort to play a minor role in the proceedings, "were introduced," a School report noted, "and made short talks."[30]

The program itself, in spirit and content was quite characteristically a Highlander Folk School program. The weekly workers' education evening classes combined several kinds of activities which had become an integral part of Highlander resident sessions. These included, at the opening of each class, the singing of labor songs led by Zilphia Horton; practice sessions on "How to run a union meeting" guided by Ralph Tefferteller and a series of broadly-defined lecture-discussions on the history of trade unionism presented by James Dombrowski. The singing was a notable success with the song leader, as she had done at Highlander, developing a mimeographed song book which featured a number of mountain ballads with labor words"[31] already familiar to the group. The sessions on "How to run a union meeting," relating as they did to the needs of the inexperienced union membership and requested by the education committee, were also well received. But the lecture-discussions, even when the topic was the Amalgamated Clothing Workers and even when Dombrowski utilized "graphic charts," which had been especially prepared for the La Follette School to help in "maintaining interest,"[32] did not do so. The Highlander staff was uncomfortably aware that the changing group of shirtworkers and miners who gathered for an evening a week in the union hall at La Follette or Careyville did not have the background or the readiness to be found in a small and involved group of resident students. "The membership of the union," the report lamented in retrospect, "was woefully ignorant about the basic facts of their own union . . . not one person in a discussion group of fifty knew the name of the national president..." And it added, "Even the miners did not know what CIO meant . . ."[33]

Other activities in Highlander's La Follette program included the production of a weekly Local 95 newspaper, *Shirt Tale* which in format and style was remarkably similar to the *Fighting Eaglet* and other "shop papers" produced by resident students in a course on Labor Journalism. In this case the paper performed a very practical function of publicizing coming events with a view to attracting the many newcomers who had little understanding of the labor movement beyond their own experience and even less understanding of workers' education. A workers' education library, consisting of "two hundred books and pamphlets from the Folk School Library," was brought to La Follette since, a report explained, there was no public library in the town and the only rental collection had "no books with a labor point of view." Here again, there was some question as to the workers' readiness for the service. There were requests for "children's books and light fiction" (which had to be borrowed from another community) but the circulation of books and pamphlets "with a labor point of view" was slight.[34]

The newly-organized Shirtworkers, their brother Mine Workers and their friends and families had the greatest readiness for the informal social and recreational aspects of the program. Each week brought a spirited and well-supported softball game between a team of girls from local 95 and other teams in the city league. Each week, too, included an evening of "play party games and folk dancing" with the dancing and traditional games participated in by young and old. The most memorable events (as recorded in such diverse publications as *Shirt Tale*, *The Chattanooga Times* and *Advance*, national paper of the Amalgamated Clothing Workers edited by J. B. S. Hardman) were a one-day Union Label Fair and an enormous Fourth of July celebration and Labor Rally. The Fair was described in *Advance* as featuring "exhibits of union-made goods, a union fortune teller and a tobacco-spitting contest with only union-made tobacco."[35] The Fourth of July celebration, closing event of the five-week school, was climaxed by an historic parade of 4,000 workers and their families—on foot, in old cars, carrying flags and banners—who assembled in the local fairgrounds to hear speeches by Zilla Hawes and other veterans of the TWOC campaign; by William Turnblazer,

President of District 19 of the United Mine Workers; by Dr. Arthur Morgan, Chairman of the TVA, and by Brother-teacher James Dombrowski. The parade was immortalized not only in the press and the memories of participants but in "People of the Cumberlands,"[36] a much-acclaimed, significant documentary film about the emerging union movement in the mountains and the School which was working with it. Its young writer-narrator-photographer team, made up of Erskine Caldwell, Elia Kazan and Ralph Steiner, caught the spirit of the day, of the movement and of the Highlander Folk School. "A new saying has come to the mountains," narrator Caldwell explained as pictures of impoverished Tennessee mountain villages were followed by pictures of miners gathered for a union meeting, "Don't mourn! Organize!" The film moved on from the "men with hands as hard as shovels" to the bright faces of a holiday parade

> July 4, 1937. The town of La Follette shut down for the Labor Rally. A new kind of Independence Day! No more terror! No more insecurity . . . The people are the unions! The unions are the people!

The paraders moved on to the fairgrounds and to the speeches they had come to hear

> A miners "rep" says "AFL or CIO we've got to get together. That's what union means." A speaker from the Highlander Folk School promises the people of La Follette that the School will continue to answer their needs . . . that the School is answerable only to the people of Tennessee. Then he introduces the textile organizer who is a graduate of the School. But no more speeches! This is a holiday!

When the Highlander Folk School announced, at the close of the Independence Day Rally, that this had been "one of the finest demonstrations of labor solidarity ever seen in this part of the country" its pride was probably justified. It could take satisfaction, too, from the way in which union leadership from the local to the national levels had become identified with the La Follette School—so much so that they considered the program a union program. Thus a feature article in *Advance* following the five-workers' education school began:

> Again the Amalgamated leads the way, this time with workers' own education in the South. A type of education which has brought hundreds of Shirtworkers—new unionists, Amalgamated members . . . a better and broader vision of their union and their labor movement.[37]

Response to the workers' education classes had fallen short of expectations. Barely a beginning had been made in reaching perhaps 200 of the 1,000 Shirtworkers and their fellow unionists with one or more lecture-discussion sessions for which most of these unionists were ill-prepared. Yet, in spite of this, there is evidence that interest had been stimulated in continuing a local program. At an "Evaluation Conference" toward the end of the last week, the girls attending were described as "enthusiastic in their comments and unanimous in wanting all the activities to go on."[38]

Whether the interest in education in La Follette was sufficiently sustained to result in the continuation of some or all of the activities is not indicated in the sparse Highlander reports for 1937. It is clear, however, that the summer school program which its planners had hoped would be updated and used by other newly-organized unions was never repeated. A full report and analysis of the program including a section on "Suggestions for Another School" was mimeographed and made available in labor and workers' education circles. At the request of the Southern Regional Director of the TWOC, specific plans were drawn up for a two-week institute to be offered for 200 Textile Workers "based on the experience at La Follette."[39] Later, a letter from James Dombrowski to Myles Horton, on-leave to the TWOC, indicates that the institute was cancelled by the Regional Director.[40] Although the reasons were never specified, it would seem likely that the demands of immediate history—of the far-flung and understaffed organizing campaign which the TWOC had undertaken in the South-had crowded out the classes on the history of American trade unionism.

Reports from Greenville, South Carolina and Lumberton, North Carolina

In contrast to the publicized school at La Follette, the various educational activities undertaken by Zilla Hawes and Myles Horton as TWOC organizers throughout most of 1937 seem not to have been noted by labor leadership or the press or, if noted, were not considered education. They had been hired, above all, for their ability to organize and it was in recognition of this ability that the Regional Director of the TWOC said, "If I had a half-dozen men like Myles Horton, I would have the South organized."[41] The periodic field reports of the two itinerant Highlander staff members, however, and especially Horton's reports, were always those of an educator although the context of the educational efforts was the organizing campaign and the main criteria of effective education were the workers, the locals, the mills which were organized.

Zilla Hawes, TWOC organizer in charge of the Greenville, South Carolina area, devoted a considerable part of her final report to the sometimes overwhelming problems which she faced in attempting to organize seven Deep South counties containing fifty-three mills, three shirt factories, 18,000 workers and an unknown number of Ku Klux Klansmen who had been reactivated to fight the union.[42] Yet even in the midst of her formidable job she was able to cite the beginnings of an educational program. As in Highlander's program in Grundy County, the most important setting for her workers' education was the union meeting—in this case, periodic district meetings of local leaders and volunteer organizers and the weekly membership meetings for new union recruits. Similarly, the subject matter consisted of the problems confronting inexperienced leaders and members—the problem of organizing tactics and collective bargaining, on the one hand and of learning how to participate in meetings and make use of union machinery on the other.

Myles Horton's reports from the mill towns of Bennettsville and McColl in South Carolina and Laurinburg and Lumberton in North Carolina also described many of the problems faced by an organizer, including the problem of unhappy workers, with little or no union experience, who were more eager to strike than to organize and of mill managers ready and willing to replace strikers with cheaper, more docile non-union labor. Yet almost from the beginning, he viewed the problems and the process of organizing as an education. Using the situation at Bennettsville as a training ground for developing volunteer organizers to assist him in McColl and the McColl situation to educate volunteers to work with him in Laurinburg, he was able to make rapid progress in organizing hundreds of workers for the TWOC and in developing competent and committed local leadership from among his volunteer staff.

In Lumberton, where the company had a tougher and more determined history of resistance to unions and union organizers and operated in close cooperation with the sheriff, progress was slower and costlier. New union members were fired from their jobs and when they picketed to dissuade others from taking their jobs, they were arrested for trespassing and for resisting arrest. Here again, Horton used the situation to educate. Having requested a federal Labor Board hearing to protest discrimination against union workers, he brought in groups of these striking workers to witness the procedure. Of this unorthodox approach to workers' education, he recalled later

> We took the pickets off the picket line and carried them to the trial . . . I went down there to deliberately let the people in the plant hear their superintendent and their foreman, and all, get up there and lie under oath. They all testified under oath that they hadn't tried to stop the union, that they hadn't given out literature against the union, fired people for union activities . . . threatened to throw people out of their homes when they joined the union. All the union people knew that this wasn't true; so the process of showing the company for what it was and building up the confidence of workers . . . was accomplished at the Labor Board Hearing.[43]

Horton developed another non-traditional program for strikers and their supporters in the community of Lumberton. Five nights a week during a month of the prolonged strike, there were two-hour mass meetings which opened with local entertainment by "some of the kids in the mill village" who could "play and sing," followed by informal workers' education talks by Horton who would begin by discussing local problems confronting the strikers and move from there to a broader perspective. As he described it

> After about a half an hour of talking about their problems, I would say, "Now this is related to the whole struggle of workers." Then I would give them a little labor history . . . Every night I would bring them up to the next chapter in connection with their problems. A course in Labor History would be one week, then the next time we would talk about the need for political action . . . . We had a regular Highlander Folk School course right there with discussion on the part of some of the people I would bring up on the platform—the leaders.[44]

The results of this kind of workers' education, according to the teacher, included an enjoyable time for strikers and their families who had nothing else to do, the communication of a certain amount of relevant knowledge and, above all, the building up of their morale, my main job was to build up their sense of power,"[45] Horton emphasized.

The longer term result was a matter of public record. Some months later, a TWOC release announced that agreements had been signed with the Jennings and Mansfield mills of Lumberton, North Carolina, establishing the union as the sole bargaining agent for some 800 employees and confirming their right to an eight hour day, forty hour week and the prevailing minimum.[46] Horton, the pragmatic educator-organizer who had by this time returned to the Highlander Folk School and his job as educational director, could take satisfaction from the way in which his evolving workers' education program had "worked." The strikers, armed with a new sense of power, had stood their ground and won.

Effects of Highlander's Movement Participation: Increasing Attacks, Increasing Support

By the end of 1937, the Highlander staff, minus one member, Zilla Hawes (who had decided to resign in favor of full-time organizing), was reunited and making plans for a winter resident term in 1938. As before, the independent workers school, whose identity for a large part of the year had almost merged with the southern labor movement, was again charting its course in relation to the perceived educational needs of the movement. Out of its direct involvement in the organizing drive and its varied extension services to new unions had come increasing recognition and support as a southern labor school, on the one hand, and increasing attacks by anti-labor groups on the other.

The year 1937 saw the beginning of a series of sensational accusations and investigations of the School which were to increase in number and virulence over the next several years. A group of articles in 1937, appearing largely in Chattanooga newspapers, reported a mysterious investigation of the School by a Tennessee highway patrolman who posed as a newspaper reporter. The investigation, revealed by a state American Legion leader who refused to say who had ordered it, alluded to a vague charge of "immorality" and emphasized, "The school is not a school, but is used as an instrument for fomenting class consciousness and teaching strike techniques."[47] Subsequent articles contained a withdrawal of the charge of immorality but introduced new charges about courses taught at the School, including a course on "How to organize and lead strikes"; about the intoxicants said to be served at social gatherings (resulting in a banner headline: "Drunkenness Frequent at Folk School")[48] and about an apparently damaging claim that "the school drew . . . finances from a Socialist bank in New York City."[49]

Neither the leadership of the vigorous young institution nor the movement were deterred by such attacks. The Central Trades and Labor Council of Chattanooga promptly responded to the charges with a widely circulated resolution in which they asserted "Such attacks on the Highlander Folk School [are] indirect attacks on the Chattanooga labor movement and organized labor in general." The Council went on to pay tribute to the School for its "commendable piece of work in the interest of labor in this section" and to express confidence in the conduct of the School and in the quality of its work.[50]

The School itself viewed these attacks as a measure of its effectiveness.[51] Two of its staff had proved to be successful organizer-educators in the recent TWOC drive. As a result, some long resistant southern mill owners in North and South Carolina had been forced to accept unionism, to recognize the rights of their workers to organize and bargain collectively. A number of its field-trained students were now in positions of local and southwide leadership in the new industrial union movement. It had developed an extension program of study groups, local workers' education classes and a Labor Chautauqua which was giving support to those former students. And, if some of the efforts, such as the La Follette School, had been only partially effective in reaching the broad membership, its involvement of local leadership in developing the program and of leadership at other levels in carrying it out had been an educative interaction which gave promise of being a continuing and creative one.

EIGHT

Helping to Strengthen The Movement: A Residential Program for New Union Leadership

The Highlander Folk School staff which met to plan the winter term for 1938 was both hopeful and confident. It was hopeful, in spite of a recession in the fall of 1937 which brought the textile organizing drive to a halt,[1] that southern labor under CIO leadership would develop a viable, broadly-inclusive movement, a movement which would adapt the kinds of social change goals espoused by the School's leadership since 1932. It was confident in its unique relationship to the new industrial union movement—a relationship built on its early services to besieged locals in mining, mill and factory towns and on the recent contributions of its staff and former students to the southern organizing campaign—which put it in a key position to serve the movement's educational needs.

The Highlander staff could find evidence for the hope of a broad movement within current CIO pronouncements. "A CIO victory," the official CIO newspaper predicted of the organizing drive, "will lay the groundwork for a mass labor movement among the most underpaid workers in the country—workers on tenant farms and those employed in power, paper, chemicals, fertilizers, lumber, meat, packing, furniture, pants, hosiery, dresses, fruit orchards, department stores and other retail establishments."[2] This same *CIO News* devoted considerable space and attention to southern problems and to southern organizations working for change. Thus, for example, in early 1938, along with treating events in the organizing drive, it spoke of the need for anti-lynching legislation,[3] hailed southern farmer-labor pacts,[4] urged political action through Labor's Nonpartisan League, called attention to the founding of state leagues in the South[5] and gave editorial recognition to the Fellowship of Southern Churchmen (which a Highlander staff member had helped to found) for their "intelligent appreciation of the role of the CIO and industrial unionism."[6] It paid special attention, too, to the "Tennessee Labor School" where eighteen students from six southern states were engaged in "a six-week intensive training course for activity in the labor movement."[7]

In addition, the independent southern labor school was aware that its position was made more important because of the paucity of southern labor's own educational resources and of other resources available to the growing movement. Although education within trade unions had been growing elsewhere in the nation throughout the thirties,[8] in the South responsibility for whatever education was developed within unions fell primarily on overworked regional and local officials and organizers.[9] They, in turn, or those among them with a belief in workers' education as a means of union building, looked increasingly to Highlander which had demonstrated its usefulness to the movement.

The Residential Program, 1938-1942

The Highlander Folk School's residential workers' education program, beginning in 1938 and until 1942 (when the war made such programs infeasible), was shaped primarily in response to the immediate, practical needs of the CIO's organizing drive and the new unions which it brought into being. At the same time, the School continued to project with greater assurance the development of a politically and socially oriented labor movement which would include Negroes and whites, farm and factory workers, employed and unemployed, American workers and workers from other countries. This projection of an ultimate goal was reflected in the kinds of students included in the resident terms as well as in the educational activities offered during these years.

In Service of Immediate Union Needs

Since the program was, first, a program to develop union leadership, the student body for the winter of 1938 (and thereafter) was made up primarily of local organizers, officers and members of CIO unions, each with immediate, practical needs and problems. It included a TWOC organizer from Greenville, South Carolina, wanting to learn about running meetings and getting out a shop paper; a member of the Garment Workers' Union in Atlanta, eager to get a broader perspective on the movement and ideas on how to deal with local problems; a president of a Textile Workers' local in Tupelo, Mississippi, concerned with acquiring knowledge of economics which could be related to the problems of low-paid Mississippi workers. It included, too, a member of a Clothing Workers' local from Nashville, interested in dramatics as it might he used to present the problems of workers "in a clear, convincing manner"; a former tobacco worker and student at the Southern Summer School for Women Workers from Durham, North Carolina, hoping to find a useful role in workers' education, and a textile worker from Louisville confronted with the problem of being black-listed after assisting with both the Textile Workers and the Steel Workers Organizing Committee drives in his area.[10]

In the following years, students in the resident terms came from other unions with which the School was working—local officers from the United Construction Workers Organizing Committee or the United Sugar Workers in New Orleans, for example, or promising members of the United Auto Workers or the National Maritime Union in Memphis. In addition, a School report in this period observed, "Carloads of rubber workers from Gadsden, shirt workers from Nashville, textile workers from Dalton and other groups . . . came to Monteagle during the term."[11] Whatever their affiliation or the length of their stay, they came eagerly with practical needs growing out of their recent experience.

The visiting speakers and special teachers, too, were drawn primarily from the industrial union movement. Speakers in the winter of 1938 included: the International Vice President of the American Federation of Hosiery Workers; the Amalgamated Clothing Workers' organizer, Nashville, later Southern Regional Director; the Steel Workers Organizing Committee (SWOC) Representative, Birmingham; the Executive Assistant to the TWOC, Atlanta; the Regional Director of the CIO and the Southern Director of the International Ladies' Garment Workers Union. These and other movement leaders met with resident students, term after term, sharing with them the thinking and strategy of their several unions as well as consulting with students on local union problems.

As in previous years, basic tool and background courses—Parliamentary Law, Labor Journalism, Union Problems, Labor History and Economics—continued to he offered. Reports indicate, however, that they underwent frequent revisions to make them more relevant to the needs of the labor movement which was becoming more structured and more sophisticated in awareness of its role and concern for its rights. Thus, for example, in 1938, Roberts' *Rules of Order* was replaced by the Amalgamated Clothing Workers' *Rules of Order* as the authoritative source on parliamentary procedure. Labor History began with three weeks of lively discussions about current labor developments and developments affecting labor, including, it was noted, "the AFL and CIO Peace Conference, the attack on the NLRB and the Wage and Hours Bill."[12] The Labor Journalism class not only wrote and put together a student newspaper as in the past, but, an enthusiastic student report in this period notes, "We wrote news articles to the labor press and learned how to properly slant the articles to suit the various presses."[13]

The problems discussed in the Union Problems class continued to be redefined by each incoming group. However, the nature of the problems and the way in which they were dealt with changed. Whether specific ones such as "How to run a clubroom" and "What to say to workers who think the CIO is 'red'" or broad ones such as "Handling AFL-CIO fights in cities" and "Negro and white workers in the same union," they were the problems of task-oriented, experienced union members, eager to get on with the job. Drawing on this experience, the class engaged in rigorous discussions where, as students in one term observed, "We never took one man's opinion or experience on the subject" and when "we couldn't arrive at a sure-fire conclusion or any definite answer . . . we waited for the visiting speaker who was an expert on the particular subject under debate."[14]

Beginning in 1938, at the request of union officials and students, new courses and training sessions were added which sought to provide some of the specialized skills and knowledge demanded of local leaders in their role as organizers, negotiators and general administrators of union affairs. Among these was a short course on Labor Law, taught by an attorney for the TWOC, which dealt with "injunctions in strike situations, the National Labor Relations Act and other laws affecting organized labor"; a group of training sessions on Duties of a Business Agent led by visiting organizers and business agents, and another set of special sessions on Collective Bargaining with the southern representative of the Typographical Union, described as "one of the country's ablest negotiators," as the chief resource person.[15]

In 1939, a so-called Workshop Course was introduced (as it was in other labor schools at about this time) in which students could learn mimeographing and the making of posters, charts and other visual materials. Unlike other labor schools, however, what the students learned was immediately put to use in the service of the School, the community and nearby union groups. Thus, for example, their mimeographic skills were utilized in putting out the *Highlander Fling* and student newspapers which had a growing circulation in labor and workers' education circles. Their poster and handbill-making talents were used to publicize local protest meetings of WPA workers or labor-sponsored political rallies in the county. Charts and other educational materials were "tested" in local workers' education classes before being carried back to their own unions.

Music and Drama as Movement Tools

Even music and drama in the form of labor songs and labor plays were viewed in terms of how they could be used by local unions and the larger movement. The School appreciated the value of encouraging individual creative self-expression among worker-students (which other workers' schools, including the Bryn Mawr Summer School and the Southern Summer School for Women Workers had been seeking to foster and encourage for some years through their classes in writing and drama).[16] Yet it was determined, beyond this, to teach its students how to be play producers and song leaders—how to carry their songs and plays and those of other workers back to their locals, back into the movement. Thus, in an announcement for the winter and summer terms of 1939, dramatics at the Highlander Folk School was described as a means by which "workers learn to build the union . . . to carry the message of Labor through drama"; music and, specifically, workers songs, as a means of helping students learn "to liven up meetings and picket lines."[17] It was for this practical contribution that the Highlander Folk School and its music and drama teacher, Zilphia Horton, were singled out for special mention in a major contemporary survey of promising developments in workers' education.[18]

Worthy of examination is the process of transforming workers-turned students (deeply involved in the day-to-day problems of their unions, accustomed to putting their feelings into words and inclined to believe, as one resident group expressed it, "that art is something 'high falutin'") into actors, writers and producers of labor plays. From the point of view of the activist students, the process was a simple one, involving as they described it, two steps: one, "Be sure of the purpose," of what "you are going to do or say" and, two, "Do it, or say it—and keep on trying."[19] As viewed by the drama teacher and other members of the staff responsible for what Dewey called the "educative environment," the process began with helping students to appreciate the interest and importance of their lives as workers and members of the movement. The Highlander experience seems clearly to have strengthened that individual and collective sense of worth and of worthiness. By the end of the winter term of 1938, for example, the students asserted in their report on "Dramatics and Writing":

> Workers' lives have much more drama in them than the average middle class person's. People who live easy, comfortable, sheltered lives get so they can't do very much or think very hard or believe in anything very strongly . . . It is out of the lives of workers, out of strikes, out of picket lines, out of union meetings . . . that drama and art grow.[20]

Within this encouraging environment where workers, who in the larger Southern environment were often harassed and reviled for their union activity, were given recognition for their activities and encouraged to tell about them, the creative process could more readily get underway. Students were helped, first, to identify problems or situations, usually derived from their own thinking and experience, which would lend themselves to acting out in a spontaneous improvisation. After two weeks of improvising and criticizing their improvisations, Zilphia Horton explained, "Each student was asked to consider himself a director working with his home organization." At this point the student assumed the role which he had observed the teacher assuming. Having identified an appropriate problem, he selected a cast, discussed briefly the plans for the dramatization and, without a rehearsal, "shouted 'curtain' and the scene was on."[21]

A number of plays were developed from the student-directed improvisations. In the summer of 1939, for example, when a somewhat smaller student group made it possible to devote more time to experimenting with labor drama, a group of short plays, *Five Plays About Labor* was evolved. Each play was "made up in about eight hours before it was written down."[22] Four of these plays, "North-South," "Look Ahead Dixie," "Stretch Out," and "Dues Blues" dealt in bold, simple terms with the problems confronting local CIO leaders in their battles against the perpetrators of anti-union propaganda, injunctions against picketing and arbitrary wage cuts. The fifth, "Lolly Pop Pappa," was a musical farce with a cast which included a mill boss named "Mr. Squeezum" and four young girls who "worked long hours for little that's ours" but "he gives us lolly pops."[23] But whether the familiar plots were seriously or lightly treated, all of the plays were explicitly planned "to be used by union performers for union audiences." To facilitate their use, they contained instructions for austerely simple settings, "if you don't have a curtain the actors simply walk on and off the stage at the beginning of and end of each scene carrying their properties" and a warning to the overly-demanding director that the scripts should not be taken word-for-word because "no busy worker could be expected to learn some of the long speeches by heart."[24]

There is evidence that the Highlander plays were widely used by local union groups and others although no systematic effort was made to ascertain how widely. The plays were made available by the School in a usable form and at a price—twenty five cents per mimeographed collection—which was modest enough for the poorest local to afford. They were publicized and circulated through southern labor contacts and various institutions engaged in workers' education. They were performed before a number of audiences by resident student groups.[25] The surest evidence of their use, however, is the School's correspondence with former students during this period who wrote from many parts of the South to request copies of the various plays, to tell of their plans for presenting them, and occasionally, to tell of plays which they had written. Following the winter term of 1938, for example, a young textile worker from Nashville with a small amount of schooling but a large amount of enthusiasm wrote back to report that he had organized "a class in draminics" [sic] and requesting copies of "all three acts of 'Labor Spy'" which he and his brothers had already scheduled for a union meeting the following month.[26]

Another student from the same term, a middle-aged organizer for the International Ladies' Garment Workers whose territory included Atlanta and a several state area, wrote to the staff in some detail of her hectic and harrowing organizing experiences and then asked in a post script, "Have you seen a copy of the play I wrote?"[27] And a letter from an Amalgamated

Clothing Workers representative in Kentucky describes various uses being made of Highlander plays and skits in her area. "I want to thank you for sending us the skit," she begins, "so that we were able to use it in the strike program." Referring to three clothing workers who had recently returned from the summer resident term, she reported "Under the direction of Elizabeth, Catherine and Hazel, the members of Local 362 rehearsed 'Lolly Pop' and 'Stretch Out.' . . . Hazel is now writing a play based on some things the women in Winchester told her."[28]

It was, however, Highlander's labor songs which were most readily and widely shared. Gathered from and inspired by the movement; sung, collected and taken back to local unions by many groups of worker-students and, finally, published in union-sponsored song books, they traveled across the South. The singing, song-writing and song collection process began almost when the School began—community evenings of hymn singing and mountain ballads; depression songs such as "My Country 'Tis of Thee, Land of Mass Misery" written by co-founder and poet Don West.[29] The process continued with the discovery of original strike songs on visits to picket lines, the Wilder mines and the Harriman mills.[30]

The singing of labor songs reached a culmination with the arrival at Highlander of Zilphia Horton. As a resident student in 1935, she had immediately initiated the practice of mimeographing song sheets which were carried on field trips and distributed to striking mill workers in the nearby towns of Soddy and Daisy, Tennessee. As the staff member in charge of music and drama, she made evening song sessions an integral part of the program. Of these sessions, one group of resident students wrote, "Now, after eating for thirty minutes, Zilphia passes out the song books and it's likely we'll start with 'Arise You Workers' and finish with 'Whirlwinds of Danger.' Well, it's dishes again, but we don't mind them this time."[31] More important for the development of music within the movement, she encouraged students to share songs out of their backgrounds, to write songs, or the words for songs, out of their experience and to lead the group in singing them. Of her successful efforts to encourage many of the union member-students of this period to become song leaders, she explained that their interest "seemed to be based on the growing realization of the need for group singing at meetings and consequently the need for leaders."[32]

As the School moved increasingly into the field with its staff and students participating in labor rallies and strike situations and taking Chautauqua-type programs to workers' organizations between terms, its reputation as a center for labor songs in the South grew. By 1938 and 1939, Highlander students, with Zilphia Horton as song leader, were frequently invited to sing and lead singing at local and state meetings of the new CIO unions and at workers' education conferences. In their report on trips during the winter's resident term in 1939, students indicated that they entertained with songs and also presented for the first time their mass chant 'Tom Mooney Lives Again' at a southern conference for workers' education in Chattanooga; "took an active part in the meeting" and "entertained the huge gathering with songs of social significance and our mass chant" at the Tennessee TWOC Conference and attended the TWOC conference in Huntsville, Alabama, "in the company of our song leader."[33]

In 1939, the school received national union recognition as a singing labor school. In May, Zilphia Horton led southern delegates to the Constitutional Convention of the new Textile Workers Union of America in Philadelphia in the singing of labor songs.[34] A few months later, *Labor Songs*, a book of workers' songs which she had collected and arranged for Highlander use, was published by the TWUA with introductory statements heralding the song book and the importance of music to the movement by CIO leaders John L. Lewis, Sidney Hillman and Emil Rieve.[35]

Workers' Stories as Movement History

Of the creative efforts which the School sought to stimulate during the resident terms in the late thirties and early forties, probably the least widely known and shared were the mimeographed collections of stories written by worker-students about their recent experiences in the southern labor movement, including *Let Southern Labor Speak*, *We the Students*, and *I Know What It Means*.

Some of these stories such as "My First Working Experience"[36] or "The Life of an Organizer's Wife"[37] are almost completely personal accounts. Others, for example, a striking textile worker's vivid description of one local's struggle to get organized entitled simply, "It Happened to Us in Louisville,"[38] served to document the kinds of threats and fear tactics which were being used on workers in mills and factories over the South. A smaller number, including a South Carolina textile worker's personal yet universal saga, "How I became interested in the Labor Movement,"[39] managed to a remarkable degree to express the hopes and disappointments of a generation of southern textile workers.

Whatever the levels of sophistication of the several writers, these stories are, as the Labor Education Service observes of Highlander's first such collection, "useful as first-hand experiences of southern industrial workers in their struggle to organize."[40] More than this (for the School was eager to give its students not only utilitarian skills and knowledge but a larger view of the movement and its potential), the setting down for all to read of their stories as workers represented a kind of dignifying of their obscure lives and the struggle in which they were collectively involved. It gave them, what one early enthusiast for workers' stories called "perspective and power with which to accomplish other ends."[41]

Toward a Broader Movement, a More Democratic South

In other ways the Highlander Folk School sought, year by year, term by term, to give its students, leaders and potential leaders of the new unions in the South, a broader view of the movement and a larger perspective on their roles and responsibilities within it. The idea of an inclusive labor movement was taught, as much else was taught in this adult progressive education center, experientially. Thus, although the large majority of students were industrial workers from CIO unions, the participation of other kinds of workers was invited. In its 1940 announcement, as it had earlier, the School continued to state explicitly that resident terms were "open to southern workers recommended by unions, co-operatives or farm organizations." And although few representatives of farm organizations were students at Highlander during these years, the terms generally included a few young mountain workers, members of unemployed and relief workers' unions who brought with them something of their independent rural tradition and outlook which two generations of poverty somehow had not destroyed. In the winter of 1939, for example, a young farmer-miner, son of an unemployed mountain family in Grundy County and leader of a WPA workers' Hod Carriers' local, joined the resident term to learn how to "urge unity in a better way."[42] So, too, did another son of an impoverished mountain family, chairman of a Workers' Alliance local who gave as his trade "WPA" and as his purpose for participating in a Highlander resident term "to get Grundy Co. and ajoining [sic] counties solid [sic] organized."[43] The spirited WPA worker unionists and their families apparently had an educative effect on some of their brothers among industrial workers, two of whom wired back from their TWOC local in Lumberton, North Carolina, after the term, "We arrived and found bad situation . . . Getting men to show some spirit as relief workers in Tracy City."[44]

During this period, especially in the summer, the resident terms tended to include one or more teachers, college students and professional persons with an intellectual commitment to the labor movement and sometimes with a working class background. In the summer of 1939, they included a young teacher from a small town in Georgia whose first contact with the labor movement began when he came to Atlanta to teach WPA classes for textile workers; a Berea College student with a Christian-Socialist orientation hoping to find a place in the labor movement and a Lynchburg, Virginia, YWCA Secretary of working class parents who was planning to "go back into the community into some kind of work which will put me in contact with industrial people."[45] Highlander staff members themselves were representatives of white collar unionism as founding members of an American Federation of Teachers local in Monteagle and active participants in the State Federation. There were also visiting speakers during every term from white collar unions—from the Newspaper Guild, from the TVA Federal Workers' Union and from the TWOC, Lucy Randolph Mason, Southern Public Relations Director, who spoke on such subjects as "Working with the Middle Class."[46]

Throughout the School's history, resident terms included an occasional worker-student from another country. Thus, in the winter term of 1938, along with seventeen industrial workers from CIO unions in Georgia, Tennessee, Kentucky, the Carolinas and Mississippi, there was a Swedish transport worker who had been given a scholarship by the Swedish labor movement to study in an American labor school. In the winter of 1939, a Mexican-born leader[47] of a local Pecan Workers' Union in San Antonio, Texas, was among the group. And, during 1940 and 1941, trade union representatives from Mexico and Columbia attended Highlander resident sessions, sponsored by the Pan American Union. These students were able through talks and class discussions, but especially in a personal and informal way, to provide their brother unionists with a different and broader view of the labor movement.

Ironically, although southern white workers might meet a Swedish or a Columbian worker among their fellow students at Highlander in these prewar years, they did not meet southern Negro workers. The School's policy, as painfully and carefully expressed in this period—"It has not been deemed advisable up to the present to have colored students at our regular workers' term"[48]—did not mean that the Highlander staff was any less determined to confront the issue of Negro workers as a part of the southern labor movement. The subject was very much in their minds and they dealt with it in many ways and contexts. In classes and informal sessions, students were encouraged to face the issue, the reasons underlying segregated unionism. They learned very soon that educational director Myles Horton, who had been working with the TWOC to organize locals and to develop workers' education classes for white textile workers in North Carolina was also working with the Southern Tenant Farmers Union to build local unions and educational programs for Negro and white sharecroppers in Arkansas. Under music director Zilphia Horton, they were taught the songs of Negro sharecroppers such as "No More Mourning" along with the songs of white working people. In addition to being challenged by Highlander staff members, in and out of the classroom, to rethink their positions, they were challenged by some of the visiting union leaders. James Terry, International Representative of the United Mine Workers, for example, speaking on "Organization of the Negro in the South" during the 1939 winter term put the case squarely to his fellow white unionists, "If we raise the Negro, we raise ourselves."[49]

There were opportunities provided as well for students to listen to and interact with visiting Negro speakers. As Zilphia Horton interpreted the policy of having Negro speakers, but not Negro worker-students, "We have thought it a more practical way to attack the problem of racial relations in the southern unions by having students meet and talk with Negro guests who visit the school and [by] making it a point to have as lecturers during the term distinguished Negroes."[50] Such statements, however, are not necessarily evidence that the Highlander staff was persuaded of its position educationally, only tactically. It was dealing as best it could with union unreadiness to accept an integrated resident student group.

To stimulate its students to become alive to and concerned with larger problems and issues affecting society and the labor movement, the School brought them in contact with representatives of many of the organizations in the South of the thirties working earnestly for democratic social change. And because Highlander staff members had helped to found several of these organizations or were actively involved in them, this interaction was not difficult to arrange. At almost every resident term, leading spokesmen for the Southern Tenant Farmers Union, the Fellowship of Southern Churchmen, the Committee on Economic and Racial Justice, the National Committee for People's Rights, Labor's Non-partisan League and the Southern Conference on Human Welfare came to the School to tell about the work of their organizations and report on current problems and developments.

In some instances, the School was able to educate its students through direct involvement in the activities of these groups. This was true of Labor's Non-partisan League and other political action organizations. In 1938, students not only heard the League's southern director, Alton Lawrence describe the way in which the organization was helping to elect New Deal candidates to office in Georgia and Alabama, but they were present when local unions in Grundy County came together in a coalition known as Labor's Political Conference. They had a behind-the-scenes view, too, of the historic county election of 1938 which brought the total slate of labor candidates into office. Subsequent resident students gained equally important firsthand knowledge of how and why these labor-backed officials were defeated for re-election and they attended meetings where plans were made to strengthen and broaden labor's base in the county and state.

In 1940, students as well as staff participated in the southwide deliberations of the Southern Conference for Human Welfare which was held in nearby Chattanooga. Here basic problems of farm tenancy, civil rights, education, labor relations, employment, suffrage and race relations were discussed. And, as social scientist W. T. Coach observed of the founding meeting of the Conference in 1938, they were discussed "not only by the professional and academic classes which usually consider these subjects," but by "tenant farmers, day laborers, farm-union and labor-union organizers and southern business men."[51] Here, also, students met with speaker and guest of honor Mrs. Eleanor Roosevelt at a Highlander-arranged supper meeting. This meeting, of course, was a major event in the expanding world of southern industrial worker-students. It also marked the beginning of a continuing interest in and support of the work of the School by Mrs. Roosevelt.[52]

Week-end Institutes for Expanding Industrial Unions

In the late thirties, there was a growing effort by unions (especially the older unions with a tradition of education such as the Garment Workers and the Hosiery Workers and some of the newer unions, including the Auto Workers who readily espoused this tradition) to reach at least a part of their expanding membership through short-term institutes and conferences. In support of this effort, the Highlander Folk School greatly expanded its short-term educational offerings, both those developed to serve specific unions and those developed around broad issues and problems.

Beginning in 1938, the School became the setting for annual institutes of the American Federation of Hosiery Workers' locals in the Tri-State area of Tennessee, Georgia and Alabama and, in 1939 and 1940, for annual institutes of the International Ladies' Garment Workers and the United Auto Workers in the South. The Southern Summer School in Asheville, North Carolina, and resident labor schools in the North were also the scene of such institutes.[53] All performed the same essential function of giving groups of union members, officials and organizers in a region, the opportunity to meet together for a week-end of education and recreation with problem-centered classes on such subjects as "Grievance Procedures" or "Building the Union." Sponsored by various unions, these institutes were developed by their national educational directors in cooperation with regional officials and staffs of the labor schools. Thus, in general format as well as in purpose, the institutes for a given union tended to be similar wherever they were offered.

The institutes held at Highlander, however, differed from those held at other resident schools in an important way, just as its relationship to the labor movement differed. Because of its early organizing and educational activities in mill and factory towns and its services to a growing group of former students and their locals over the years, the Highlander institutes were part of an on-going program in relation to the several unions rather than a brief, one week-end-a-year educational offering. In the case of the Hosiery Workers, for example, the School had begun going out to besieged locals near the School in 1934 and 1935, lending support to their strikes and organizing educational and recreational activities. Out of these activities had developed the support of union leaders such as Edward Callaghan, Regional Director of the American Federation of Hosiery Workers, who became convinced of the value of workers' education and specifically Highlander's workers' education program. Callaghan not only sent promising local leaders to the School for training beginning in 1935, but he came to the School himself as a guest speaker and resource person for resident sessions. Thus, by 1938, Callaghan and Highlander alumnus Matt Lynch, who had become a southern organizer for the Hosiery Workers, were not only actively involved in planning and carrying out the Highlander-based institutes, but they were involved in helping to plan follow up activities. More than this, southern leaders such as Lynch and Callaghan tended to become increasingly involved in the larger field of workers' education, in helping, for example, to plan a Southern Conference on Workers' Education held in Chattanooga in February 1938. As a result, the Conference featured major labor leader speakers as well as major educators: George Googe, Southern Representative of the AFL, and John Martin, Southern Director of the Garment Workers as well as Hilda Smith, WPA specialist on workers' education, and President Frank Graham of the University of North Carolina.[54]

Nor is it surprising that out of these short-term Highlander-based institutes, in combination with and reinforced by other kinds of educational activities, it was possible to develop increasing enthusiasm and support for education at the local level. One notes, therefore, at a Hosiery Workers' convention in 1938, that southern delegates, pointing proudly to the educational work which "has already been carried on particularly in the Tri-State area in co-operation with the Highlander Folk School," urged that education be "a vital part of the union, as much a part of union activities as the holding of a meeting."[55]

Highlander Folk School's residential program in the years 1938-1942 represented a response to the practical needs of the new southern industrial union movement with union leadership participating not only in defining the needs but in carrying out the program to meet them. At the same time, it was peculiarly a Highlander program. Music and drama, for example, were elevated to subjects of major importance in the education of local movement leadership. The projected movement was transformed and expanded, in the course of successive resident terms, to include professional and white collar workers, unemployed mountaineers, European and Latin American trade unionists and members of organizations working for racial and social justice as well as white industrial workers.

With the advent of the war period, there was a greatly increased demand for mass services to new unions. In the wartime extension program developed in response to this demand as in its earlier extension program, the liberal elements so characteristic of Highlander's resident program were notably absent. It is this extension program which will he examined in the following chapter.

NINE

Serving Organizational Needs: A Field Program for New Union Members

With the national defense boom of 1940 came a growing number of government contracts to southern industry and a concerted and renewed CIO organizing drive in major southern industrial areas. Lucy Randolph Mason reviewing the rapid growth in union membership which followed in the next year and a half in Birmingham, New Orleans, Atlanta, Memphis and Knoxville, the tens of thousands of new members and the new locals "springing up in every direction," concluded in an article in the *CIO News*, "It's not the same old South!"[1] Along with the vast new membership and the new locals "springing up" were many new contracts to be negotiated and hosts of new grievances to be handled. The week-end institutes as sponsored by the Federation of Hosiery Workers or the United Auto Workers could train only a few of the inexperienced leaders and reach only a few of the newly recruited members. The great majority had to be reached in some other way. Some unions, such as the Steel Workers Organizing Committee held classes for training union representatives in various regions. Others, such as the Rubber Workers, developed manuals on negotiating procedures and on handling grievances.[2] However, the scope and urgency and complexity of the educational needs of both new members and new leaders could not be met by manuals and a few regional classes. For the Highlander Folk School, very aware of these widespread needs, but committed to continuing its intensive residential terms for developing liberally as well as technically-educated union leadership and to an expanding program of field

129

services to alumni and their locals, the problem was one of finding new ways to maximize the use of its limited resources.

Between 1940 and 1944, a series of large-scale extension programs was developed; beginning with a short-lived effort in Alcoa, Tennessee, and followed by a major program in New Orleans which provided the pattern for subsequent programs in Memphis, Atlanta and Knoxville. In each of these areas, a Highlander staff member, working closely with an industrial union council, planned and carried out an educational program for many hundreds of rank and file members, their officers and stewards. In the process, several of the School's younger staff members became skilled and sought after as educational directors for unions, materials which they developed were widely used and some of the more promising volunteer teachers discovered through these programs emerged, after an apprenticeship in the field and a term at Highlander, as workers' education leaders in their unions.

The Education of an Extension Director

The first and most important of these members of the School's extension staff to be developed in the field was Mary Lawrence. Coming to Highlander in 1938 after being graduated from Duke University (where she was a leader in campus-industrial YWCA activities), she became, in 1944, Highlander extension director. Her initial assignment was working with community groups and teaching WPA workers' classes in Grundy County. Out of this experience, as described in her Highlander-published handbook on union education, *Education Unlimited*, she became convinced that an educational program should be based "on personal knowledge" of a given group of people and situation, "on their experiences and not your theories."[3]

Her only other preparation for her role as a member of Highlander's extension staff was several months' experience working directly with the labor movement. Through the School, she obtained a job which combined serving as an office worker for an AFL Teamsters' local in Louisville and helping to set up its workers' education classes. This job was of brief duration, in part because the Teamster president's idea of workers' education was "making speeches." Thereafter, she worked for a short time with the Workers' Education Committee of Louisville and with a CIO Textile Workers' Local, helping, again, to set up classes and also establishing a mimeographed local paper, *The Textile Times*. In both of these instances the setting up of classes proved difficult because the membership evidenced little interest. "I spent all my energy," she later confessed, "convincing a few staunch union members to be stauncher members."[4] Out of this Louisville training-in-the-field, however, came another basic conviction: that an educational program should be identified "with the growth of the union," and classes should be organized "only where there is a demand for them and where you have succeeded in organizing a program for the whole membership."[5]

A Program for One Union, Alcoa, Tennessee

In the summer of 1940, Mary Lawrence was sent by Highlander on her first six-weeks field assignment to a huge Aluminum Workers' local in Alcoa, Tennessee, where officials had requested the School's help in stimulating the interest of new members in the union. From reports, it is apparent that she sought, with little success, to involve the Executive Board of the local in finding ways to reach the new members. She also attempted to get to know and involve a defunct Women's Auxiliary in union affairs and met with a separate group of wives of Negro members. When these efforts proved unrewarding, she analyzed the problems involved in the situation—the racial divisions, a widely scattered membership, poor transportation facilities, a basically rural rather than industrial orientation on the part of many members and an uncooperative Board—and organized volunteer committees to help deal with them. The ensuing efforts over the next weeks to reach the membership through enlivening and publicizing union meetings, developing an informal recreation and dramatics program and producing and circulating a shop paper did not "solve" any of the problems. A few more of the 8,000 workers began to attend meetings.[6] The meetings themselves became more lively when popular speeches, a string band and skits by a young people's drama group were added to the business agenda. The shop paper, the *AWA News*, written primarily by the educational director assisted by a small and inexperienced union committee, reached some 500 members and helped them, presumably, to become more informed about their local. But it promptly collapsed when Mary Lawrence left the scene. Yet in spite of the limited results, the Alcoa program was a stimulating rather than a discouraging experience for the young educator. She firmly believed, with all of the many problems inherent in the situation, that over a longer period of time elements of an on-going program could have been developed.[7]

A Program for an Industrial Area: New Orleans, 1941-1942

In contrast to Alcoa, various positive factors were implicit in the New Orleans situation where Highlander and Mary Lawrence undertook an extension program in the spring of 1941. With a CIO membership which had grown, according to the Regional Director Fred Pieper, from 675 in 1939 to 15,000 in 1941,[8] the need for a practical educational program to reach the unreached membership and train the untrained local officers was clear. The New Orleans Industrial Union council not only eagerly approached the Highlander Folk School for assistance in developing such a program,[9] but it stood ready to support and work with the staff assigned. When Mary Lawrence arrived, the Council immediately selected a representative committee of Negro and white leaders of locals and gave it "full power to arrange meetings . . . and draft programs."[10] And, although the resources, institutional and staff, which the School brought to the situation were obviously small in relation to the size of the task, they were peculiarly well suited to it.

Highlander's characteristically pragmatic approach was needed in finding ways to relate to diverse unions in an area whose locals "spread from the water front through the industrial life of the city and out to cities fifty miles away."[11] So, too, was its practical method of identifying and developing new educational leadership in a field setting. Defined in terms of traditional workers' education classes and teaching loads, all of the School's staff and more could have been absorbed in a program for the New Orleans area alone. Time, of course, was required—time to get acquainted with the special needs and problems of the various groups to be reached and time to test out ways of reaching them. Here, with a sense of the size and scope of the proposed program, Highlander offered the services of Mary Lawrence for a year along with the resources of the residential School to train small groups of local leaders.

Training for Union Officers and Other Classes

If the School in its residential terms had come to allocate increasing time to utilitarian kinds of educational activities such as workshop courses and special training sessions for business agents, the Highlander extension program as developed in cooperation with the New Orleans Union Council was totally so. In projecting the year-long[12] program to meet a variety of urgent, practical needs, the Regional Director and Council-appointed Education Committee decided that priority in the first phase of the program must be given to training local officers in their essential tasks related to holding the new unions together with priority in later classes to be given to basic education of the rank and file about their union rights and responsibilities.

The initial four weeks Officers' Training School, quite properly called "training," illustrates the extent to which the educational experiences were selected in terms of the single criterion of usefulness to the union. In planning the school, Mary Lawrence carefully "screened" the kinds of activities to be offered by discussing them with her committee and other union leaders and by visiting locals to observe their needs. As a final test of the usefulness of the proposed offerings, she gave a demonstration of the various classes at a meeting of local union leaders. In this way, they could judge for themselves whether they wanted or needed a class in Union Problems, Labor History, Parliamentary Law or Union Publicity. Based on their responses, the program was defined and scheduled weekly.[13]

Within these several classes whose goal was, in the teacher's words, "how to set up a more efficient organization within their union" the emphasis was on helping the 120 officers, committeemen and stewards to deal with current problems confronting their locals.[14] "Actual grievances to be taken up with management are discussed," she explained in the first months report; "local presidents use the parliamentary law in conducting meetings; posters are made for picket lines; outlines of speeches to be made at union meetings are worked out in class."[15] If this did not sufficiently insure the usefulness of the several learning activities, toward the end of the four weeks' school, the officer, steward and committeeman-students "drew up a plan to put into practice what they have been taught."[16]

Two other kinds of practical purposes were indirectly served by this initial areawide Officers' School. In the course of their intensive four weeks' training, local leaders became well acquainted with the Council's workers' education program and what it hoped to accomplish. Officer-students, in turn, were able to interpret the program to members of their unions. In addition, where they evidenced special interest and aptitude, these leaders were invited to assist in developing and carrying out the educational program for their locals.

With a view to enlarging her pool of volunteer teachers in the many and far-flung locals, the New Orleans educational director noted in her first month's report that she was conducting a class for a small group from the Inland Boatman Division of the National Maritime Union "who desire to learn how to give the membership as a whole a better understanding of their organization." Here again, the local union leaders defined what they needed and wanted to learn to take back their members. "The class started with an analysis of their contract,"[17] she indicated.

Another class, a stewards' training class for a large Sugar Workers' local in Reserve, Louisiana, was based, in large part, on helping the stewards prepare to negotiate an adequate contract as well as coping with their jobs. Initiated a few months before the contract for the newly-organized local was to be written, the class was enthusiastically received. In preparing to write the contract, considerable learning apparently occurred. The group studied typical clauses from other union contracts to see which fitted their needs. They also prepared to defend their version of the contract by making a cost of living survey to justify their wage demands.[18] Based on this class experience which reinforced her already strong belief that union education should help students deal with immediate problems, Mary Lawrence recommended to other educational directors that as part of their preparation they should "visit the plant where the students work" and "where possible, sit in on negotiation of contracts."[19]

In addition to such classes tailored to the needs of individual locals, several area classes were offered in 1941 in Parliamentary Law, Public Speaking and General Union Education. However, the broad membership was reached, not through classes, but through informal activities.

Education Through Union Meetings and Other Informal Activities

Beginning very early, the ambitious area director engaged in various kinds of informal education by "attending Hosiery Workers' meetings and calling attention to mistakes in parliamentary procedure"; "helping the Furniture Workers' Union draw picket signs, mimeograph a bulletin and put up a display at strike headquarters"; and "meeting with the girls' departments of the Sugar Workers and discussing the duties of shop stewards with them."[20]

Increasingly throughout the year, the areawide program was carried on within meetings—executive board meetings, department meetings, committee meetings and general membership meetings, rather than in classes. Mary Lawrence adopted this familiar Highlander approach both because she was able to reach many "class shy" leaders as well as members. She had also become convinced through her recent experience that "the best education in new locals is carried on within the framework of the union structure itself."[21] Even newly elected officers and stewards, she found, were very often loath to attend classes which would assist them in their duties. In one large plant, for example, new stewards who freely admitted the difficulties which they were encountering in settling grievances did not respond to her repeated efforts to set up special classes for them. Observing that some 70 per cent of these stewards were attending Stewards' Council meetings, she simply changed the locus. "Thereafter," she concluded, "an educational program was carried on at every Cellotex Steward Council Meeting."[22] Other kinds of activities and services were also undertaken by the educational director and her growing staff of volunteers whose talents were augmented by attending Highlander resident terms.[23] Among these activities were informal talks at union meetings, writing weekly articles for the local labor paper, starting an area labor library, helping locals to set up legislative committees to acquaint members with issues and candidates important to labor and developing a union handbook, *How to Build Your Union*[24] and other widely used educational materials.

Wartime Efforts to Reach the Membership

By the beginning of 1942, with the entry of the United States into World War II, most classes were discontinued. The decision was a reality dictated one: even highly motivated workers found attendance difficult due to the pressure of their jobs. In place of classes, the educational director worked with local union officials to make informal adult education a part of all departmental and general membership meetings. The primary purpose of this program, as defined by Mary Lawrence and the Industrial Union Council Education Committee, was to combat the apathy of the membership toward the war and war-related union problems. It was welcomed by overworked local leaders whose ranks were being diminished by the war and who were concerned about the "unions-as-usual, let-the-officers-do-it" attitude which they were encountering.

In attempting to make effective use of the half hour allocated to education on the agenda of general union meetings, two kinds of approaches were used. First, Mary Lawrence reported to the Highlander staff, there was "an introductory discussion of the gravity of the world situation and threat to the labor movement" and "the necessity of more rank and file members taking part in the union." Second, there was a recommendation regarding "some very practical way in which the membership could become active."[25]

The success of the thirty minute effort to give a new union members a national and even an international appreciation of the wartime crisis as it affected the labor movement was doubtful—even when supplemented by an occasional one-day institute. A letter from Mary Lawrence to a national union official asking him to serve as keynote speaker for an institute on "Your Local Has a Part in This War" suggests that she was keenly aware of the size of the task

> Organization in New Orleans is fairly new, and they do not have much background in unionism to fall back on to meet the problems of the war situation. They are having many difficulties because their trained leaders are rapidly leaving for the army and for the shipyards . . . In addition, there is little understanding of the war. Most members are rather apathetic.[26]

Some effects of the Overall Program

As the one Highlander staff person working with a volunteer union committee and a volunteer teaching staff to develop a diverse leadership and membership program, Mary Lawrence did not attempt a systematic evaluation of the program. Of the kinds of practical, behavioral changes which she observed growing out of the functionally-conceived and evolved program, she indicated

> . . . progress was made in getting the rank and file members on their feet and expressing themselves. . . some officers are presiding over meetings and carrying on their jobs better. . . stewards are doing a better job of taking up grievances and getting more cooperation from their members and, in general, quite a few members have a better understanding of the possibilities of unionism and how to build their organizations more efficiently.[27]

Evaluating the significance of the New Orleans program some five years later in her study of workers' education in the South, she emphasized the importance of the close interrelationship between the School's resident and extension programs. Of the union members who demonstrated "special leadership qualities" and had been selected to attend a workers' education term, a good many proved able to assume increased responsibility in the educational program and new roles within their unions. This readiness to take on new leadership responsibilities which she observed in some union member-students as soon as they returned from Highlander[28] remained characteristic of the alumni group. Thus, of the twenty-four New Orleans area union members who attended resident terms in 1941 and 1942, she found, eighteen continued to take a notably active part in workers' education and union affairs, seven as fulltime organizers and business agents.[29]

The interrelationship had its positive effects, as well, on the School itself. As the New Orleans educational director moved between the field situation and Highlander, she was able to bring to the resident group, both students and staff, a current perspective on problems and developments in the movement and to share some of the educational techniques and materials evolved and tested in the field. And, based on the New Orleans experience, the School planned and carried out other such extension programs with industrial union councils—with the Memphis Industrial Council, beginning in 1941; with the Atlanta Industrial Union Council, beginning in 1942; and with the Knoxville Council, beginning in the spring of 1943.

The School as Viewed by Itself and Others

Assessing its ten-year record in workers' education in 1942, the Highlander Folk School stated with some pride, "We may safely say that the School has been a significant factor in the development of the southern labor movement." As proof of this statement it noted, "About ninety percent of Highlander's alumni are international union officials, local union officials or organizers in the South. Last year alone, the number of students trained in resident, community and extension classes totaled 425." It noted, too, its endorsement by "numerous CIO and AF of L international unions" and by the CIO National Convention. "The most active cooperation, however," the report emphasized, "comes from twelve southern CIO, AF of L and Railroad Brotherhood officials on Highlander's Executive Council. These men and women not only make policy, but assist in carrying it out."[30]

The same report also emphasized Highlander's independent status and its broad social role and purpose. "Independently organized, with no political affiliations," it declared, "the school works with all branches of organized labor." And because of its relationship to various groups within the movement, the report concluded, "Highlander has become a center for progressive action," assuming leadership, it pointed out, in "the fight against the reactionary . . . poll tax congressmen and senators."[31]

Some educators and students of workers' education in this period, looking at this labor-allied institution which both noted with pride its closeness to the labor movement and avowed its independence, found it difficult to know where to place the School, how to categorize it. Florence Schneider, author of a well-documented study, *Patterns of Workers' Education*,[32] was unable to fit Highlander into any one of the patterns which she discerned. She discusses the School, therefore, not only in her chapter on resident schools (along with the Bryn Mawr Summer School for Women Workers and others),[33] but also in her chapter on education "within the trade union movement" where she describes Highlander's summer school in La Follette, Tennessee, as developed with and for the Amalgamated Clothing Workers.[34]

The author of another contemporary study, T.R. Adam in the *Workers' Road to Learning*, viewed the Highlander Folk School, along with Commonwealth College, as totally and, from his vantage point, dangerously tied to the trade union movement. "These schools," he observed, "commit the future of workers' education in the South to the political and economic fate of unionism." In consequence, he warned, "reactionary oppression of the cultural life of the people is invited whenever the labor movement suffers a reverse."[35]

One educator, John Dewey, whose educational thinking, directly and indirectly, had influenced the co-founder of the Highlander Folk School and whose hopes for a broadly-based labor movement were also Highlander's hopes, was unequivocal in his enthusiastic assessment of the independent workers' school. In replying to allegations against the School in the *Nashville Banner*, he wrote

> The organized labor movement is one of the most important, if not the most important, bulwark of democracy. In helping southern unions to educate an intelligent native leadership, and in promoting a better understanding of the essentials of collective bargaining, the Highlander Folk School is making a considerable contribution to democratic institutions.[36]

It is not surprising that several educators looking at Highlander's role in relation to the southern labor movement in 1940 saw "different institutions."

One could see, looking at Highlander, a residential workers' school with a program which included (along with music and drama and spokesmen for radical social change) courses in Parliamentary Law, Labor History and Labor Economics not unlike those offered at other workers' schools of the period. One could see, looking at Highlander's Executive Council, made up almost entirely of southern union leaders, and its growing extension program for industrial union councils, a kind of service agency for the union movement.

One could also see, as Highlander did and as John Dewey apparently did an independent and dynamic radical institution which in its interactions with the southern labor movement was both affecting and being affected by it—was both responding to immediate organizational needs of new unions and seeking to develop a more inclusive labor movement, a more democratic South. Thus, the extension program in New Orleans as viewed by Highlander, produced, along with officers "presiding over meetings and carrying out their jobs better" and members with "a better understanding of the possibilities of unionism," a group of local leaders who returned home from resident terms with a larger view of workers' education, of the movement and of their roles within it. The program produced, too, a regional CIO director who, in the process of helping to develop the Industrial Union Council program for New Orleans became sufficiently interested in workers' education to become more broadly involved. Thus, Louisiana CIO Director Pieper served as a major speaker and resource person for Highlander resident terms beginning in the fall of 1941 and became a member of the program planning Executive Council by the end of the year.

This last view of the School and of the labor movement was an optimistic one. It presupposed a school able to continue to respond to the movement's changing needs and a movement willing to remain open and responsive to the radically democratic school which sought quite honestly to influence it. For some years, in the war and early postwar years, this optimism was to prove well-founded. Thereafter, as the industrial union movement became increasingly institutionalized and its goals more narrowly and conservatively defined, it no longer was willing to interact freely with the School which had developed many of its early leaders and supported its early struggles. The growth and deterioration of Highlander's educational relationship to the Southern CIO will be considered in the chapter which follows.

TEN

A Program and a Movement Become Institutionalized: The Southern CIO Schools

"In 1942," a Highlander report predicted, "all of the resources of labor and the country will be directed to the defeat of the Axis and the destruction of Fascism. The energies of Highlander will be geared into that great effort."[1] In 1942 and 1943, too, the resources of the Highlander Folk School were devoted almost entirely to union education activities in support of the war effort.[2] Even the School's restatement of its purpose in this period—"to assist in the defense and expansion of political and economic democracy"[3]—although as broad as ever, reflected in its terminology the thinking of a war period. By 1944, although its unions-in-wartime programs and services continued, the School and its policy-making Executive Council of southern labor leaders and educators began to concern itself increasingly with the kind of labor movement, the kind of South and nation, even the kind of world to emerge after the war. The minutes of the Highlander Executive Council in January 1944 suggest the broad, politically and socially active postwar labor movement which the School projected and proposed to encourage. They also suggest the strong convictions of labor members of the Council regarding the importance of workers' education in the creation of that movement ("with the CIO," as they noted, "still young and growing in the South") and their discontent with the meager funds available for educational staff and program. The National CIO, they lamented, "doesn't realize the demand in the South."[4] The main focus of the Council's discussion was on how to help meet that need by developing the first CIO School in the South to be held at the Highlander Folk School in May.

Like Sidney Hillman who, in the midst of an organizing drive in the late thirties, urged delegates to a Clothing Workers' convention, "Let us not become too practical . . . let us dedicate ourselves to new dreams of the future . . . where men and women will be economically secure and politically free,"[5] Highlander's leadership was allowing itself to dream. And there was some basis for those dreams. In July 1943 the CIO formed the Political Action Committee (PAC), headed by Hillman which was authorized to organize labor and friends of labor politically on a year-around basis with a view to effective action in state and national elections and to achieving legislation in the broad interests of working people and their families. In the same period, James Patton of the National Farmers Union was calling for "a people's peace" with small farmers, organized labor, church groups and others coming together in one great coalition.[6] And in the spring of 1944, The *Highlander Fling* hailed, as the first step in this people's coalition, the formation of the Federated Labor Committee for Political Action in Tennessee, with CIO members of Highlander's Executive Council taking active leadership along with representatives from the AF of L, the Farmers Union and the PAC in the southeast.[7]

The Southern CIO School, 1944: A Labor-proposed Cooperatively-developed Program

The idea for the Southern CIO School was first introduced by delegates to the CIO Convention in Philadelphia in 1943. Minutes of a Highlander staff meeting shortly thereafter record its beginning

> Myles wrote that the Southern CIO Regional Directors met at the CIO Convention and proposed a four-weeks workers' term to be held at Highlander in the spring. They plan to attend our next Executive Council meeting.[8]

Preceding the proposal, of course, had been three years of frequent interaction between Highlander staff members and Southern CIO leaders as members of the School's Executive Council. Preceding the proposal, too, had been a series of interactions between the Highlander field staff and representatives of industrial union councils who had together produced

142

educational programs for new CIO locals in New Orleans, Atlanta, Memphis and elsewhere. And in the background of the proposal for a Highlander-CIO school was the longer history of Highlander's interactions with the movement. It was in those difficult early years when the southern labor movement was struggling to get underway that the Tennessee Director and other conveners of the Southern Regional Directors meeting came to know and work with Myles Horton and the Highlander staff. The proposed Southern School, having originated with the Southern Directors, found ready approval from the National CIO Director of Organization, Allen Haywood, as well as from J. Raymond Walsh of the Research and Education Department who expressed a readiness to "cooperate to the fullest extent."[9]

In the course of the two-day Highlander Executive Council meeting (to which other CIO representatives, southern and national had been invited), basic plans were formulated for financing, staffing and recruiting students for the one-month School as well as for the educational program. Regional leaders present agreed to assume joint direction of the School, along with representatives from the National CIO office and the Highlander Folk School; to share in its financing through an appeal for funds to their several international unions; to assist in recruiting and approving students working through state and local organizations in their region and to serve as speakers and resource persons with one regional director serving as teacher for a course on CIO Policy during each of the four weeks of the term. Commenting on these plans as "a significant development in the field of workers' education," a Highlander report observed, "As far as we know no similar group of labor officials have [sic] ever requested, worked out details, and offered to finance such a program."[10]

The outlines of an educational program which came out of this Highlander-Southern CIO leader planning meetings clearly represented the thinking of both. In the interest of serving the immediate and practical needs of unions, the program was to include a central course on "CIO Policy and Program, based on the CIO Convention proceedings" and courses such as Parliamentary Law, Public Speaking and the production of mimeographed shop papers. Looking toward a more democratic South, there was to be a strong emphasis on "the CIO Political Action and Legislative Program," with a one-day conference on political action to be headed, if possible, by Sidney Hillman and a group of lecture-discussions on "the relations between farmers and workers and the need for farmer-labor unity" with, it was proposed, President James Patton of the National Farmers Union.[11]

Viewed quantitatively, the first Southern CIO School must be considered a failure. Only eight students from CIO locals and industrial union councils in Tennessee, Alabama, Georgia, Louisiana and Texas were fulltime participants and they, according to a follow-up study, were "hand-picked" by the southern directors who helped to plan the program. (It would seem apparent, in retrospect, that launching the new southwide program in wartime with the expectation that busy regional directors would be able to involve busy state and local officials, with only a slight notion of the new CIO School, in finding promising war worker-students willing and able to take a month away from their jobs was, at best, an optimistic undertaking.) Viewed qualitatively, however, as an educational experience for the resident students and for the labor leader planners and viewed as the first such cooperative venture, it was a significant beginning.

The educational activities offered to the little group of eight potential union leader-students[12] in the course of the one-month School of May 1944 were scaled down from the initial planning session, but they still represented an ambitious array. As agreed, there were newly-defined courses on CIO policy and on political action, as well as Labor Economics, Parliamentary Law and Labor Journalism. There was also a new course on union-community relations as well as several Highlander courses related to the war effort including Labor and Government Agencies. In all, some thirty National and Southern CIO leaders, government officials and representatives of the Cooperative League and the PAC participated as visiting teachers, speakers and resource persons.

By involving CIO leaders new to teaching and other teachers new to their subjects, the School was, in a real sense, a learning experience for staff as well as students. The course on Community Relations was taught by a member of the International Ladies' Garment Workers education staff in Knoxville who indicated in her evaluation that the course was necessarily an "experiment" since it was the first time it was being offered. She also pointed out that she had been unable to find materials for the students to read in helping them to understand the process of "integrating the union into the life of the community." (This was, perhaps, a reflection of the fact that unions, especially CIO unions in the South, had been preoccupied with establishing their right merely to exist in the community.) By pooling her experiences and ideas with those of students whose locals had begun to participate on community boards and committees and by drawing on the experiences of visiting speakers, the teacher reported, the class was able to develop its own projects and guidelines for building good community relations. "I want to express my appreciation," she wrote back to Myles Horton, "for having been on the staff in May. I learned many things in a short period."[13]

Notes on a Highlander staff evaluation session indicate that Southern CIO leader-teachers, however authoritative and current their union information, needed more assistance than they received in assuming their unfamiliar roles. Especially in 1944, when the CIO Regional Directors had not yet developed any sort of outline for their newly-conceived four-week course, "CIO Policy and Organization," several of the teachers were apparently given to repetition and "rambling about their personal experiences." To avoid these pitfalls and to assist in conducting discussions, it was agreed that "experienced staff members should sit in on their classes and help them out if necessary."[14]

Because of the small size of the resident group, it was possible for the Highlander staff to give the students a number of opportunities for field experiences to supplement their formal courses. They assisted the staff in planning and carrying out a weekend conference on farmer-labor problems and cooperation which was attended by 100 area farmer and labor representatives. They also assumed responsibility, with the Highlander staff, for a conference on "Political Action and Postwar Employment" which was held in Chattanooga under the auspices of the Chattanooga Industrial Union Council. The one-day gathering, in which students participated on panels and in discussions and led group singing of labor songs, was, in effect, a one-day training session in workers' education. At the end of the term when students were asked to look critically at their experience and make recommendations for future terms, they emphasized the value to them as future leaders of learning to run such conferences.

Students also emphasized the value of participating in a democratically-managed resident community where staff and student representatives were members of a governing council which functioned as a sort of grievance committee, hearing and acting on criticisms and suggestions regarding the on-going educational, recreational and work activities. Valued, too, as an idea to be taken back to their locals, was the Workers' Cooperative Store, set up at the beginning of the term, where students and staff purchased various supplies and later received a small rebate.

In evaluating the effects of the first CIO Term, one might cite, as did a Highlander Folk School report for 1944, the fact that four of the eight union member-students were put on the organizing staffs of their international unions and that the other four were officers in their locals.[15] Since these students were admittedly "hand-picked," however, they might well have achieved their positions, if at a somewhat later date, without participating in the School. Of more far-reaching effect was the active support which they and the regional directors gave to subsequent CIO Schools.[16]

The Southern CIO School, 1945: Labor's Increased Participation

Minutes of planning meetings and reports on the 1945 Southern CIO School indicate that additional regional directors and international representatives participated in developing and carrying out the second school and that four of these union leaders subsequently became members of Highlander's Executive Council. With more labor officials assuming an active role in planning the 1945 School, the program, in various ways, was "their program." Thus, in spite of the strong feelings expressed by some Highlander staff members that Labor History and Labor Economics should continue to be offered, both were dropped. The educational director later explained with regard to the economics course that regional directors requested that it be omitted because, in their words, "most people don't know what economics would include and are against it."[17] The regional directors were also responsible for adding Training for Shop Stewards and Fundamentals of Collective Bargaining to the program.

On the other hand, in part because of Highlander's influence, but also because this self-selected group of labor officials were themselves more broadly concerned with workers' education and the problems of the world-after-the-war, the program which they helped to develop was devoted to other problems and issues as well. Thus, the CIO policy against discrimination was a major focus of attention throughout the term. Highlander staff members and the regional directors dealt with the policy and encouraged students to discuss its implications for their local unions. A number of visiting speakers also addressed themselves to the subject including George Weaver, Director of the National CIO Committee to Abolish Racial Discrimination, and James Dombrowski, new Executive Secretary of the Southern Conference for Human Welfare after many years as a Highlander staff member. More important for the education (or re-education) of future southern labor leaders, several Negroes were among the twenty-six CIO member students in the second CIO school.[18]

Political action continued to be emphasized in the 1945 CIO term. A course on Legislation and Political Action, taught by Highlander staff members, was supplemented by special sessions led by George Mitchell, Regional Director of the CIO-PAC, who was also a member of the Highlander Executive Council and by a representative of the National Committee to Abolish the Poll Tax. The Union-Community Relations course also continued to be offered, taught by the Highlander staff and Executive Council member-CIO Public Relations Representative Lucy Randolph Mason. Beyond the courses, there were two series of lecture-discussions: one on labor and international affairs led by an executive of the Industrial Division of the National YWCA and the other on labor education led by Kermit Eby, Director of the Education and Research Department of the National CIO.

Evaluative reports and articles by staff and students indicate that the second school, like the first, was an educative experience for labor officials and staff as well as for union member-students. CIO Educational Director Eby candidly admitted, looking back at his lecture-discussions on "Workers' Education, Why and What Is It?" that teaching southern workers at Highlander educated him to some of the shortcomings of his overly academic approach. In a conference with a group of students after one of his early sessions, he recalled, "Very politely, but very firmly, I was asked to modify my vocabulary." This he readily promised to do, "But," he added, "translation of my ideas was no easy task!"[19] Others, too, had their difficulties in communication. One of these was a New York oriented workers' education teacher-in-training, chairman of his local Maritime Union Education Committee, who had come to the Highlander Folk School to learn more about techniques of workers' education. The CIO regional directors on the staff, three of whom had never taught before, continued to have their problems as teachers.

The problems related to the development of workers' education teachers were met by the Highlander staff with no special concern. However, concern was expressed about problems related to integration of the term. One student who had come "with the usual prejudice," the staff noted, "went back unprejudiced." Two others, in spite of efforts to dissuade them, "left at the end of two weeks because the term was integrated." This raised a policy question in the minds of the staff as to whether to "select" Negro students and "limit the number" in the interest of educating prejudiced whites or to have "many Negro students and therefore have as white students only the unprejudiced." It was decided, with some differences of opinion expressed, that Highlander, in the near future at least, should recommend that CIO regional directors send "just selected Negroes" each term.[20] This decision for the School which a few years later was to be a southwide center for civil rights education would seem surprisingly cautious. The decision, however, represented a forward step for southern CIO co-sponsors, many of whose local leaders were strongly resistant to integrated unions, much less living and learning together in an intimate, informal residential setting.[21]

There are other indications that the Highlander staff found it necessary to make accommodations to the wishes of its co-sponsors. Not only were some of the broader courses such as Labor History omitted, but it was agreed that, in the future, the month-long School would be planned around five-day weeks since "People who come from a long distance want to see this section of the country and are determined to leave for the weekend."[22] This decision represented far more of an accommodation than merely rescheduling activities because, as Myles Horton explained when he first rejected the idea, he considered weekends during the resident term "a most important part of the program."[23]

However critically the staff may have viewed the term's shortcomings, the students seem to have been highly motivated and inspired by their experience. Typical of the feelings which they expressed was the concluding paragraph in a story entitled "Autobiography," one of a collection of stories written during the term, by the President of an Oil Workers' local from El Dorado, Arkansas. "My union," he wrote, "sent me to Highlander to get and bring back to it the knowledge and spirit of unionism which is not to be obtained elsewhere. If I am able to take back to them only a small part of the fire, enthusiasm and militancy which has been instilled in me here, I will consider it a job well done."[24]

Not so typical, but suggesting that some students, at least, gained a broad view of labor's future role and responsibility through their participation in the Highlander-CIO School, was an article in *The International Oil Worker* by a local officer-student. "Labor needs just this type of School," he asserted. "Our problems are not merely local but of world importance because the peace and prosperity of the world are going to be determined by the part that labor plays in keeping the welfare of workers of all nations."[25]

There is some evidence, other than enthusiastic articles, that students in the 1945 CIO Term did, in fact, respond to the broader goals which the Highlander staff and others sought to project for the southern labor movement. A School report following the term indicates that along with students who had assumed new offices within their several unions, some had become involved in workers' education, political action and community organizations. Some, for example, had become members or chairman of local Political Action Committees. One student was writing a regular PAC column for the state CIO paper. Still others were teaching classes in job relations, parliamentary law and world events. One had helped to organize a so-called "City Forum of the Air." Some, for the first time, had joined the board of such organizations as the Community Chest and the Urban League as union representatives.[26]

In assuring the continuation of the Southern CIO School, the most important evaluation, as after the first School, was the official approval and support which was forthcoming. Thus, the Education Committee of the Tennessee State Industrial Union Council not only gave special recognition to "the Annual Southern CIO Term held at Highlander Folk School" for its "tremendous value in training our best leadership" but recommended that the State Council "give its full support to the third Annual CIO Term," and "make scholarships available for outstanding leaders of Tennessee CIO unions."[27]

The Southern CIO School, 1946: Labor's Lack of Participation

In 1946, with the Southern CIO Term at the Highlander Folk School already established as the "Annual Southern CIO Term," its continued existence was made difficult and the full and free participation of the CIO Regional Directors impossible. Only brief mention appears in the Highlander Executive Council minutes of the events which impinged on plans for the Third Annual Term and led, finally, to a basically changed and diminished relationship between the School and the Southern industrial union movement. "This year the CIO Term is late in getting started," the minutes note, "because of the various strikes and the fact that the CIO is tied up with plans for a Southern Organizing Drive."[28]

The program for the Third CIO Term as "put together" by the Highlander staff was notable for its lack of participation, in any significant way, by CIO leadership. Although a committee of Regional Directors had helped draw up plans before the beginning of the organizing drive in April and although Myles Horton invited the Director of the drive to visit the Term,[29] hoping to relate the program directly to it, few of the Southern Directors were able to take part, even for a day and there is no record of any response to the educational director's invitation. As a result, most of the courses were taught by the Highlander staff members: Union Problems by Myles Horton; Shop Steward Training and Labor Legislation by Mary Lawrence; Music and Singing by Zilphia Horton and other courses, Current Events, Parliamentary Law and Public Speaking by wartime arrivals to the Highlander staff. A group of sessions on farmer-labor unity were also led by a Highlander staff member who had come to the School a few months before to help develop a Farmers Union program in Tennessee.[30] Only a course in Labor History and a Workshop on Union Publicity[31] were taught by members of the National CIO staff and one of them, Aleine Austin, teacher of Labor History, was, in a sense, a returned Highlander staff member for she had received her orientation to workers' education as an Antioch student-trainee at the School several years before.[32] Myles Horton did manage occasionally to involve a Southern CIO leader as speaker in his Union Problems class and Lucy Randolph Mason led several discussions on "Labor and Community" but otherwise it was a Highlander rather than a CIO Term.

Nor did CIO leaders, "knee deep in the Southern Organizing Drive," assist in recruiting potential union leader-students for the Term. Of the nineteen students who enrolled, a later analysis indicates, "All but four students came from locals that had benefited from the Highlander program during the previous year." Actually, as was pointed out, "the students from the 1946 Term were recruited by former students."[33]

Reports and articles about the term are rather brief. They indicate that life at the School, as in the previous term, was governed by a staff-student council and that committees of the council planned recreation, put out a mimeographed weekly paper and a book of student stories and ran a workers' Co-operative Store. They also indicate that a steering committee was formed which worked closely with educational director Myles Horton in shaping and modifying the program to make it as relevant as possible to the needs of the organizing drive. In response, for example, to an Oil Worker student who, along with others explained, "When I get home I'm going to do some volunteer organizing in the oil fields . . . and I need more information about how to organize," the committee decided that additional time should be devoted to teaching these techniques as well as collective bargaining.[34]

The 1946 Southern CIO Drive: Highlander's Lack of Participation

In view of the heavy demands of the Southern Organizing Drive, it as not surprising that the 1946 CIO School was primarily Highlander-staffed. With an announced goal of organizing 500,000 textile workers alone[35] and with $1 million being pledged to the operation by affiliated international unions,[36] all of the southern leadership which could be mustered was needed and more. What was surprising, however, and painfully so to the southern labor school which had been heavily involved in the 1937 CIO drive, was its exclusion from any useful educational role in the postwar drive. Minutes of a Highlander Executive Council meeting as the drive was getting underway suggest that the staff had been attempting vainly and for some time to make the School's educational resources available. One Council member, a CIO Regional Director, recommended that other Regional Directors and International Representatives should be encouraged to put pressure on the CIO to use the School in specific ways. After some discussion a motion was made authorizing a staff member to work up a definite proposal regarding the relationship of the School with the Southern Organizing Drive and submit his Proposal personally to the leaders of the drive.[37]

The official response to the Highlander Folk School's offer to develop educational programs "for organizers or new members before bargaining-rights are won" amounted to a dismissal of the offer. It was explained by one of the assistants to the Director of the Southern Drive that all programs "should be requested by the State Director of the CIO Drive."[38] The cool reaction of drive leadership to the School's offer of assistance might be interpreted as preoccupied, bureaucratic behavior. The CIO had grown considerably larger and inevitably more bureaucratic in the decade since its first all-join-in drive. Educationally, too, the CIO was becoming increasingly institutionalized with the staff of its Research and Education Department holding regional meetings with the educational staffs of affiliated unions and developing its own programs and materials for the use of affiliates.

However, underlying the basic change in the relationship of Highlander Folk School to the leadership of the Southern Organizing Drives in 1937 and 1946 was not merely a change in the structure of the CIO but a change

151

in the general social climate. From the thirties and early forties when critics of American capitalism, of the ailing social order, spoke out freely and frequently whether as concerned Christians, Communists, Socialists or independent radicals, the nation in the mid-forties entered rather suddenly into a postwar, cold war period when as historian Van Woodward has described it, "The floodstream of criticism dwindled to a trickle and very nearly ceased altogether . . . as if some giant sluice gate had been firmly shut."[39] The cold war climate which served generally to silence social critics, stifle debate and suppress political differences (ironically in the name of protecting a free society) was not without its effect upon the climate within the southern labor movement.

As the Southern CIO began its drive, complicated as always by the hostility of paternalist, racist and fundamentalist elements traditionally arrayed with the mill and factory owners against the unions, the AF of L also launched a postwar drive in the South, making the situation even more difficult. "Neither reactionary employers nor Communists within the CIO," President Green announced to an opening rally, "can stop the campaign of the Federation of Labor to enroll 1,000,000 unorganized southern workers in the next twelve months."[40]

Given this sort of climate within and outside of the movement, it is not surprising, as Avrahm Mezerik, free lance writer for *The Nation*, observed of the CIO Southern Organizing Drive, "It has ignored the entire left including the constructive Southern Conference for Human Welfare. It is not even going along with the PAC which is hard to take."[41] Nor is it surprising that the leaders of the Southern Organizing Drive chose to ignore the Highlander Folk School which not only insisted on continuing to advocate political action and democratic social change in the South, but fought actively with and through its students and organizations such as the PAC and the Southern Conference for Human Welfare to bring about that change.

At the same time that the School refused to compromise in its broad goals for political and social as well as economic democracy in the South, it evidenced increasing flexibility in the ways in which it sought to bring these goals about. When the Director of the Southern Organizing Drive was unresponsive to Highlander's offer of educational assistance, the School worked increasingly with individual unions and with non-union groups. This flexibility is evident in the Highlander Folk School agenda for 1946 which included, along with the Highlander-run CIO Term, special one-week terms and weekend institutes for five international unions—the Food, Tobacco and

Agricultural Workers (FTA), the American Federation of Hosiery Workers, the United Packinghouse Workers, the Steelworkers and the Auto Workers. In addition, it included a Labor Journalism term and various exploratory meetings with veteran and Negro groups. It also included an expanded new program with a fulltime Highlander staff member for the Tennessee Farmers Union.[42]

In the midst of developing new programs and relating its programs to new groups, the School continued to offer its General Term "open to all union members endorsed by their unions" and weekly extension classes sponsored by local industrial union councils in Tennessee. Within the several terms and institutes there was a discernible continuity. They invariably included Political Action as well as Parliamentary Law. They tended to include Current Events whether the term was for members of the FTA or students of Labor journalism. And, whatever their affiliation, there was singing of labor songs with Zilphia Horton teaching worker-students to lead their own groups.[43]

The Southern CIO School, 1947: A National CIO School with a Highlander Staff and Setting

The 1946 Southern CIO School had been characterized by very limited participation of Southern CIO leadership. The 1947 School, in turn, was characterized by considerable participation on the part of National CIO leadership. However, although the 1947 School was referred to as "the National CIO Term for Southerners," it cannot be so described when one examines the program and the roles of the National and Highlander staffs.[44] Officially, the term was headed by CIO Assistant Director of Education George Guernsey whose signature appeared on all communications which went out to international unions to recruit students. He also selected and scheduled the various National CIO officials who were featured as speakers and special teachers, including the Director of the CIO Committee to Abolish Discrimination, the Assistant Director of the Industrial Union Council Division, the Assistant Legal Council, two National Representatives of the PAC, the Director of the Department of Education and Research and Guernsey himself. But none of these national officials were a part of the day-by-day program, part of the life of the self-governed community made up of Highlander staff, the twenty-two students recruited by the CIO and a group of five college student-apprentices who assisted with various phases of the resident and community programs while learning about workers' education and the southern labor movement. Thus, for example, the weekly student-edited newspaper lists Guernsey among the "visiting speakers" along with the other CIO officials. In contrast, a paragraph and a cartoon in the same paper are devoted to Zilphia Horton, "the lady who sings." Another paragraph was devoted to welcoming "Brother Wilder," a Steelworker student from Chattanooga who was a late-arrival in the resident group.[45]

In spite of a recommendation from the CIO Department of Education that Highlander "draw up an hour-by-hour schedule of each day,"[46] its scheduling was about as flexible as in other Highlander terms where students participated in the on-going planning and evaluation. Students roundly if respectfully criticized the Assistant Director of the Industrial Union Councils Division for his initial lecture on "Long Range Implications of Labor's Legislative and Political Programs." They indicated that it was "too broad a field for [the] length of time he had to go." They also suggested that "discussion would wake up everybody and we would listen."[47]

Thereafter, the Assistant Director was scheduled at an earlier hour, more conducive to students remaining alert, and time was allocated for discussion. Program reports and records also indicate that considerable time beyond the several hours scheduled for speakers from the PAC was devoted to discussions of local political action in the South and to immediate steps to be taken in relation to the punitive Taft-Hartley labor law enacted by Congress during the term. A sheaf of student and staff-signed telegrams to their various senators gives evidence of the kind of practical action in which they engaged.

Further evidence that the term was not just another in a group of National CIO Summer Schools is indicated by the fact that one weekend of the term was devoted to a Farmer-Labor Conference with the President of the Tennessee Territorial Farmers Union among the major speakers along with CIO Research and Education Director Kermit Eby.

The closing talk to the departing southern union member-students by Zilphia Horton perhaps best represents the kind of thinking which made the National CIO School a Highlander-CIO School. Dwelling, first, on various aspects of their communal life, she moved on to what she felt had made both staff and students feel that the group and the month-long experience had been a significant one. "I think it's because we've been interested in the same things and have been thinking big thoughts—big ideas," she suggested; "ideas which you probably didn't know you had when you came here. And

its not, " she emphasized, "that we have the same ideas or that we all agree
. . ." she went on to add one more "big idea" to the group's thinking by
reading to them from the United Nations Charter and relating its world
goals to their jobs as leaders of CIO locals and citizens in southern
communities. "We know that Jack in Texas, Clay in Knoxville, Bart in
Memphis, Slick in Arkansas . . . that none of you," she stressed, "can do the
job alone, but that each of you has a job to do to get your unions to help
you." She closed, appropriately for the song leader, with the title of a song
which students had recently learned, a song which had been brought to the
School by members of a Negro Food and Tobacco Workers local in
Charleston, South Carolina, soon to be sung across the South, "We Will
Overcome."[48]

Student stories written during the term combined in a mimeographed
collection, *We're on the Freedom Trail*, suggest that many of the ideas and
experiences which emerged as significant to union member-students during
the term were not necessarily related to CIO policy or how to handle
grievances. A song, "Freedom Trail," written by a Chemical Worker-student
from Louisiana with stanzas on winning the peace, brotherhood within the
movement and farmer-labor unity introduces the unorthodox collection.[49] A
story entitled "Is He a Lot Different?" by another member of a Chemical
Workers' local from Tennessee points out, "People of all colors, races and
religions worked together during the war and it didn't hurt any of us. If it
will work one time why then won't it work all the time?" The author
concludes with an observation which may well have come out of his recent
experience as a southern white living for the first time in a setting with
southern Negro union members. "When people get together and talk over
their problems, we find out that we all have about the same problems in
life."[50]

Serving as Chairman of the Student Steering Committee was clearly a
central learning experience for a member of an Oil Workers' local from
Texas. In his story, "My Experience and Opinions Formed While Acting
Chairman of the Steering Committee of the Highlander Folk School," he
describes the value of the democratic decision-making process employed by
the Committee and ends with an appeal to his fellow representatives of CIO
locals. "I, by placing this, my own experience before you, urge one and all
to place and test a Steering Committee in your local, now."[51]

A visiting staff member during the 1948 CIO Term at the Highlander
Folk School, university labor education specialist A. A. Liveright, also made

special mention of the kinds and quality of informal learning activities which be observed. In his volume, *Union Leadership Training*, he noted the two-way education involved in the Student Steering Committee's rigorous evaluation sessions which stimulated them to think critically and caused a distinguished speaker during the term, James P. Warburg, to completely revise his approach to his subject.[52] Liveright noted, too, the role of the long and probing, late-night discussions by staff and students on the problems of prejudice affecting their locals and the southern union movement, problems identified but not fully dealt with in class sessions.[53]

Union Education by Unions: Highlander Faces up to a Diminishing Role

Whatever the capacity of the Highlander Folk School to influence the quality of education within a given union-sponsored term, its role as a center for southern workers' education was inevitably affected by the growing trend toward unions developing their own educational programs to meet their own institutionally-defined leadership needs. In a very real sense the Highlander Folk School had encouraged the growth of that trend in the South: by preparing its students to assume professional and volunteer responsibilities on union staffs and with local education committees; by involving union officials in educational programming for their own unions or industrial union councils and, later, for the South through membership on the Highlander Executive Council; by making available its programs and materials for use by various labor organizations, local and regional, and, finally, by helping those organizations to run their own programs, utilizing the School's residential facilities and staff and drawing on its educational experience.

Yet in spite of taking some pride in having assisted and encouraged the trend, the educational director and staff had to face up to its negative effects which included the narrowing of the School's programming for labor. More and more, Highlander became a center for special terms and institutes for various international unions. And, as these special terms and institutes increased, it offered fewer and fewer general workers' education terms in service of the larger movement and the School's larger goals for society.

Another effect of the trend toward unions sponsoring and, later, organizing and running their own residential terms was the narrowing of the School's role within those terms. So unhappy was the staff after one such experience, in the summer of 1947, when it acquiesced to the UAW's request to "run their term," that it decided, "Since very few of the UAW students knew they were at Highlander Folk School . . . they should not be listed as Highlander alumni."[54] In a more practical effort to guard against complete domination by unions of all aspects of their educational programs held at the School, the staff defined a new policy regarding the areas of educational decision-making to be shared with or retained by Highlander. They agreed to recommend to the Executive Council that "someone from the staff work with people in charge of any session" and sit in on their meetings "to coordinate, help, plan and interpret School policy." They also agreed that "there should be an orientation by a Highlander staff member on the opening night" of a union-sponsored term and that the staff member, working with union representatives, should "point out that Highlander staff members are available for teaching and that they will have to know in advance if they are to be used."[55]

The Executive Council meeting in January, 1948 was historically significant in that the School's leadership faced the full implications of Highlander's diminishing role in relation to the institutionalized labor movement. Minutes of the meeting begin with the forthright assertion, "It was felt necessary by the Council to broaden the program of the School to include all branches of organized labor, farmers and sympathetic non-labor."[56] (This broadening of the program, of course, had already been initiated as early as 1944 when Myles Horton was instrumental in organizing the first Farmers Union local in Tennessee. Highlander staff members had also been holding exploratory meetings with Negro and liberal veterans' groups.)

In officially articulating its move toward broader educational programming the School also faced the fact of decreasing labor participation on its Executive Council. Some labor leadership had already resigned from the Council. At the 1948 meeting, the Council Chairman for three years, Steelworkers District Director W. H. Crawford, resigned as did three CIO officials, two of them CIO Regional Directors for Alabama and Louisiana who had worked with the School in developing its CIO terms and other programs.

Chairman Crawford's resignation reflects as well another postwar trend—more slow to develop in the South—toward expanding participation by universities and colleges in serving the needs of the institutionalized labor movement.[57] As Crawford explained in his letter of resignation to Myles Horton

As you have no doubt learned, the United Steelworkers of America is concentrating their efforts in the field of education to working within the structure of the land-grant colleges. Such a program has been indicated in the South and I deem it necessary to work with this program.[58]

In keeping with the broadened definition of Highlander's program, the Steelworker Chairman was replaced by Dr. George Mitchell, Director of the Southern Regional Council, author of books and articles on the problems of tenant farmers and Negroes in the southern labor movement and a firm believer that the greatest contribution which the Highlander Folk School could make would be in bringing together labor and other groups in an "overall movement in the South."[59] At the same time, new members elected to the Council included a representative of the Farmers Union and a faculty member of Morehouse College, a Negro college in Atlanta.

The redefinition of Highlander's role and program did not mean that the School would no longer serve the CIO and other labor organizations. It was agreed, however, that the School "must concentrate on work with unions with less developed educational programs."[60] In 1948, therefore, the program included, as it had in the previous year, residential terms and field services for the Mine, Mill and Smelter Workers, the United Rubber Workers and the Food, Tobacco and Agricultural Workers, all with considerable new Negro membership and limited, if any, local educational programs.[61]

The Council's major action to implement its decision broadening the School's program was to respond positively to an expressed interest of the National Farmers Union "in establishing an official connection with Highlander and using the School as the center for their educational program in the South." It was further noted that the Farmers Union would "contribute to the School's budget,"[62] part of which for some years had come from unions in the form of tuition and contributions. These several actions and decisions taken together—related to the School's leadership, its program emphasis and its sources of support—served to change rather basically the southern labor school which for ten years had been a "CIO School," in its allocation of staff and other resources if not in its overall goals.[63]

The Worsening Climate: Highlander's Break with the Movement is Hastened

In view of the growing and irreversible trend of the CIO and its several international unions toward running their own educational programs or allocating them to universities and colleges, the Highlander Folk School's decision to broaden and redirect its program efforts was probably, at some point, an inevitable one. That decision, however, was hastened and the School's close relationship to the southern industrial union movement undermined by the steadily worsening social climate. The heresy hunters and loyalty investigators who patrolled the national scene, causing public reactions from caution to conformity, were having a growing impact on organized labor. This tendency toward narrow conformity was especially true after the death in 1946 of Sidney Hillman, chief proponent among the CIO's founders of an all inclusive labor movement. (As a biographer pointed out, Hillman was accused by conservative Republicans of being "red" and by Communists of being "an agent of the old bosses" because he was "not a doctrinaire of any sort and would not allow the labor movement to be used by doctrinaires.")[64] Increasingly, the strongest voices within the CIO were those who called, first, for the disciplining of the minority of "Communist-line leadership" and later for expelling it—in order, as Walter Reuther expressed it at the 1949 convention where the expulsion was completed, "to cut the cancer out and save the body of the CIO."[65]

Many friends of labor who were not, like Myles Horton, resistant to any rigidly doctrinaire positions and policies (whether for Highlander or the labor movement), considered the action inevitable and necessary. Yet even among these, concern was expressed that a dangerous precedent had been set. "The danger is," observed an editorial writer for *The New Republic*, "that authority will advance too far. Then leadership becomes an unrepresentative clique, self-serving and self-perpetuating."[66]

The immediate problem for the School related to its deteriorating relationship with Van Bittner, the single-minded Director of the CIO southern organizing drive. Not only had the School been excluded from any educational role, but when one of the abler CIO organizers, Louis Krainock, decided to leave the drive and take a position with the Highlander staff in the fall of 1947, Van Bittner became actively hostile, threatening that the organizer's departure would result in the "withdrawal of all CIO support" and that there would be "no more official connection with the School."[67] Although Krainock and the School believed firmly that by helping to build a broad program for farm and labor groups, they would assist in building a stronger southern labor movement,[68] the Director of the faltering CIO drive and those around him were unable to appreciate the action or the point of view. Myles Horton, writing to Executive Council Chairman George Mitchell regarding the way in which Van Bittner's hostility had communicated itself to the new Director of the CIO's Research and Education Department and was threatening the School's relationship to CIO leadership in the South, observed, "Such an attitude on his part makes it almost impossible to have a successful CIO Term, since he is in a position to limit the support given by southern directors."[69]

In the same letter, the Highlander educational director complained that the School was encountering increasing pressure to conform to changes in the National CIO policy. "For example," he wrote, "I was informed in Washington that we should not have run sessions for FTA or MM and SW since they are officially on the CIO's black list."[70] To the founder of the outspokenly independent school whose staff and later its staff and Executive Council had steered a determined course throughout its sixteen year history of not allowing any political or other outside organization to determine or interfere with its policy, this kind of directive, formal or informal, was unacceptable.

Even more unacceptable was an effort on the part of the CIO leadership beginning in 1949 to get the School to amend its statement of purpose by "declaring that the Highlander Folk School is opposed to all kinds of totalitarianism including communism, fascism and nazism" [sic].[71] The School was itself split on the matter with one of the remaining CIO members explaining at the January 1949 meeting, "There is no question on the part of any Board member as to the nature of the School's policy or program, but only a question of whether the School should try to satisfy those groups which demand a public statement."[72]

The matter continued to be at issue until a 1950 Executive Council meeting. In the interim period, the CIO Educational Director wrote to Myles Horton communicating the decision of the National office "not to hold any institute at Highlander Folk School this year." He indicated that "while I personally may be convinced of the fallaciousness of the statement," two or three southern directors "have the opinion that at Highlander there exists some left-wing 'Communist' influence." He stressed in closing, "I feel that we could once again establish very favorable relations with Highlander if such a statement of policy as suggested, were approved by your Board."[73]

In explaining to the Executive Council why he believed the demand of the CIO to be an unwarranted and dangerous intrusion, the co-founder-educational director of the Highlander Folk School traced the School's history as an independent institution "resisting the efforts of those who try to restrict the School's program by insisting that their policy alone be followed."[74] He pointed out that as early as 1934 "we stated: 'The School is in no way connected with any political party, either in an official capacity' or as a recipient of financial aid' . . ." Looking ahead, he expressed grave concern as to the consequences of agreeing to the CIO's requested amendment

> The South is still largely unorganized, and the opportunity to serve southern workers and farmers cannot be limited to any particular organization. Even if we should decide at this time to let one organization determine the policy of the School, and thus limit our services to that organization, there would be little likelihood of Highlander's survival.[75]

At the January 1950 meeting of the Highlander Executive Council, a majority of members voted to reject the negatively-conceived amendment. Instead the Council set forth its own positive restatement of Highlander's purpose and policy

> We affirm our faith in democracy as a goal that will bring dignity and freedom to all; in democracy as an expanding concept encompassing human relations from the smallest community organization to international structure; and permeating all economic, social and political activities. We hold that democracy is inactive unless workers are given a full voice in industry through unions; or farmers are given a voice in the market place through co-operatives; or where freedom of thought and discussion is limited . . .[76]

In spite of the independent institution's firm refusal to modify its policies, its purposes or even its statement of those purposes, the National CIO continued, after a lapse in 1949, to hold its Southern Summer Schools at Highlander Folk School for three more years. But the creative relationship of the Highlander Folk School to the southern labor movement had ceased to exist.

In some ways, the short-lived Annual CIO School represented the culmination as well as the end of Highlander's longtime relationship to the southern labor movement. The regional CIO leaders who sat on Highlander's Executive Council and who, with the staff, were responsible for planning and carrying out the first such School in the South (or in the nation) had themselves been educated by that relationship. A few were early Highlander resident students. Others had come to know and work with the School through its many movement-supporting and building extension activities. All had participated in residential terms as teachers, speakers and resource persons. And out of these several kinds of interactions, they had become convinced of the value of Highlander's workers' education programs for the developing of local and southwide union leadership—so convinced, in fact, that they were willing to become involved in program development themselves. Moreover, as major labor spokesmen for workers' education in the South, they were able to involve their fellow labor leaders—not only in recruiting promising students from their international unions and helping to finance the cooperative venture, but, some of them, in teaching courses on CIO policy and program.

The four CIO Schools developed in the years 1944-1947, including the so-called "National CIO Term for Southerners" were, to a remarkable degree, "Highlander Schools" for all that they featured a number of CIO staff members and speakers and omitted traditional Highlander courses such as Labor History and Economics in favor of training for shop stewards and fundamentals of collective bargaining. At a time when the leadership of the CIO postwar southern organizing drive was concentrating on the narrow goal of "unionizing," the Highlander-Southern CIO Schools were providing local leader-students with a variety of social and educational experiences to help them gain a broader view of the labor movement and its role in society. And, along with discussing the CIO's national policy against discrimination and its implications for southern locals, the School, beginning in 1945, included Negro union members. Along with discussing the desirability of farmer-labor unity, students had the opportunity, at weekend conferences, to meet with other union and farm representatives and consider ways of achieving that unity. Along with discussing the idea of union-owned cooperatives, they were members of a Workers' Cooperative Store run by staff and students in the one month School.

The fact that the CIO Schools very soon ceased to be held at Highlander was not a measure of their effectiveness. The response of most of the students who participated in them and of educators such as CIO Education Director Kermit Eby and University of Chicago labor education specialist A.A. Liveright, who observed and assisted the program, was enthusiastic. The decision of the National CIO to end its relationship to Highlander was, instead, a measure of the growing postwar conservatism in the nation and

162

within the institutionalized labor movement. It was a measure, too, of the determination of the independent, radically democratic School not to give up any of its independence or radicalism to gain acceptance.

Since there was real doubt, in any event, whether the Highlander Folk School could have survived as a labor school in view of the trend of union education by unions, the decision to relate its educational resources to the development of "an overall movement in the South" must have appeared institutionally as well as ideologically sound. The effort to help build a broad movement working with and through the Farmers Union will be examined in Part IV which follows.

Photographs

1. Southern Farmers Union School, 1947 or 1948. Myles Horton is in the left front (with pipe) and beside him is J.D. Mott, South Alabama Farmers Union leader. Photograph: Emil Willimetz.

2. School Desegregation Workshop, August, 1955. From left to right (at table): Septima Clark, Dr. Parrish, University of Louisville, Dr. Fred Patterson, President of Tuskegee Institute, and Rosa Parks. It was only several months later that Mrs. Parks was to refuse to give up her seat on a Montgomery bus, the action that began the boycott. Photograph: Emil Willimetz.

3. Eleanor Roosevelt speaking at Highlander 25th anniversary. With her are Myles Horton and May Justus. Photograph: State Historical Society of Wisconsin.

4. Civil rights group in front of Highlander Library. Septima Clark is at the left. Photograph: State Historical Society of Wisconsin.

5. Johns Island, South Carolina. Left to right: Esau Jenkins, Aimee Horton, and Guy Carawan, the folk singer and Highlander staff member who taught students in the movement to sing *We Shall Overcome*. Photograph: Thorsten Horton.

6. Johns Island Workshop, July/August 1964. Left to right: Esau Jenkins (Johns Island leader who came to Highlander as a student and asked the school to teach his neighbors to read and write so that they could be "first-class citizens." Subsequently, he became a Highlander Board Member.); B.R. Brazeal (Dean, Morehouse College and President of the Highlander Board); and Myles Horton. Photograph: Thorsten Horton.

PART FOUR

Education and Organization for the Farmers Union in the South

ELEVEN

A Program
in Search of
a Movement

The Institution Seeks a New Role

Unlike Highlander's programs related to the mountain poor of Grundy County and to the southern labor movement which were developed in response to group-perceived needs, the School's leadership decided that it would be both institutionally and socially desirable to attempt to develop a Farmers union program in the South which, it was hoped, would lead to the development of a broad, farmer-labor people's movement. From 1944 until 1950, Highlander served as the organizing and educational center for the Farmers Union in Tennessee and, later, in Virginia and Alabama. For reasons to be examined, the Southern Farmers Union program was short-lived and the people's movement was never achieved.

In the brief period of partial development, the School never devoted more than one third of its staff and resources to the program and, in the exploratory first two years, a fraction of that.[1] No Highlander staff members devoted full-time to the Farmers Union program until 1946 when a Field Representative was hired to work with the newly-organized Tennessee Farmers Union.[2] No Farmers Union resident terms were offered until 1947. Although some 5,100 farmers and their families in Tennessee, Alabama and Virginia became members of the Farmers Union in the years from 1944 to 1950[3] and participated in local meetings and educational activities, only 102 of the farmers attended a total of four Farmers Union resident terms held at Highlander between 1947 and 1949.[4]

Highlander continued during these years to serve the workers' education needs of some industrial unions, including several primarily Negro unions, and it began to seek new bases for relating to Negro Southerners. In addition, the School set up a Film Center in 1949 to produce films, film strips and other visual aids for farm, labor, race relations and other liberal groups in the South.[5]

The make-up of the Executive Council in this period reflects the several groups with whom the School was working. Thus, the Executive Council in 1947 included three Farmers Union representatives, representatives of the Urban League and the NAACP and three liberal white Southerners from church and social action organizations along with a majority of labor members.[6]

The building and land improvement projects in this period also reflect the several groups served by the School. The last two major buildings were added: the Harry Lasker Library,[7] used by farmer, worker (and later civil rights leader) resident students and the so-called Community Building used by the Summerfield nursery school and a sewing cooperative. Executive Council minutes also indicate that a farm demonstration project was embarked upon including "experimentation with permanent pasture" and the planting of nut trees "added to previous plantings of 7,000 pine and poplar seedlings."[8]

Immediate and Historical Bases for the Farmers Union Program

The proposal, at the Highlander Executive Council meeting in January 1944 to promote the Farmers Union in Tennessee was initiated by one of the labor members. As State Legislative Representative for a small Railroad Brotherhood, Council member Hollis Reid pointed out that farmers represented a potentially valuable ally. "The farmers would be a big asset to the labor group," he indicated. "Our strength is largely in the big centers and a lot of our difficulty comes with men in rural areas."[9]

The idea, in fact, of building a farmer-labor coalition in Tennessee working with and through the Farmers Union had first been introduced to the Council by Myles Horton in 1943. He perceived not only an immediate potential for electing "some really progressive men," but an ultimate potential for building the kind of broadly-based movement which he and others of the School's early leadership had envisioned before there was a widespread industrial union movement in the South. For various reasons, including insufficient exploration, the proposal had not been acted upon. In the interim, Horton consulted further with the National Farmers Union and with a number of labor officials including CIO, AF of L and Railroad Brotherhood officials who, like Highlander Council member Reid, could appreciate the desirability of building a Farmers Union organization in Tennessee as a basis for a liberal political coalition.

The decision to work with the Farmers Union was a response to the founding purposes of the School by Horton and his fellow Southerner, Don West, in 1932: "to provide an educational center . . . for the training of rural and industrial leaders." It represented the most recent of the School's efforts to relate its educational programs to farmers as well as industrial workers beginning with its first organizing and educational program for impoverished rural people in the surrounding community and county. The School, of course, had always sought to encourage interaction between rural and industrial workers. It invited the participation of young leaders from neighboring mountain communities in workers' education terms. Later, it sponsored farmer-labor conferences. And, perhaps most important of all as precedent for working with a radically democratic farm organization, Myles and Zilphia Horton had, almost from its founding in the mid-thirties, assisted the Southern Tenant Farmers Union in building an educational program for Negro and white sharecropper members in Arkansas and other Deep South states. Out of this experience, they brought to Highlander and the School's worker-students an understanding of the problems and an appreciation of the songs of the sharecroppers.

Beyond the immediate political coalition reasons and the reasons traceable to the School's founding purposes, the notion of farmers and workers joining together in a common movement was, as a biographer of Southern Populist leader Tom Watson observed, an appealing one among intellectuals of the "neo-Populist" New Deal period.[10] It was especially appealing to Myles Horton who could find in early Populism an example of a native radical movement of small farmers who aligned themselves with workers and who for, for a brief time at least, identified with and spoke out courageously for the rights of Negroes.[11]

That the Highlander Folk School selected the Farmers Union as the farm organization with which to work in building a state farmer-labor coalition and a broader southwide movement could hardly have been more appropriate. The Farmers Union had, in fact, been founded in the South, in Rains County, Texas, in 1902, by a former Populist organizer and a little group of populists, Socialists, Democrats and Independents[12] who were keenly aware of their "rural sense of disadvantage" and the need for a political alliance with organized labor.[13] And, although the Farmers Union had flourished in the South for only a decade, and then moved northward to the prairie and wheat-producing states (where it became more of a liberal pressure group and less of a farm protest movement),[14] it continued to advocate an alliance with organized labor. Especially after 1940, when James Patton became National Farmers Union president, its social and economic concerns broadened and its political activities accelerated. Thus, a student of the organization and its leadership, at about the time that Highlander proposed to promote it, noted that the National Farmers Union was not only taking a stand in behalf of extending the Wage and Hours Act and the National Labor Relations Act to include farm workers, but was joining other progressive groups to work for the preservation of civil liberties and the protection of the rights of minorities.[15] The Farmers Union of the 1940s, therefore, represented a particularly hopeful and congenial ally to an outspokenly independent adult school seeking to relate to industrial unionists, small farmers and Negroes in a South where organized labor was a minority, small farmers were a generally disadvantaged group and Negroes, whether small farmers or industrial workers, were both disadvantaged and discriminated against.

Not only was the Farmers Union an ideologically congenial ally, but, as its official name, the Farmers Educational and Cooperative Union of America, and its official emblem, a triangle with "education" as the base and "cooperation" and "legislation" the two sides), clearly suggest, it was an ally committed to education as a means of achieving its goals. And, just as its educational and social goals were broadly defined, its educational goals and program, rather than being vocationally oriented, were concerned with teaching "the principles, ideals and philosophy of cooperation," with creating "an interest in and a consciousness of the social and economic forces at work in the world against which the rural people of the world must pit their brains" and with developing "a sense of social responsibility among farmers, toward one another and the rest of society."[16]

Summerfield, a Symbolic Beginning

In setting out to promote the Farmers Union in Tennessee as the basis for a farmer-labor coalition and a "people's movement" the Highlander educational director began in 1944 in the same local community of

Summerfield where he and a little company of pragmatic educators and seekers after a new social order had undertaken the School's first exploratory community and workers' education efforts. However, in the case of the Farmers Union, Summerfield represented more of a symbol than a real beginning. It was a convenient place, in terms of a physical setting and the existence of a nucleus of Highlander-educated, organization-oriented mountain people with a long-time "sense of rural disadvantage" in which to announce the formation of "the first Farmers Union local in Tennessee."[17] Among this little nucleus was a deeply committed and articulate spokesman for militant farm and labor organizations, Henry Thomas, leader of the 1933 Bugwood Strike and son of a Farmers' Alliance member who urged his Cumberland mountain neighbors

Organized labor is working in war plants for the victory and peace that is soon to come. Farmers should unite themselves and make plans to help bring victory and peace. We at home have got a row to weed to have a free democracy for all races of people.[18]

Summerfield also afforded an immediate and tangible situation and setting in which to involve organized labor with a view to securing its financial support as well as its espousal of the coalition. Thus, although it may have been unusual and perhaps unprecedented for the CIO Regional Director of the state to present the charter to the first Farmers Union local, it was, in this case, quite understandable. The first Southern CIO-School which got underway soon after the Summerfield Farmers Union local had been organized provided another opportunity for interaction and a show of labor support. CIO worker-students together with visiting representatives of CIO locals in Tennessee, Alabama and Georgia, some 100 in all, participated in a fund-raising Farmers Union carnival and listened to the Secretary of the Southeastern Cooperative League tell how Farmers Union and CIO members in the Atlanta area were working together to solve their marketing and buying problems through cooperative organization.[19]

The Summerfield Farmers Union local, in spite of its historic, labor-heralded beginning, remained more of a symbol than a fully functioning organization. During 1944, the forty-eight member local set up education and political action committees; the former committee sponsoring a Highlander-led study group and the latter carrying on a determined campaign to get Grundy County residents to pay their poll taxes and vote for the re-election of Franklin Roosevelt.[20] But by the end of 1945, except for "Marlowe's Mountain Musicians" (a Farmers Union band made up of members of the Summerfield local which furnished entertainment as a part of the state organizing campaign) and periodic inspired letters to the editor of the *Tennessee Union Farmer* by ever-loyal Henry Thomas, the first Farmers Union chapter was rarely heard from; its membership growing ever smaller as returning veterans and their families left the community.

Along with the beginnings of an organization in Tennessee, the Farmers Union received official labor support in 1944. At the initiative of Railroad Brotherhood Representative Reid, a state committee for the promotion of the Tennessee Farmers Union was formed made up of legislative representatives of the AF of L, the CIO and the Brotherhoods. Under his leadership, the committee announced, "Farmers are our kind of people . . . They need our help and we need theirs," and urged fellow unionists to send the committee names of "interested farmers," potential members of the Farmers Union.[21] Labor's financial backing was slower to develop. As a first step, the unions in Tennessee paid for 2,000 subscriptions to the *National Union Farmer*, official Farmers Union publication, to be distributed to farmers throughout the state.[22] These subscriptions, in turn, furnished the basis for a poll among a sample of farmer readers by Myles Horton to ascertain and publicize potential interest in the Farmers Union.

Greenhaw, the Beginning of an Organization

As an educator with a background in sociology, Myles Horton could make use of a poll to get some notion of how small farmers might be expected to respond to the idea of a Tennessee Farmers Union. As an educator who believed that a sound program of education and organization had to be built around farmer-defined needs, he found it necessary to obtain firsthand knowledge of their perceived needs and the relevance of the Farmers Union to those needs. Early in 1945, therefore, he arbitrarily selected Greenhaw, a farming community near the Highlander Folk School, but with no previous relationship to it, as the place in which to begin obtaining this firsthand knowledge by interacting informally with community leaders. Among those who expressed interest was a local teacher who offered to bring together a group of farmers to discuss their problems and explore the role of the Farmers Union. There are no reports in the School files of that first Greenhaw meeting or those which followed in the winter and spring of

1945. However, it is clear from Myles Horton's correspondence with the National Farmers Union and from his frequent correspondence over the next two years with a local farmer-community leader that this exploratory effort was of consequence in the development of the Tennessee Farmers Union. Writing to the National office after the first successful meeting in a rural schoolhouse, Horton described local discontent with the conservative Farm Bureau and with low prices received for farm products and indicated that the group had invited him to come back to talk about the Farmers Union and "seemed anxious to start a potato cooperative."[23] Along with finding a mood of discontent, the labor educator-turned-farmer educator, who had always sought to identify promising local leadership around which to build, wrote the Regional Farmers Union representative

> You'll be impressed with Homer Crabtree who is taking the lead in organizing the local, which now includes nine of the best farm families in the county . . . . His father was an old Farmers' Alliance member in Alabama around 1900 and he knows what to expect in the way of opposition.[24]

Working with Crabtree, he could report just two months later that a thriving local and a potato cooperative were underway. "The Greenhaw local," he wrote, "has made arrangements to sell their potato crop . . . at fifteen cents per hundred above the market price." And, he noted, "Some of the biggest farmers in the county are joining so that they can take advantage of this contract."[25]

In spite of the growing membership and able leadership, the kind of narrow economic self-interest issue which brought the farmers of Greenhaw together did not furnish the basis for building a broad movement or even a broad new educational program. In terms of Highlander's immediate goal, however, of promoting the Farmers Union in Tennessee, the Greenhaw local provided the basis for publicizing the Farmers Union and developing interest in other parts of the state. A flier headed "Tennessee Farmers Are Organizing" announced, "This is the beginning of a people's movement by the farmers of Tennessee." It described the organization of the Greenhaw Farmers Union rooted in the community and democratically run by the members" and told farmers how to start their own locals. An open letter signed by Homer Crabtree, Secretary of a new "Tennessee Organizing Committee" attested to the power of small farmers coming together and invited fellow farmers to write to the Committee for more information.[26]

Education as a Part of Organization

With only the beginning of an organization and a "paper movement," the Highlander Folk School during the years 1945 and 1946 offered few formal educational activities related to its Tennessee Farmers Union Program. The Annual Reports during these years, describing residential terms and field activities for the CIO and the various international unions, barely mention the Farmers Union. The only activities cited are a Leadership Training Institute held at Greenhaw and some classes on cooperatives.[27] The one-week institute was primarily organization-serving. Typical, apparently, of Farmers Union Institutes elsewhere, it emphasized recreation and youth activities together with some discussion of cooperatives and rural community leadership.[28]

Yet from progress reports in the Tennessee Union Farmer, beginning in the fall of 1945, it is clear that the Greenhaw message together with the energetic follow-up activities of the little Highlander-staffed, farmer-led organizing committee were finding a response. Various kinds of cooperative organizations—a dairy cooperative in East Tennessee, a marketing cooperative in Chattanooga and cooperative grist and feed mills in West Tennessee were being established in five counties across the state "from the Smoky Mountains in East Tennessee to the Western part of the state near the Mississippi River."[29] During this period, too, a seven-member state Farmers Union committee was formed which endorsed the broad National Farmers Union legislative program and proposed a boldly expanded state program of farmer-led cooperative enterprises. There was some encouraging evidence, as well, of farmer-labor cooperation in several local situations. And, stimulated and encouraged by Highlander's early progress in building a Farmers Union base in the state, the Brotherhood of Railroad Trainmen made a $3,750 contribution to the work of the Tennessee Organizing Committee of the Farmers Union for 1945-1946.[30]

An examination of how the organization of the several locals and a statewide organization with labor support were achieved reveals the elements of a nontraditional educational program. That these elements did not find their way into the School's Annual Reports is understandable. The educational activities as carried on by Tennessee Farmers Union Representative Myles Horton and the Highlander staff member who assisted him[31] were often so interwoven with the organizing activities as to be indistinguishable. Then, too, the program was still an exploratory one, very secondary in terms of staff time and funds to the School's labor education program.

Most of the education took place during field visits and meetings with local farmers and in the considerable correspondence which developed between Horton and the key farmers around whom the organizing program was built. In view of the vast length of the state, the hundreds of miles to be covered by the two staff members, and the limited funds available for the new program, education-by-correspondence was of vital importance. Thus, for example, the Farmers Union program in Greene County in East Tennessee began with a field visit by Myles Horton in the summer of 1945 at the invitation of a former college classmate and "poor people's lawyer" who was concerned about the plight of local farmers. After talking with individual farmers and holding a public meeting to consider their grievances against a large condensed milk company, much of the planning and organizing which followed was facilitated through letters between Horton and two farmer-leaders whom he came to know on his initial visit. Through this process of correspondence and a limited number of follow-up visits, the farmers were able to establish the East Tennessee Dairy Cooperative and several Farmers Union locals. Subsequent correspondence with the two men (who were elected president and secretary-treasurer of the new dairy cooperative) deals with the many problems confronting them. It is concerned first with the problems of setting up a "going organization" with Horton sending the new officers alternative sets of by-laws from Farmers Union organizations in other states together with instructions for the by-laws committee.[32] It is concerned, too, with the problems of public education: how to answer charges of agrarian radicalism. Here, Horton supplied the hard-put local leaders with information for the conservative local press about a statewide committee of rural ministers, organized with Highlander's help, in support of the Tennessee Farmers Union. And the correspondence is concerned with longer term problems such as how to build a relationship of mutual understanding and support between state and local labor organizations and the Farmers Union. (Even in these early letters, therefore, soon after the establishment of the new East Tennessee dairy cooperative, plans are discussed for meetings between Greeneville cooperative leaders and the State Director of the CIO[33] and between cooperative leaders and the Regional Director of the United Packinghouse Workers.[34])

Meetings, of course, had always been utilized by Highlander as a setting in which to carry on education, whether a protest meeting of WPA workers in Grundy County or a business meeting of a Sugarworkers local in New Orleans. Along with holding meetings to consider the broad goals and problems of the Farmers Union as related to small farmers in a given area, Highlander-Farmers Union staff members presented talks and led discussions on the development of cooperative enterprises for farmers "about which," a staff report notes, "so little is understood by rank and file or leaders from farm organizations in the South."[35] Membership meetings of the new locals and cooperative organizations were also utilized to introduce non-Farmers Union speakers representing various progressive groups and points of view. An anti-Crump Machine candidate for United States Senator and a member of the Tennessee Valley Authority Board of Directors, for example, were among the featured speakers at meetings of the new East Tennessee cooperative. Farmers Union meetings were also addressed by labor speakers, including labor members of the Highlander Executive Council. In Carroll County in West Tennessee, the Legislative Representative of the Brotherhood of Railroad Trainmen "made the first contacts and arranged for the organizing meeting" in that area.[36]

Along with these kinds of education, the *Tennessee Union Farmer* was very consciously employed as a vehicle for education. By the summer of 1946, with a growing readership and membership, it was changed from a modest sort of national newsletter to a full-sized eight-page newspaper featuring regular columns by farmer leaders as well as gadfly editorials by Highlander staff member-editor Tom Ludwig. Under his energetic leadership, it served not only as a means of indoctrinating members and potential members with the importance of the Farmers Union as the champion of small farmers in Tennessee and the nation, but as an educational forum where local Farmers Union leaders, labor union spokesmen, rural ministers, the Highlander staff and others could present their views on the Farm Bureau, Henry Wallace, the Guaranteed Annual Wage, race relations in the South, or pending state and national legislation affecting farmers and workers.

To facilitate farmer-labor understanding and joint action, Highlander, as has been indicated, also sought to educate its labor union students. These educational efforts are reflected in the content of the residential workers' education program during this period whether of the Southern CIO Schools or the several terms for international unions. In addition, publicly and behind the scenes, Highlander staff and Executive Council members were instrumental is arranging farmer-labor conferences and informal meetings between farm and labor leaders.

By the end of 1946, Myles Horton stated with some confidence what he had indicated tentatively in an early issue of the little mimeographed *Union* paper, "a basis has been laid for a large and permanent Farmers Union in Tennessee." In verification of this hopeful outlook, National Farmers Union President James Patton wrote to Myles Horton, Tennessee Representative of the National Farmers Union, that the Board of Directors had "designated the State of Tennessee as a territory."[37] This designation, however modest-sounding, was significant historically for it meant that after a full generation in decline the Farmers Union was once again coming alive in Tennessee. It meant, too, the promise of much needed funds to expand the program in Tennessee and to move into other southern states.

The promise very soon began to become a reality. In December 1946 the Director of Rural Education for the Rosenwald Fund announced a grant of $15,000 to the Highlander Folk School over a three-year period "for the development of a rural program."[38]

Beyond Organization: Education for a People's Movement

Three major Farmers Union and farmer-labor resident terms were held at the Highlander Folk School in 1947. Having established a Farmers Union base in Tennessee which was recognized by both the National Farmers Union and organized labor in the state, and having received a modest grant, the School was in a position to begin to develop an intensive educational program committed to strengthening the state and local Farmers Union and helping its leadership look beyond the present organization to the development of a farmer-labor coalition and a broad people's movement in the South.

The First Tennessee Farmers Union School

The Farmers Union School in February, sponsored by the new Tennessee Territorial Farmers Union for their local leaders, was clearly designed with the coalition and movement as well as organizational goals in mind. Thus, the Tennessee School, described in the *Highlander Fling* as "the first of its kind in the South for a generation," included a small number of Negro as well as white Farmers Union members.[39] (It was, therefore, probably the first of its kind in the South ever.)

In order to bring to the twenty-three farmer and three rural minister-students, representing six counties and a number of little Farmers Union locals and cooperative organizations across Tennessee, some larger notion of the farmers movement and the potential for a broader movement in the South, Highlander involved speakers and visiting staff members with a variety of backgrounds and vantage points.[40] Students listened to and talked informally with a radical southern theologian who was a long-time friend of organized labor, the Farmers Union and the Highlander Folk School; a political analyst and columnist for *The Nashville Tennessean*; the Chairman of Highlander's Executive Council who was both a former regional administrator for the Farm Security Administration and a former regional director for the CIO-PAC; a widely known and outspoken Alabama Farmers Union leader and a less known but no less outspoken Mississippi-born Farmers Union leader who urged an attack on the problems of low income Negro farmers. The group also had daily discussion sessions led by two members of the National staff—the editor of the *National Union Farmer* and the Assistant Director of Education. Problems and questions ranged from how to get farmers interested in attending local meetings to the position of the National Farmers Union on the poll tax and on fair employment and how to interpret those issues locally.

In addition to the farmers and rural ministers, at least one Tennessee labor representative participated in the term. Judging by the letters sent to her and her union by her fellow students, the young woman representing the American Federation of Hosiery Workers made a significant contribution to their experience. In thanking the Hosiery Workers' officials who made it possible for her to be with us," they wrote, "We feel that we've gained in our understanding of the interdependence of farmers and workers during the School and begun to better appreciate that working people, field or factory, must stand together."[41]

They probably gained, too, in their understanding of the political process and their role in it. As in other Highlander terms, the staff and students sent telegrams to a key group of senators—in this case, urging confirmation of TVA Administrator Lilienthal as Chairman of the Atomic Energy Commission because "We know and trust him without reservation."[42] Thus, in their week together, Farmers Union members, whether from the new Spring Hill local in West Tennessee, the Negro farming community of Bakewell or the growing East Tennessee Dairy Cooperative, explored whole new areas of thought and experience.

The Highlander staff evaluation of the Tennessee Farmers Union School, as contained in minutes of a meeting shortly thereafter, indicates general approval of the broadly-defined program. It was suggested by one of the staff that "the religious movement," meaning, apparently, church organizations concerned with rural problems, "be tied into the Farmers Union movement a little more closely."[43] The National staff was also, apparently, in accord with the broad program for, in the course of the Tennessee School, the National Farmers Union proposed to co-sponsor the first Southern Farmers Union School with Highlander and the Farmers Educational Foundation.[44]

With the National Farmers Union making it clear that it wanted Highlander to serve as the center for its educational work in the South, the School began to project an increasing role for itself as a "movement meeting place," a center for stimulating farmer-labor political action. And at an Executive Council meeting in January, 1947, there was even some mention of helping to build a political party. "Working together toward a farmer-labor party is the logical goal,"[45] it was suggested.

If Highlander planners were optimistic, they could cite as a basis for their optimism the School's unique relationship to both the industrial union movement and the Farmers Union in the South. They could and did cite a growing number of instances of farmer-labor cooperation in those parts of Tennessee where the School had been developing a local Farmers Union program. Council minutes note that in West Tennessee the farmers had been holding farmer-labor meetings to demonstrate their support for a Clothing Workers organizing drive after two organizers were driven out of town. "The Farmers Union," the minutes indicate, "has taken the heat off the union down there." The minutes note also that the East Tennessee Dairy Cooperative, with organized labor support, had finally won its struggle with the condensed milk company to have a farmer representative check the weighing and testing of milk. "The Farmers Union leadership feels definitely," the report stresses, "that the only reason they succeeded is because the CIO is in the plant." And, as further evidence of the promising future for a political coalition, the Council cited a recent example of organized labor in Tennessee rallying to the support of legislation exempting farmers from paying road tax on gasoline used in their farm machinery. "This help," minutes observed, "has done a lot to convince the farmers that labor is going to work with them."[46]

The First Southern Farmers Union School

Amidst these hopeful coalition stirrings, the first Southern Farmers Union School was convened in July, 1947. To the Cumberland Mountain came Negro and white Farmers Union members representing new and revived locals and cooperatives in Virginia, Alabama, Mississippi, Louisiana and various parts of Tennessee. Also in the group that came to Highlander were a small number of representatives of labor unions and rural church and community organizations. In all the participants numbered some fifty Farmers Union members and fellow believers.

The five-day resident term was led by National Farmers Union, Farmers Educational Fund and Highlander staff members, and was highlighted by an array of visiting speakers including the National Farmers Union President, the Alabama Farmers Union President and Southern Farmer editor, the Agricultural Relations Director of the TVA and several Regional Representatives of the CIO. The program, as in the case of the recent Tennessee Farmers Union School, was far-ranging and sought to deal with both organizational needs and problems related to achieving a more democratic South. It included, according to an article in the *Tennessee Union Farmer*, "classes, discussions and forums on co-operatives, political action, farmer-labor relationships, religion, farm problems and parliamentary law."[47] But more important than the formal program, judging by the accounts of Negro and white farmer and labor participants was the experience of coming together—out of their far-flung Farmers Union locals, out of a southern society where economic and social prejudices had kept them apart. In a special staff-student newspaper on the term, they made some very personal comments about their experiences. An East Tennessee dairy farmer observed of a state labor leader whom he came to know

> I have been very much impressed by the interest shown by Mr. White in the farmers movement and by my association with him during the week I spent at Highlander. He is just another good old farmer at heart even though he is an executive in the Brotherhood of Railroad Trainmen.[48]

A labor leader who had brought with him the group views and judgments of a lifetime wrote, "After some forty years of observation and struggle in the labor movement, I see and hear these leaders of farmers repudiate the destructive policy, practiced down through the years of oftentimes bitter opposition to labor unions . . ."[49]

A Negro Farmers Union member from a recently organized Tennessee local spoke in religious terms. You are all my brothers," he said. "And I yours. We cannot live together with the barriers of religious and racial prejudices keeping God's spirit of cooperation from our daily living."[50]

The chairman of a hard-pressed Farmers Union local in Louisiana, who came seeking answers to immediate problems, received, along with suggestions for dealing with those problems, a much larger notion of what his organization's goals should be. "The people of Louisiana," he stated, "must learn to organize a Farmers Union as many other states have. To win the full fight for their freedom, strictly they must fight to elect people both in the Legislature and the Governorship, who will help support a democratic way of living."[51]

A South Alabama Farmers Union leader, after coming together with leaders of isolated Farmers Union locals and representatives of labor and other groups, discovered that they had many common problems and hopes. "The possibility of a strong progressive farm-labor movement arising in this country has certainly become clear in my mind during this week at Highlander."[52] Myles Horton, perhaps inspired by the movement environment which had been created, predicted hopefully in the last session together, "There's [sic] enough of you right here in this room to set the whole South on fire . . ."[53]

Only one member of the National Farmers Union staff, more organization than movement-minded, spoke in quite other terms to participants ln Southern Farmers Union School

> We must remember that back in our home communities we must again plant our feet on the ground. Those around us were not at Highlander. They have not felt the inspirational uplift we have received. That may shock some of us. It will be discouraging and that will be the real test.[54]

The First Farmer-Labor School

The first Farmer-Labor School to be held at the Highlander Folk School in the fall of 1947 was also its last. Highlander announcements described it as the term that "will climax a series of twelve separate sessions for industrial workers and farmers." It was widely publicized in the labor press as "the first Farmer-Labor School in the South" with articles and pictures featuring its integrated farmer-labor student body and its recommendations for joint political and legislative action.[55]

In spite of the apparently bright potential, the Farmer-Labor School was in difficulty even in the planning stages. The Highlander Executive Council had recommended that the term be co-sponsored by the National Farmers Union and the CIO.[56] This joint sponsorship, for whatever reasons, was not achieved. But sponsorship was only the initial problem. The underlying problem was what kind of educational program, what issues would make the School relevant to industrial workers as well as farmers. "The only thing that strikes fire," Horton observed to fellow staff members "is the political action idea. There should be," he emphasized, "an economic counterpart."[57] The counterpart selected was producer and consumer cooperatives. But some of the staff was itself not very clear about why workers should become excited about farmers' fertilizer cooperatives. (It was pointed out that the kind and quality of fertilizer produced was related to the "workers' need for vitamins.") The staff agreed to encourage workers to appreciate the importance of producer cooperatives and, at the same time, to give them a firsthand understanding of consumer cooperatives by running their own store.

Efforts to publicize the Farmer-Labor School to prospective students on the grounds that "the farmer gets so little for what he produces and pays so much for the machinery he buys" and "the laborer gets so little for what he produces and pays so much for the food he buys"[58] did not "strike fire." A total of sixteen representatives of Farmers Union and industrial union locals were recruited for the southwide School.[59] Of these, all of the Farmers Union representatives had participated in one or both of the previous Farmers Union terms. There were labor participants from six unions but staff meeting minutes suggest that many unions which the School had hoped would send students failed to do so and those which did responded, in large part, on the basis of personal contact.[60]

The ten-day Farmer-Labor School, like the Farmers Union Schools, dealt with a number of broad problems including the political and economic bases for a farmer-labor coalition. Among the visiting staff members and teachers were Farmers Union and labor union leaders and specialists on cooperatives from the TVA and the Cooperative Federation of Philadelphia, the President of the Chattanooga NAACP, the Director of the Southern Regional Council and the Chairman of the Association of Oak Ridge Engineers and Scientists.

Minutes of several student-led meetings of an organization known as the "Highlander Farmer-Labor Cooperative" indicate that it not only functioned with some effectiveness, producing a modest profit for its members, but provided an opportunity for the Director of the Philadelphia Cooperative Federation to teach the group the difference between a cooperative and a corporation and to explain the Rochdale principles. However, although the Highlander staff subsequently prepared and sent all participants in the term an illustrated pamphlet, "How to Plan for a Consumer Services Cooperative," there is no evidence that labor union students returned home to help establish local cooperatives or demonstrated a new and enlightened interest in producer cooperatives.

The most heralded result of the ten-day terms, according to the *Tennessee Union Farmer*, was a so-called "preliminary draft for economic and political co-operation" as proposed by a committee of Farmers Union and labor union students. In addition, according to the paper, industrial worker students "returned with plans for setting up Farm Relations committees in their locals" and farmer-students "pledged their support in setting up Farmer-Labor Councils."[61] Again, there seems to be no record of whether, in fact, they acted on these intentions.

What is clear is that although the leadership of the Highlander Folk School continued to advocate the idea of a farmer-labor coalition (urging through *The Union Farmer* joint action in the election of liberal candidates to state and federal office and encouraging farmer-labor cooperation at the local level in Tennessee and, later, in Alabama and Virginia), it never again attempted to hold a Farmer-Labor School. One might well assume that was because the first such School did not "strike fire." But viewing the educational effort in relation to the southern labor movement of the late forties (increasingly institutionalized, increasingly running its own educational programs to serve its own narrowing goals; its leadership, notably in the Southern CIO Organizing Drive, less and less inclined to be involved in political and social action), it would seem that not only Highlander's Farmer-Labor School but the whole broad movement idea failed to "strike fire."

Education in Service of the Southern Farmers Union

What lay ahead, therefore, for the pragmatic, would-be farmer-labor school was to work with the Farmers Union, not as part of a movement but as an organization with congenial goals and program. As Myles Horton explained the School's organization-serving role in a 1949 letter to a former staff member

> The situation in the South is still a puzzling mixture of hopefulness and the worst kind of reaction. The labor picture doesn't add up to much at present. That's why we are working so hard organizing farmers.[62]

Viewed as a program in service of an organization, Highlander's organizing and educational activities in behalf of the Farmers Union were not ineffective. Its efforts were warmly praised in an article, "Rural Awakening in the Near South," which appeared in *The Nation* in the summer of 1948. "Stimulated by the school," the agricultural economist author reported, "interest in farm organization is heightening. The Greeneville Cooperative is expanding into the livestock market. A Southern States Cooperative Fertilizer Factory is being organized." He cited examples as well in East Tennessee of labor and farmers supporting one another. "These things," he admitted, "are just a beginning," but Tennessee represents "an opening wedge." The example "of East Tennessee farmers meeting their problems successfully through cooperation, learning to make common cause with labor," he concluded, ". . . augers well for the future of the South."[63]

Highlander's report for 1948[64] indicates that the territorial jurisdiction of Tennessee Farmers Union Representative Myles Horton had been extended to include Southwestern Virginia and that in the new area six new locals had been organized as well as a brokerage cooperative to sell feed, seed and equipment to members. The report also indicates that Highlander staff member and *Tennessee Union Farmer* editor Tom Ludwig had enlarged the scope of his activities, devoting much of his time to working with the Alabama Farmers Union in organizing and guiding the development of a fertilizer cooperative in South Alabama. In keeping with the School's expanding Farmers Union program, the Farmers Union newspaper itself was expanded to southwide edition, henceforth to be known as the *Union Farmer* with special late sections for Virginia and Alabama as well as Tennessee.

Parallel to its organizing activities the Highlander staff, assisted by visiting National Farmers Union staff members, offered a series of community institutes in Tennessee and Alabama and a resident school for Farmers Union representatives from old and new locals in Tennessee, Alabama and Virginia. A staff report on the 1948 Southern Farmers Union School indicates that it was informal and problem-centered and guided by a "farmers steering committee" which met each day to decide what problems would be discussed. With a small group of white and Negro farmer leaders as students, fourteen in all, and a minimum of visiting speakers, the program was one of "concentrated discussion and thinking" both on immediate questions such as "how to get young people and women interested in the organization" and on long-term questions related to "farmer-labor cooperation" and "cooperation between the races."[65] The community institutes, planned jointly by Highlander and local Farmers Union representatives, varied from place to place. Generally they combined day-long leadership sessions where a key group from the local area met with visiting Highlander and National Farmers Union staff and inspirational-recreational-type meetings for Farmers Union members and their families. These evening meetings, including drama by a junior group and singing led by Zilphia Horton, brought together as many as 125 in a little Farmers Union hall in Andalusia, Alabama.[66] National Farmers Union staff members who visited local communities in Tennessee and Alabama and took part in the educational institutes were impressed with the spirit and the interest which they encountered. Education Director Gladys Talbott Edwards, after participating in several community institutes, wrote with admiration in the *National Union Farmer* of the way in which men, women and children came out to meetings "even though the season was a very busy one" and of their broad concerns. Not only, she observed, were they eager to obtain "better health care, recreation and education for their children" but "all of them want world peace." Most of all she was impressed with the determination of South Alabama Farmers Union members in the face of poverty and efforts to divide them. "The courage of the little band of folks in the South who are building this cooperative out of their dollar shares, she observed, "is like nothing else I have ever known except the courage of the drought destroyed families in the Northwest . . ."[67]

The Movement Spirit in South Alabama

What was most heartening to Highlander, along with the organization of new locals and cooperatives and the development of broader goals and interests growing out of the jointly planned educational program, was the fact that these activities were shared by both Negro and white farmers and their families. A special issue of the *Highlander Fling* in 1948 was devoted to "Highlander's Program in Civil Rights" and featured a picture of an integrated residential session along with the words of a white South Alabama Farmers Union leader, J. D. Mott

> The second colored man that I had ever shaken hands with was at Highlander Folk School. It encouraged me to see this being done, and I figured if it could be done at Monteagle it could be done at Covington County, Alabama. And now after one year since going to Highlander everyone knows that it can be done. I'll bet I've shaken hands with five hundred colored farmers—and organized them into the Farmers Union. We are all getting together as farmers to solve our problems.[68]

An effort had been made in Tennessee to seek out and include Negro farmers in the Farmers Union. This effort had been limited by the limited number of Negro farmers in the several areas where the organization was underway. In South Alabama, however, there were numerous Negro as well as white small farmers and other factors encouraged the process. Historically, of course, the Farmers Union founded in the South at the turn of the century had been an organization of white farmers. Not only did whites reject ideas that they change their constitution and admit Negroes, but "some even questioned the wisdom of encouraging the Negro to form his own organization."[69] However, when the depression of the thirties gave to many a common sense of misery, the Farmers Union revived in Alabama and (especially in the areas influenced by industrial unionism) some locals included Negro as well as white sharecroppers and independent farm operators.[70] In addition to this precedent, the Alabama Farmers Union was headed by *Southern Farmer* editor and Highlander Board member Aubrey Williams who was one of the staunchest voices for integrated farm, labor and other organizations in the South. Thus, when J.D. Mott returned from the Southern Farmers Union School at Highlander in the summer of 1947, inspired by his "hand-shaking" integrated living experience, he had support within his home environment. The story of what he and Highlander staff member Tom Ludwig were able to accomplish in three South Alabama counties, building an educational program and bringing together Negro and white small farmers in some twenty locals and a Farmers Union fertilizer cooperative is well documented, month by month, in *Union Farmer*. Pictures of leading Negro and white farmers selling shares and building a structure to house their cooperative appear in a number of issues during 1948. The pictures together with stories about the "rain or shine volunteers" were featured not only to give recognition, but to say to Farmers Union members in other parts of Alabama and other parts of the South, "Look what can be accomplished by working together!"

The spirit of the South Alabama Farmers Union did, apparently, communicate itself for when delegates gathered for the annual Alabama Farmers Union convention in the northern town of Center in December 1948, the theme was unity. "We need unity of all working people," they affirmed, whether farmers in the field or hands in the factory, whether one religion or another, whether of one color or another." And, inspired perhaps by the national leaders who addressed them, including President James Patton and Secretary of Agriculture Charles Brannon, they spoke not just for the Alabama Farmers Union or even the South, "The people of the world want peace," they asserted, "and it is the responsibility and duty of our leaders to find ways to realize this."[71]

The End of Highlander's Farmers Union Program

If the "people's movement" spirit of this small but growing group of Negro and white Farmers Union members was hopeful, the economic future of the Farmers Union also seemed to be hopeful. In the spring of 1949, a National Farmers Union advisor close to President Patton made a careful analysis of progress in the South and recommended the establishment of a "regional wholesale supply service as the first step in developing a fully rounded Farmers Union organization in the South." He noted that in carrying out these new services and in building a southwide organization, "South Alabama offers an example of a pattern which has many advantages and which may well be adaptable to other communities of the South."[72] Some two months later, after meetings with numerous leaders of Farmers Union organizations in Tennessee, Alabama and Virginia, the same National Farmers Union advisor reported that all were in favor of joining a regional wholesale service and that "steps have been taken" towards its early establishment. He concluded by urging strongly "the strategic importance of this southern program," pointing out that "this area contains about forty per cent of all the farmers in the United States . . ." He added further, "It is our belief that the present leadership in the South is fully competent to guide a strong and effective Farmers Union and the latent leadership in these communities cannot be excelled."[73]

Reports indicate that in 1949 and 1950, its last years of association with the Farmers Union, the Highlander Folk School continued to assist local Farmers Union organizations in Alabama, Virginia and Tennessee through the services of its field staff and jointly planned leadership institutes and through the one-week Southern Farmers Union resident terms,[74] bringing together local leadership from the three states. Reports also indicate that even in 1950, new plans were being made and new local programs were getting underway.

Thus, for example, in the Altoona area, near Gadsden, Alabama, "a coordinated Farmers Union program" was being developed combining "cooperatives, organizations, education and insurance." Noting that "This may set the pattern for building the Farmers Union in the state," a Highlander staff report outlines some of the elements including " a strong union spirit among both farmers and industrial workers in the area," which were contributing to the success of the venture.[75]

Yet, in spite of promising beginnings and parent potential for building an organization in the southeast, the National Farmers Union never acted on these recommendations. Instead, less than two years later, it made a policy decision to withdraw from the region and to concentrate its efforts and resources in the grain-producing West where its strength and influence had long been established.[76]

All of the factors and thinking which led to the National Farmers Union decision in 1951 to quit the region may never be known. Publicly, President James Patton explained that it was necessary to revoke the Alabama State Charter "in compliance with requirements of the National Farmers Union Constitution and By-laws" providing that the Charter is to be revoked "whenever . . . state membership falls below one thousand." However, Patton's painstaking reiteration in the same letter to an Alabama Farmers Union leader that the action had "absolutely nothing to do with your political or social views on any subject" and his ardent avowal, "You and I are both non-Communist liberals"[77] suggests the kind of pressures on liberal organizations and leaders which may have helped to bring that action about.

Avraham Mezerik, author of books and articles on the South and articles on the Farmers Union,[78] has indicated that in his judgment there were two elements in the Farmers Union "pull out." The first, as he assessed it, was that "no organizing successes emerged." The second, he believes, was related to the political climate of the Korean War period which took the National Farmers Union leadership, in his words, "out of the ranks of Populist radicalism and made them into Truman patriots tinged with virulent anti-Communism, so much a part of that era." He points out that none of the organizational leaders, including the President of the Alabama Farmers Union and Myles Horton and his Highlander-Farmers Union staff, whose "anti-hot war and anti-cold war" views were contrary to the national position, survived the period.[79]

Two Highlander staff members who worked with the Farmers Union are convinced, but for somewhat different reasons, that the decision to withdraw was a political one. The staff member who worked with J. D. Mott in building a fertilizer cooperative and integrated locals in South Alabama cites the destructive effects of the Dixiecrats—the increasing accusations and smear attacks against the Farmers Union in the South and the resulting caution and conservatism among some within the organization. "But before politics intervened," he emphasizes, "we dignified people who had lost their self-dignity."[80]

The other staff member and former CIO organizer who served as part-time Farmers Union field representative for Virginia and Tennessee states, "We were ahead of our time . . . working together in spite of political, racial and other issues." In retrospect, he remains convinced of the soundness of the program. "It wasn't," he asserts, "the Virginia or the Tennessee or the Alabama Farmers Union that failed. It was the National Farmers Union."[81]

Whatever the judgments of future students of southern history regarding the short-lived revival of the Farmers Union in the South, in the view of Highlander's educational director, the program which he originally promised had failed. The program represented an effort, working with and through the Farmers Union to build a farmer-labor people's movement in the South. Looking back, some two decades later, Myles Horton concludes that the School which had built its earlier programs in response to movement related needs failed because "We were trying to create something to respond to."[82]

It should be added that the Southern Farmers Union program which failed to create a movement made an indirect contribution to the civil rights movement which was to follow. The program helped to establish Highlander's status, southwide and beyond, as a residential center where Negro and white farmers as well as industrial workers could come together to discuss their problems.[83] And among the local Farmers Union leaders who came to the School from South Alabama was one young Negro farmer-school teacher who was to become the director of the first Highlander workshops on school desegregation[84] and an active participant in the civil rights movement in the deep South. These workshops and subsequent programs related to the voter education movement and the student movement will be examined in Part V.

PART FIVE

Education for Leadership in the Southwide Civil Rights Movement

PREFACE

Between 1953 and 1961, as Negro Southerners sought with increasing determination to achieve their full rights as citizens, the Highlander Folk School developed three major educational programs to encourage and strengthen their efforts. The first of these was a series of workshops on desegregation for Negro and white community leaders. The workshops began in 1953 in anticipation of the Supreme Court decision outlawing public school segregation and continued until 1957 when Highlander former students were among the leaders of a southern movement to desegregate all public facilities. Its second major program, the Citizenship School Program, 1957-1961, was developed in the South Carolina Sea Islands in response to the desire of illiterate Negro islanders to read and write in order to qualify as voters. From there, in the wake of the mounting voter registration drive of the late fifties, the program was carried by Highlander Citizenship School teachers to communities from the Upper to the Deep South. The third and last major civil rights program of the Highlander Folk School was a series of workshops related to the southern student movement, 1960-1961, beginning with the first workshop for local sit-in leaders and followed by several workshops for leaders of the rapidly growing southwide movement. These programs will be examined, in turn, in the three chapters which follow.

TWELVE

Community Leadership for an Emerging Movement: First Workshops on School Desegregation

The Highlander Folk School as an Institution, 1953-1961

The School was never so concertedly under attack as in the years when it served as the educational center for the southern civil rights movement. At the same time, it was never stronger or more effective, measured in terms of financial support, internal organization and functioning and the number and variety of students served.

In the fiscal year ending September 30, 1953, Highlander's income, derived from foundation grants as well as individual contributions, was more than $59,000[1]—the largest amount for a single year in the School's history. And it continued to grow. (Only in 1957, when its tax exempt status was temporarily revoked, did Highlander's income drop drastically; in that year it was $39,000[2]) In 1958, 1959 and 1960—the last years before the School was closed by action of the Tennessee courts—its annual income, again from foundation grants and individual contributions, rose to well over $100,000.[3]

Administratively, much of the burden of day-to-day responsibility was transferred to two new staff assistants during these years. The small educational staff of four to six members, therefore, was able to concentrate on educational problems related to planning and carrying out a growing number of workshops and on fund-raising to underwrite those workshops. One of the administrative assistants, formerly a student at the University of Arkansas, was responsible for office management and record keeping[4] at a time when the School's records were under frequent scrutiny by investigative bodies. The other, who came to Highlander originally as a student intern from Antioch College, served as administrative assistant to Myles Horton and helped in the development of workshops related to the student movement.[5]

Highlander's educational staff as well as members of its Executive Council, beginning in 1953, included Negro civil rights leaders.[6] One of these leaders, Mrs. Septima Clark, who attended early Highlander workshops on desegregation, became Director of Workshops in 1955. Two others, Mrs. Bernice Robinson and Esau Jenkins, served as Coordinators of Highlander's citizenship School Program in the Sea Islands of South Carolina. In their combined roles as civil rights leaders and Highlander staff members, they strengthened the School's relationship to the movement.

The growth in the number of participants in Highlander's civil rights workshops and the growth in the number of workshops—from seventy-one community leaders who attended three school desegregation workshops in the summer of 1953[7] to 728 adult and student movement leaders who attended eighteen workshops in 1960 and 1961[8]—was unequalled in the School's history. The diversity of their backgrounds was also unequalled: Negro and white professional persons, Negro and white churchmen, Negro and white college students met together with Negro and white farmers and industrial workers and Negro day laborers and domestic workers. The "broad movement" which Highlander had long projected seemed, for a brief time, at least, a reality.

In Preparation for the Movement, 1932-1952

Although the Highlander Folk School did not hold integrated residential terms for labor unions until 1944 or for the Farmers Union until 1947, it began very early to get ready for its role as a center to develop leadership for school integration and the southwide civil rights movement. Its founder could be said to have been "getting ready" even before the unorthodox institution came into being. In Denmark, in the winter of 1931, he wrote of the school that its primarily southern students would come from the mountains and from the factories and, he noted explicitly, "Negroes should be among the students."[9]

There is evidence that as early as 1933 an effort was made to integrate the small and struggling residential school. A staff member from Knoxville College, a Tennessee Negro college, wrote in response to an inquiry from Myles Horton, "At this time we know of no student or graduate of our school who would be a good candidate or who would be desirous of enrolling with you." He added in closing, "A number of us are extremely interested in your work."[10]

The early effort to integrate this student body was subsequently deferred, in large part, records of staff meetings indicated, because of concern about the reaction of the all-white mountain community and county where the School was beginning to build a program. The staff was in full agreement, however, that "some sort of interracial work was . . . necessary"[11]—for the education of the local community and leaders of a future southern labor movement.

In the summer of 1934, after some discussion with mountain neighbors, Negro speakers and college groups[12] began to visit the School during resident terms. The first speaker, Knoxville College professor Herman Daves was invited, according to a Highlander memorandum, at the suggestion of a group of resident students and community members. The memorandum addressed to "Our friends in Summerfield and neighboring communities" carefully explained

A few students who . . . have families to support and live in towns where Negroes are unorganized, wanted first-hand information as to how Negro workers could be organized . . . Following a discussion several people from the community said that the students should get the Negroes' side.[13]

The most distinguished of the early visiting speakers and friends of the School was Dr. Charles S. Johnson, Fisk University sociologist, later founder of the Race Relations Institute and, still later, President of the University. Correspondence between Charles Johnson and Myles Horton over the years indicates the deep regard of each for the other's efforts and the efforts of their two Tennessee institutions[14] to enlarge understanding and facilitate change in the South. With the coming of the CIO visiting speakers began to include, for the first time, Negro as well as white labor leaders along with Negro college professors and other professional persons.

In this period, too, the Highlander Folk School and its resident and community students participated in many depression-born, New Deal-inspired conferences and organizations of Negro and white southerners seeking to better their common lot in the land of the ill-fed, ill-clothed and ill-housed. They took an active part in regional meetings of the Negro and white unemployed. They worked with the National Committee to Abolish the Poll Tax, beginning with a suit instituted in Grundy County. They participated in the founding and subsequent meetings of the Southern Conference for Human Welfare where thousands of Negro and white southerners came together in tradition-breaking sessions to confront the problems of the problem region.

The most dramatic and unforgettable of these early meetings, at least for its more than fifty Negro and white delegates representing union, church, university, and liberal-to-radical political organizations, as well as Highlander staff and students, was the All-Southern Civil and Trade Union Rights Conference held at the Highlander Folk School in 1935. The broadly conceived interracial conference which announced as its objective "a higher standard of life in the South"[15] had to struggle for the right to meet before it could consider its agenda. Slated originally to confer in Chattanooga, the group encountered great difficulty in finding a place to meet because, a Highlander staff report noted, as soon as a hall was rented "pressure would be put on the owner and the engagement would be cancelled."[16] When a second floor hall was finally secured from a Negro proprietor, the delegates were forced to flee as a mob gathered and threatened to dynamite the building. Faced by the mob, the delegates managed to escape to Highlander, some fifty miles away, where the sessions proceeded. Zilphia Horton, in writing about the harried conference some years later, noted that a group of loyal mountain neighbors who attended the sessions "sat at the edge of the conference group and kept a watchful eye toward the road in front of the School. They were," she explained, "defending the right of the mixed group to meet at the Highlander Folk School."[17]

Non-discrimination: From a Policy to Integrated Residential Sessions

In 1940, with this kind of preparation in the local community and "feeling the urgency . . . of the inter-racial problem," Highlander's leadership decided that the time had come to put a non-discrimination policy into effect. It informed all unions, therefore, that "the School would accept Negro students" and that "unions should notify in advance all students both white and Negro that there would be no discrimination "[18] If the School was "feeling the urgency," the unions apparently were not. The first union to respond to the proposal, the United Auto Workers, did not do so until 1944. By 1945, however, aided by the persuasive efforts of a Highlander Council Member-CIO Regional Director, Paul Christopher, all of the labor terms were integrated.[19]

These first integrated resident terms were not, of course, free of problems. As Zilphia Horton pointed out, "When the white students arrive, the majority of them have the usual prejudices. It is the first experience," she pointed out, too, "for the majority of Negroes and it is likewise a difficult adjustment for them to make."[20] Yet in spite of some tension situations, especially early in a new term, and in spite of the fact that a few whites departed abruptly when they learned that they would be eating at the same tables and sharing the same cabins with Negroes, most stayed and came, surprisingly quickly, to know and accept one another.

With each new integrated labor or Farmers Union group, apparently, the assumption of the School's educational director was that students should find their own ways of interacting and relating, given an informal social setting and an agenda of common problems. Efforts were made to encourage white students to take some initiative in the process. Thus, for example, before the first Southern Farmers Union term, minutes of a planning meeting contain the following instructions to the staff

> Myles asked that white students be allowed to take the lead in making advances to the Negro students. Anyone connected with the School should take the back seat all through the term. Tom will arrange for the white students to sit at the table with Negro students and will get the farmers to take the lead.[21]

For Negro students, the experience was an amazing and unprecedented one which tended to strengthen their belief in unions and, in at least some, of their fellow southerners. A young UAW committeeman explained his feelings towards the end of a one-week term in June 1945

> When I first joined, I had an idea that there were a few people who didn't feel about Negroes like those I had been brought up with in Memphis. And when I came to Highlander, I was fully convinced there were such people. Here, it's just a matter of giving the CIO a chance to carry out its

Constitution . . . There is more religion in this union than in the average church.[22]

The relative ease of adjustment to an integrated living and learning situation after a lifetime in a segregated society amazed other people as well as the students. Executive Council member Lucy Randolph Mason, for example, a staunch believer in Highlander, in the CIO and in its non-discrimination policy, must also have been amazed. Two years before the first integrated term she had written to Myles Horton. "To work among Negro unionists seems important—I think it has to be done in the field, for if you undertake it at Highlander you will undoubtably lose your white workers."[23] Ten years later, having observed many integrated worker and farmer terms at Highlander, she could pay warm tribute to the School in her little volume, *To Win These Rights*,[24] for doing what she had warned against.

Beginning with two or three Negro students out of a total of twenty-five or thirty in a UAW or CIO term in 1944 and 1945, an increasing number of Negro students attended Highlander resident terms in the late forties and early fifties. During these years, as has been indicated, it was decided that the School should "concentrate on work with unions which have less well developed educational programs"[25] and these were frequently unions which had a high proportion of Negro members. In 1952, Myles Horton served for one year as educational director for the United Packinghouse Workers of America as well as Highlander educational director. The union had a high proportion of Negro members. Negro and white union leadership, this time from the North as well as the South, came to Highlander for their residential training.[26]

The Highlander Executive Council became an integrated body early in the 1940s. The first Negro member, Lewis Jones, Fisk University sociologist and a student of Dr. Charles Johnson, came to the Council in 1942 as a representative of the American Federation of Teachers. In 1947, a Tennessee NAACP leader and an Atlanta Urban League official were elected to the Council and in 1949 another Negro leader and educator, Dean B. R. Brazeal of Morehouse College in Atlanta was elected to the Council.

Thus, by 1953 the Highlander Folk School had considerable experience as a center for integrated residential programs. More than that, by its very existence as a viable educational institution with a growing constituency of southern Negro and white farmer, labor and community leader students and an Executive Council of Negro and white regional leaders, it represented a kind of microcosm of the democratic society which the South could become.

Negro Southerners Prepare for Full Citizenship

If Highlander had been "getting ready" for its new role for a long time, so had the South, however involuntary that preparation on the part of many. The New Deal assisted the process and organizations of Negro and white southerners begun then. So, too, did the CIO which proclaimed a new national standard of Negro and white workers together and equal—even if that standard was only glimpsed in the South. A proposed march on Washington accelerated the process. When A. Philip Randolph, backed by members of the Brotherhood of Sleeping Car Porters, North and South, made the proposal that Negroes march to end discrimination in employment and won an executive order for Fair Employment without marching, the power of a massive civil rights protest was demonstrated.

Other events and social changes hastened the process. Among these was World War II with Negro and white soldiers in one fighting force, Negro and white workers in one industrial force and all of them together defeating an enemy bent on destroying hated minorities. Among them, too, was the growing migration of Negroes from their rural isolation to the cities—with new problems, but also with new economic potential and a larger notion of the world. And out of all this experience, this social preparation, had come southern Negroes who began to view themselves and their future differently. Charles Johnson in the crisis period of the fifties sought to communicate this new view, this new self-concept which so few white southerners in positions of power and influence cared to listen to or understand. "The present day southern Negro," he stated, "does not share the belief of the southern white that he is inferior as a human being, even though he may earn lower wages and have fewer years of schooling." Of his aspirations, he observed. "There are very few if any southern Negroes who do not want full American citizenship." And of the path ahead in achieving this aspiration, he noted

> The southern Negro does not seriously expect very much change in his civil rights status through "grass roots" conversion . . . in employment and wages, voting, personal security, access to cultural facilities and other requisites of democratic living, there has been little change except that brought about by a stronger and a higher authority.[27]

1953 Workshops on School Desegregation: A Program for "the Coming Upheaval in the South"

With the rising belief among southern Negroes in themselves and in their right to full citizenship, the Highlander Folk School Executive Council determined to relate its resources to what Council member George Mitchell called "the next great problem" which he defined as "not the problem of conquering poverty, but conquering meanness, prejudice and tradition. Highlander," he predicted, "could become the place in which this is studied, a place where one could learn the art and practice the methods of brotherhood."[28] More specifically, he proposed, "The new emphasis at Highlander should be on the desegregation of public schools in the South." The reason for the immediacy of the program, he noted, "is the coming upheaval in the South" as a result of the impending Supreme Court decision "either outlawing segregation in the schools or enforcing equal facilities."[29]

In response to the challenge, the Council, together with other southern leaders invited to participate in a special planning meeting in April 1953, proposed that the Highlander Folk School develop an experimental program for preparing community leaders, Negro and white, to implement the expected decision.[30] The result was two summer workshops in July and August 1953 on "The Supreme Court Decisions and the Public Schools" and subsequent workshops on school desegregation in 1954, 1955, 1956 and 1957.

In undertaking to develop the first program in the South to assist local leaders in desegregating their schools, Highlander was acting in a manner consistent with its convictions and experience regarding the educational needs and democratic potential inherent in social crises and movements. Underlying its programs over the years had been two basic assumptions: (1) that society and, specifically the South, to become more democratic had to have more widely shared and effective community and organizational leadership, (2) that such leadership could be most readily developed and most highly motivated to learn in a time of social crisis or the emergence of social movement.

The first workshops in 1953 were undertaken in the spirit of hope and excitement. "We are at our best at Highlander," Myles Horton observed to the assembled group of planners from southern church and labor organizations and the Executive Council, "when we are pioneering." They were also undertaken in a spirit of humility with an awareness of both the vastness and complexity of the problem and the lack of any court mandate, as yet, to support action. "The proposed program dealing with segregation in primary and secondary schools of the South," Council members concluded, "is a tremendous undertaking" and one which "can only be done well and fast with the cooperation of many interested individuals and organizations."[31] The broadly defined first workshops, therefore, invited the thinking and participation of a variety of consultants and resource persons. Among the consultants were officials of the national church and welfare organizations and the American Civil Liberties Union as well as a number of national labor leaders and the President of the National Farmers Union. Among those who served as resource persons, helping southern community leader students from nine states[32] to think through the difficult process of desegregation and learn from the experience of others were Irene Osborne, American Friends Service Committee specialist on school desegregation, who was working with civic groups to change patterns in Washington, D.C.,[33] and William Van Til, Professor of Education, Peabody College, Nashville, with a broad knowledge of intergroup relations and some prior experience in coping with school desegregation problems in the North. The director of the two summer workshops was Paul Bennett, a young Negro graduate student, formerly a local Farmers Union leader and school teacher in South Alabama. More and more, beginning in 1953, the directors, resource persons and discussion leaders for Highlander programs were Negro southerners—men, women, college students who knew most about the problems of segregated citizenship and who represented the leadership of the emerging movement for a changed society.

The 1953 workshops were complicated by their size and diversity, with seventy-one[34] ministers, farmers, industrial workers, teachers, adult education leaders and members of interracial organizations from rural and urban communities in the Upper to the Deep South among the participants. In addition, they were held at a time when the Court's decision and the white South's reaction to that decision were as yet unknown. In spite of these factors, an effort was made to relate discussions and resource materials to the needs of participants in their local situations, to help them answer the questions: Who are we going to work with? How are we going to do it? Out of the general and small group discussions and aided by the Washington, D.C., experience, participants developed a guide, "Find Your Friends," and check list of suggested steps to be taken. They also generated, out of the interaction, a sense of eagerness to get on with the job in their local communities. One Negro labor leader from Columbia, South Carolina, who admitted to the group, "I was a little reluctant to come to what might be just another meeting,'" stated at the close of the sessions, "I don't know when I have gained so much that I could put to practical use." And he announced, "As soon as I get back I am calling the first meeting. In fact, I have already written my son to pass on the word for this coming Tuesday."[35]

1954 Workshop on School Desegregation: A Program to Implement a Decision

One month after the May 17, 1954, decision of the Court that "in the field of public education the doctrine of 'separate but equal' has no place," the Highlander Folk School held its second summer workshops on desegregation of the public schools. "We started our first summer workshops," the School noted, "almost a year before the Supreme Court handed down its now historic decision. We had faith that amounted to a conviction that the time had come for action. We have another conviction," it asserted, "that the acceptance of the Supreme Court decision in the South will come even more quickly and with less violence than the majority of the people believe possible."[36]

If Highlander's leadership was hopeful, so, too, were other on-the-scene observers. In an article entitled "The South Will Go Along," Harold Fleming of the Southern Regional Council praised the Court for its "unprecedented invitation to the South to help work out the implementing decrees."[37] And Charles Johnson, together with some 100 southern Negro educators, drafted a generous forward-looking statement to white fellow educators calling for a new cooperative effort

> The Court's decision makes possible a single school system with the opportunity for people in the region to marshal their educational resources and to develop a philosophy that can bring to education generally a new perspective. Let it be clearly understood that we are not pleading for Negroes alone. We are concerned about the best education that can be made available to every child in the South.[38]

In this spirit of hope the 1954 workshops were convened. Participants, about half of them Negro and many of them parents and teachers, came from some of the same communities in South Carolina, Alabama, Georgia and Tennessee from which participants in the 1953 workshop had come. They came strengthened not only by the Court's decision, but also for some of them, by having seen first steps taken locally to implement the goals set the summer before. Several sessions led by Highlander staff were devoted to describing these first steps. Participants from Oak Ridge, Tennessee, an Upper South community with many federally-employed scientists, technicians and workers, reported major progress by their active citizens' group which was looking toward integration of its schools in the fall of 1955, "the first community in Tennessee."[39] Even in Tuskegee, Alabama and Columbia, South Carolina, some steps had been taken. In Columbia, it was noted, "Highlander-trained People . . . are working quietly in the shadow of the hostile State Capitol to organize their political strength in support of integrated schools." And in Tuskegee, representatives of the all-Negro civic association could report that it was "following a plan of action which some of their members helped to develop at Highlander." With these evidences of progress before them, the community leader-participants, aided by consultants B.R. Brazeal of Morehouse College and Irene Osborne, consultant to school integration in Washington, could get down to the central task of the workshop: to develop "a program of action directly related to the needs of each community." In carrying out those programs of action, a workshop report notes, "the Highlander staff committed itself to follow up the activity in each of the communities with personal visits during the following months."[40]

1955 Workshop on School Desegregation: The Challenge of Desegregated Community Living and Learning

In planning the workshop on desegregation for 1955, an Advisory Committee,[41] including local leaders and consultants from previous workshops met the Highlander staff and Executive Council. Among these was Mrs. Anna Kelly of the Negro YWCA in Charleston who had attended the first workshop in 1953 and returned home to involve other Negro leaders in initiating a program of public education; Mrs Septima Clark also of Charleston, a Negro elementary school teacher and civic leader who, since participating in a workshop, had been assisting with the Highlander Community leadership Project in the South Carolina Sea Islands;[42] and Mr. and Mrs. Will Thomas of Bessemer, Alabama, Negro civil rights and community leaders who had made some hard-won progress in their community following attendance at a Highlander workshop in 1954. The

Advisory Committee also included Irene Osborne who had played a continuing role in the successful efforts to integrate public schools in Washington, D.C. , and Dr. Charles Gomillion of Tuskegee Institute in Alabama, educator and leader of the Tuskegee Civic Association, who had come to work with Highlander through its desegregation field activities and who subsequently joined its Executive Council.

During a workshop planning meeting, it was pointed out based on the School's previous workshops and follow-up field activities, that by "concentrating on a few communities where we have friends or former students, we can build a nucleus of informed leaders who are able to start and carry forward a plan of community action for public school integration."[43] The staff field service, it was recommended, should be continued and, if possible, staff and participants for the coming workshop should be drawn from these areas. It was also suggested that the workshop, along with providing opportunities for participants to analyze the problems and plan for school desegregation in their own communities, might analyze and propose plans for three or four typical southern communities representing different patterns and traditions of segregation.

Conceiving of both planning and evaluation as integral parts of an ongoing program development process, the pre-workshop planning meeting arranged for a post-workshop meeting of Council, staff and Advisory Committee with a threefold purpose: "1) to evaluate the past summer's workshop; 2) to plan the next year's resident programs; and 3) to make any policy decisions required."[44]

As in previous years, the Negro and white local leaders who attended the action-oriented Highlander Folk School workshops on school desegregation in 1955 tended to be highly motivated men and women. The brochure circulated to workshop applicants stated in simple but explicit terms that those eligible included anyone working with local "educational, religious, fraternal, or intercultural organizations or otherwise in a position to provide community leadership."[45] There were no academic or other requirements, and scholarships were available. Thus, persons of varied educational and socio-economic backgrounds were enabled to participate.

Most important perhaps, the majority of participants were again recruited by former participants who, because they were enthusiastic about what they had gained from the workshop experience, encouraged others who might share the local leadership responsibilities. In this way, Mrs. Anna Kelly of Charleston, South Carolina, after participating in the first workshop, had encouraged Mrs. Septima Clark to attend. Mrs. Clark, in turn, influenced Esau Jenkins, self-educated Negro small businessman and Johns Island, South Carolina, civic leader. After he had participated in several workshops, Mr. Jenkins expanded his own civil rights role in Charleston and the Sea Islands, sent numerous other island students to Highlander workshops and helped to develop local workshops.

Other participants were identified and recruited by Highlander staff on field visits to communities attempting to work out their problems of desegregation. For example, the report of a staff visit to Tuskegee, Alabama, in February 1955 indicates

> Met with school teachers, clergymen, N.A.A.C.P. leaders, Civic Association representatives and Tuskegee students who analyzed deadlock between white and Negro communities and discussed possible solutions. Visited town and rural schools and planned for the training of additional community leaders at Highlander next summer.[46]

The Problem-centered Program

In the evolving program to develop local leaders able to deal with the patterns of segregation in their several communities, the problems which they were encountering provided the basic content and focus for the educational activities. Esau Jenkins, from Johns Island, South Carolina, and several other Sea Island participants provided one complex of problems for the workshop agenda: the problems of arousing and inspiring some 2,000 Negroes, isolated, psychologically as well as physically, from changes in the nation, in the South and even in nearby Charleston; dominated, still, by the plantation world of their parents, a world where the government, the schools, the jobs, the whole system controlling the lives of Negroes, belonged to the white man. How to convince people of their rights to better schools and health services? Of their rights to vote for those schools and services by electing officials to represent their interests? Of their rights, in fact, to vote, to be citizens?

A middle-class, northern-born white couple, Anne and Ken Kennedy of Knoxville, Tennessee, presented another set of not-so-difficult problems: the problems of a Joint Citizens' Committee for School Integration attempting to activate a conservative school board in a city where Negroes were a small, inactive minority.

Other problems described were those of the Deep South community of Montgomery, Alabama, where Mrs. Rosa Parks, an NAACP official, youth advisor and over-worked civic leader, described the unchallenged patterns of segregation in schools and in all aspects of community life and observed, as she heard reports of progress in other communities, that Negroes in Montgomery were "too timid and would not act."[47]

Still others were the atypical community problems as viewed by Tuskegee Institute faculty members and Civic Association members in an area where Negroes were in a clear majority and frequently had more education and better jobs than whites (both at the Institute and at a nearby Veterans' Administration Hospital), but who were prevented from voting and whose children were forced to attend segregated schools.

And along with these were the problems brought by white ministers and university students from Tennessee and by white union members from Tennessee and Alabama who were often less clear about community problems, but were seeking to understand and define useful roles.

In the course of the workshop, each local leader described his community and its problems as he perceived them. The group, in turn, attempted to identify and analyze the common or underlying problems of the several communities. With this kind of interactive approach to learning, every participant had the opportunity to function both as a learner and a teacher. On the problems of his community, he was the first-hand authority. At the same time, in getting a different and broader perspective on the community and in dealing with its school segregation problems, he could learn from what others, whether staff or consultants or fellow participants, had succeeded in accomplishing elsewhere. Of this process, one of the consultants to the 1955 workshop, Irene Osborne wrote

> The workshop sessions rely on group discussion in which the common problems of different areas are used as material for discussion. Staff persons and invited consultants take part in the total process, lending help when needed, but not dominating the discussions and not converting the sessions into an academic routine. Participants learn, and learn a remarkable amount in a short time, because they are doing it themselves and because the work stays close to the needs which they feel.[48]

Finally, divided into two groups, participants worked to develop practical plans and guidelines for action when they returned home. One of these, *A Guide to Community Action for Public School Integration*, was a rewriting (in the light of the Court's decision of 1954 and subsequent developments) of a guide which had been developed by the members of a 1953 workshop. The other was a carefully composed series of recommendations, addressed to community leaders, entitled *Basic Policies for Presentation to Local School Boards* which included courses of action related to: (1) pupil integration; (2) teacher and administrative integration; and (3) necessary educational preparation. In composing both the *Guide* and the *Basic Policies*, each working committee presented its material to the whole group for discussion and revision before turning it over to a small committee for final editing.

Along with group discussion for identifying and analyzing problems and the use of small working committees to prepare written materials, an experimental planning project was undertaken as recommended by the Highlander Executive Council. Selected for special analysis were several typical southern communities with varied patterns of segregation: Charleston, where Negroes and whites live in the same areas; Atlanta, where Negroes live in segregated areas; and a Tennessee mountain community with only a 4 or 5 per cent Negro population. After finding out where the lines of the neighborhoods and the location of the schools were in these communities, students worked on suitable plans for desegregation. According to a summary report of the workshop, "The project provided one of the most interesting and valuable experiences of the session."[49]

Evening programs throughout the workshop offered participants a variety of other kinds of social-educational experiences and suggested ideas for programs which they might adapt to their own communities. Folk music, square-dancing, improvisations and films[50] were utilized.

What was Valued, What was Learned

As these Negro and white community leaders evaluated their Highlander workshop experience, in response to two quite different questionnaires,[51] they did so, most often, not in terms of the information and resources obtained for solving problems, but in terms of some aspect or aspects of the residential experience. Negro and white, college-educated and self-educated, their comments express with deep personal conviction what Royce Pitkin, President of Goddard College, suggests regarding the effectiveness of residential education for adults in his essay on the American residential school.[52] Pitkin points out that "when adults are in residence in relatively small groups, a considerable degree of intimacy develops fairly quickly."[53] He suggests that the resulting informality makes for ease in participation and in acquiring new ideas and outlooks.

The achievement of this kind of informality and intimacy by a group of Negroes and whites in the South was, of course, a unique experience for most participants in the Highlander desegregation workshops. Almost all of them, therefore, commented, in some way, on what it meant to them. Of the learning growing out of this experience, a workshop member from Tuskegee Institute wrote

> I have changed my attitude toward leadership from that of domination to one of companionship. I have never before had the opportunity to actually live in wholesome friendship with other groups who were interested, and unafraid, in my problems.[54]

Another Negro leader from the rural Sea Islands stated simply

> It showed me how wonderful it[is] to live, share and become co-operative with others.[55]

Noting that "learning is enhanced if emotional strain or tension is low",[56] Pitkin observes that adults in the residential school setting seem relieved of many of their tensions; seem able to respond to the various challenges to learn without embarrassment, to learn, in fact, with increasing confidence. Speaking of this atmosphere for learning, a Negro beautician explained

> . . . at times when in a group, much of the information is lost because of the tenseness of the group as a whole and you cannot relax and receive what is being offered. This is not true at Highlander for there is no tension at all and one can absorb more easily. I felt as though I had been coming there for years and years.[57]

It should be added that this same beautician acquired sufficient confidence as well as competence to be able to participate in a Highlander developed literacy and voter education program in the Sea Islands as the first teacher in a so-called Citizenship School.[58]

Another workshop participant who spoke specifically about the group atmosphere and its effects on her was Mrs. Rosa Parks, soon afterwards leader of the Montgomery Bus Boycott. Fellow participants recall that Mrs. Parks, during the first several days of the workshop was extremely shy and quiet.[59] Of this experience, she wrote

I learned about informal group participation for serious problems and become more relaxed and communicative with others working toward the same goal of freedom from racial prejudice and injustice.[60]

In considering the residential school as it contributes to the physical-emotional-intellectual learning process, Pitkin observes that in this setting "the adult is free to live, to talk . . . to be a live, active human being and not simply an occupant of a seat in a given row."[61]

Illustrative of the varied opportunities for learning during the Highlander Folk School desegregation workshops, a middle-class white couple whose contacts with Negroes had been limited primarily to formal occasions such as church-sponsored gatherings and civic meetings stated that most important in their experience was coming to know Negro workshop members, not in group discussions, but " in the kitchen, washing dishes together."[62] (For the Negro participants, the "washing dishes together" may have been quite another learning experience, as it was in the case of an earlier Highlander student, a Negro union member from the Deep South, who recalled of the session which she had attended, "It was the first time I ever worked in a kitchen where I was in charge and a white man was doing the dishes!")[63]

Another kind of educational value of the residential school, not discussed in Pitkin's essay, is cited frequently by participants in the Highlander Folk School workshops on desegregation, especially by Negroes. One woman from Alabama called it "democratic living in practice" which, she stated, "for the first time in my life . . . was mine to observe."[64]

And Esau Jenkins of the Sea Islands, looking back to when he first ventured to spend ten days in a Tennessee residential center with southern white people wrote

Whenever I want[ed] to see part of this great democracy at work, I use[d] to go to New York. It was very significant and exclamatory to me to find democracy at work in Monteagle at Highlander Folk School which place makes me feel that he is counted as a human being, and one of God's people . . .[65]

The Effects of the 1955 Workshop

In attempting to evaluate the effects of the two-week residential learning experience on the actions of participants, it seems evident that the effects were sometimes indirect or related to an individual's participation in more than one workshop. Some workshop members on returning home intensified their efforts to bring about desegregation of schools and other facilities and to encourage greater participation of others. Correspondence and reports from Knoxville, Tennessee, participants in the 1955 workshop indicate that they played the gadfly role within the Knoxville Joint Committee, made up of representatives of Negro and white civic organizations working for public school desegregation. As advocates of positive action, they brought before the Committee the ideas contained in the Highlander workshop paper, *Basic Policies for Presentation to Local School Boards* and challenged it to draw up a positive plan of desegregation for presentation to member organizations and the school board.[66] Subsequent correspondence and reports indicate that dissension within the Committee resulted in its dissolution. However, their efforts did, apparently, mobilize the more active organizations represented on the Committee. They, in turn, continued to work for and finally achieved complete school integration.

Another such behind-the-scenes effort occurred in a rural county in East Tennessee where Negroes were a tiny minority but where two participants in the 1955 workshop, a young Negro teacher and a young white Baptist minister worked together over a period of time to identify and organize support for school integration.[67] Again, positive steps were not quickly achieved, but constructive elements, within ministerial groups, the Negro community and among sympathetic white leadership, were mobilized and finally succeeded in achieving school integration.

A third example of the workshop participant who continued, but in some new ways, to work on local problems was a Negro labor union and NAACP leader from Bessemer, Alabama, who attended Highlander school desegregation workshops in 1953 and 1955. After the first workshop he set up voter registration classes, organized educational panels and forums on current events and worked with and through other organizations in his community to encourage Negroes to vote and to take an active part in desegregation efforts.[68] During the 1955 workshop, he served as a participant-resource person describing his activities as well as gathering additional ideas which strengthened his community efforts in Bessemer.

Some effects of the workshop experience were more immediately identifiable. Esau Jenkins, on returning from the workshop to Johns Island, South Carolina, wrote back to the Highlander staff that he had decided to attempt to "integrate" school leadership on the island by running as the first Negro candidate for School Trustee since the Reconstruction Period. He was defeated, but he succeeded in arousing Negro interest in qualifying to vote and in demanding improved school and community services.[69]

Certainly the most dramatic action taken by a participant in the 1955 School Desegregation Workshop was by Mrs. Rosa Parks. Her refusal, some months after she returned home, to give up her bus seat to a white passenger not only was the first act in the prolonged Montgomery Bus Boycott but was viewed by many as the first major event in the southwide civil rights movement. Although Mrs. Parks was certainly not "taught" at the workshop the action that she was to take, she was taught by her experience there the possibility of living as an equal in an integrated society. The woman responsible for sending her to Highlander wrote after the Montgomery Bus Boycott was underway

> But now comes your part . . . the effect that the School had on Mrs. Parks. When she came back she was so happy and felt so liberated and then as time went on she said the discrimination got worse and worse to bear after having, for the first time in her life, been free of it at Highlander. I am sure that had a lot to do with her daring to risk arrest as she is naturally a very quiet and retiring person . . . [70]

Thus, the residential workshop in addition to helping participants develop practical guidelines for school desegregation provided them with an example of what could be and made them more critical of what was.

Workshops on School Desegregation, 1956-1957: Beyond School Desegregation to Full Citizenship

By the beginning of 1956, the actions of a Rosa Parks and an Esau Jenkins, who had come to the Highlander Folk School to develop plans for school integration and returned to their communities to inspire a bus boycott in Montgomery, Alabama, and an eagerness to read and write and qualify to vote among illiterate Negroes on Johns Island, South Carolina, made it clear that the School's program needed to be more broadly defined. The students

211

had moved beyond the goal of integrating the primary and secondary schools of the South which had seemed a large goal in 1953. In the face of mounting white resistance, of White Citizens' Councils, the National Association for the Advancement of White People, some twenty anti-integration groups in all,[71] the minds of local civil rights leaders were, as in the old-new spiritual, "Stayed on Freedom," on the goal of full citizenship. Thus, the Highlander staff, Executive Council members and former students, including Mrs. Parks, who met to plan the school integration workshops for 1956 proposed a radically new agenda. The subjects to be considered, they agreed, should be: Passive Resistance, Registration and Voting, Transportation, Housing, Parks, and Action through Churches, along with School Integration.[72]

No new sets of guidelines were developed during the four integration workshops which were held in the summer of 1956 or during those of the following year. Instead, the Negro and white local leaders who came together out of their segregated communities heard Rosa Parks describe the development of the Bus Boycott and the Passive Resistance Movement in Montgomery, beginning with her simple but profoundly important personal decision, "This was the place for me to stop being pushed around."[73] They heard another member of the Montgomery Movement describe the effect of the protest on those who walked and on those who watched

> On December 1, 1955, every Negro around there was walking around like a little boy in knee pants. On Monday he became a grown man and had to shave. The white man knew how to handle the boy. He had handled him for ninety years. He knew how to do that. But he didn't know how to handle this man.[74]

They listened with some awe as another former Highlander student, L. A. Blackman of Elloree, South Carolina, told of standing up on his truck at a meeting of Klan members who had sworn to run him out of town and stating defiantly, "I've been here seventeen years and I have no idea of leaving."[75] He told them, too, of a counter-boycott by Negro college students and local citizens in his county who "refused to pay for segregation" and stopped buying from shopkeeper members of the White Citizens' Council.[76] They listened to these and others and out of the interaction with their "movement teachers" and their living together and learning together and washing dishes together, they fashioned their plans for achieving full citizenship in their several communities.

New Attacks on Highlander as a Civil Rights Center

During this period when Highlander held the first workshops in the South on school integration and began to establish itself as a center for developing leadership for the emerging civil rights movement, it came under increasingly frequent attack by southwide leaders of the segregationist forces. In 1954, Myles Horton was called to testify at a much-publicized hearing of the Senate Internal Security Sub-committee, on alleged Communist activity in the South, presided over by Senator James Eastland of Mississippi. Horton, who indicated a readiness to answer any questions about himself, but refused to answer questions about others and, specifically, about a former staff member, so infuriated Senator Eastland that he was ousted from the hearing. The picture and the story of his ousting appeared in newspapers across the South and the nation. *The New York Times*, along with the picture and the story[77] also published Horton's reply to the Senator following his abruptly terminated appearance at the hearing. Stating that he was not a communist but a firm believer in democracy, he told the investigation, "The hysteria spread by your committee and the McCarthy committee has made substantial contribution to the fiction that the only dynamic force in the world is Communism. This I deny . . . I believe in democracy . . ." Turning to the reason for his interrogation, he added, "I suppose in the eyes of the Chairman of the Sub-committee, opposition to segregation in the South is subversive."[78]

In 1957, a new commission, the Georgia Commission on Education was established by Governor Marvin Griffin, a leading champion of segregation. In spite of its bland title, the Commission's most celebrated contribution to education was the preparation and southwide distribution of a sensational broadside on the Highlander Folk School on the occasion of the Twenty-fifth Anniversary Workshop with the banner heading "Communist Training School, Monteagle, Tenn."[79] Pictures calculated to inflame segregationists included Negro and white participants socializing and square-dancing together and prominent civil rights leaders including Mrs. Rosa Parks and Dr. Martin Luther King, Jr. Dr. King gave a major address paying tribute to the School for its "noble purpose and creative work" and for giving the South "some of its most responsible leaders."[80]

A less well known but potentially far more serious action against the School in 1957 was the sudden revocation of its tax-exempt status which, a Highlander report[81] took note, was greeted with a statement of approval by Senator Eastland. Although the School's friends and supporters[82] responded to the emergency by making twice as many individual contributions as in the previous year and although adult education leaders came to the School's defense and helped to regain its tax-exempt status within a year,[83] the action might well have been a fatal one.[84] When Senator Eastland indicated that he was "in thorough agreement" with the revocation action, he doubtless had a thorough understanding of what it might accomplish.

There was a good reason for southern segregationists to want to put the Highlander Folk School out of existence. The workshops on school desegregation in the years 1953-1957, while they affected the public school system in only a small number of communities, provided a unique residential meeting place in which Negro and white southerners could interact freely as they exchanged ideas and made plans to change their segregated and unequal society.

The workshops after 1953, developed, as they were, with the help of a selected group of active civil rights leaders who had participated in previous workshops, were notably responsive to the changing needs and potential of the movement. Thus, the workshops in 1953, before the Court decision and the resulting local movements were underway, focused solely on schools and utilized the experience of academic and other outside specialists in drawing up guidelines for desegregation. The workshops thereafter could focus on action and planning for action in specific communities with local movement leaders from previous workshops serving as resource persons or "teacher-leaders." Beginning in 1956, when a participant in a 1955 workshop had initiated the Montgomery Bus Boycott, this action furnished the workshop focus and stimulated and inspired a variety of other kinds of peaceful protest actions in communities over the South.

Moreover, participants in two of the movement-shaped and movement-shaping desegregation workshops helped to develop a Sea Islands (and later southwide) Citizenship School Program for Negroes aspiring to read, write, and become "first-class" voting citizens. This program will be examined in the chapter which follows.

THIRTEEN

Developing Teacher-Leaders for the Voter Education Movement: The Citizenship School Program

The Sea Islands, Unlikely Setting for a New Program

Johns Island, South Carolina, home of some 2,700 poor, rural and, until the 1930s, isolated descendants of cotton plantation slaves was the unlikely place where the Highlander Folk School evolved a major new program to develop "first class citizens" and teacher-leaders for the southwide voter education movement. They were segregated physically, socially and psychologically from other Negroes as well as from whites. Mrs. Septima Clark, who helped to develop the program, first came by boat to Johns Island from mainland Charleston in 1916 to serve as youthful teaching principal in a crude, two-room school. Noting the poverty, the disease, the superstition, the high illiteracy rate, she lamented, "Being isolated for so long, these island folk knew very little about the few public service benefits that even Negroes on the mainland had come to have."[1] Returning over the years, she was distressed to find little progress in the lives of "these potentially wonderful people." A fifty-odd year old island-born woman recalled of her childhood years of the unfamiliar white man and his world

> When I was growing up, I must have seen one white man . . . And I was so scared of that white man I never see his face.[2]

In the 1930s, a bridge was built connecting Johns Island and the mainland, five miles away. By the 1950s, the white population of the island numbered some 2,000. "Now," the same woman observed, "the world is nothing but white people!"[3] Myles Horton, writing to the president of the Schwartzhaupt Foundation in 1956 to describe the School's experimental efforts to develop local leadership on the island indicated, "These people are beset by many problems rooted in a deep apathy to the responsibilities and obligations of citizenship."[4] Yet in this setting and faced with these kinds of problems related, first, to isolation and, later, to segregation, the Citizenship School program was developed. The first classes were held in the winter of 1957. The students were illiterate and semi-literate adults (including the woman "so scared of that white man" that she dared not see his face) who were learning how to read and write and become registered voters of South Carolina.

Behind this program was the Supreme Court decision outlawing public school segregation and the stirrings of a southern civil rights movement. It was this decision and these stirrings which brought Mrs. Clark, Charleston teacher who had, as she said, "spent all my life teaching citizenship to children who aren't really citizens"[5] and Esau Jenkins, striving, self-made Johns Island leader, to Highlander workshops on desegregation in the summer of 1954.

The first Highlander workshop which Esau Jenkins attended, encouraged by Mrs. Clark, was, in fact, entitled "World Problems, the United Nations and You." But like many other problem-centered Highlander workshops, it dealt with pressing problems of local communities as well as with the problems and the hopes of the world community. Looking back, Esau Jenkins recalled

> They asked each individual to give the immediate problem in his locality. My immediate problem was adult education, because so many person [sic] were here who couldn't read and write and I know this condition because I would have been almost in the same condition if I didn't [sic] go back to school.[6]

Records of the workshop indicate that there was considerable discussion by the integrated group of long-term goals for a southern society, like the United Nations, "based on equality." Each person, whether from Johns Island or Knoxville, was urged to return home and take a first step. "Our problem," Myles Horton emphasized, "is to take our step right here wherever we are. And deal in terms [of] the goals. And deal in such a way that we involve other people."[7] He predicted as a result of such local action

> . . . Once you get a lot of people marching and a lot of people in step, you quit taking steps and you run . . . Nobody is concerned about the movement against this segregation business because they see it creeping along . . . But within a year's time, within two years' time, we are going to start moving a little faster.[8]

Esau Jenkins, who had for some years attempted to get his fellow islanders, those who could read and write, to register and vote took a bold first step on his return home. As has been indicated, he ran for the office of School Trustee, the first Negro to run for office on Johns Island in ninety years!

Experiment in Community Leadership Training

The Johns Island program was undertaken as part of a three-year Community Leadership Training Project which Highlander had initiated in 1953 in one Alabama and several Tennessee rural communities. Supported by a grant from the Schwartzhaupt Foundation, its aim was "to train community leaders who will help bring about a better understanding of the nature of a democratic society." "The leaders," the proposal stated "will be given guidance in increasing participation in local and national affairs, in stimulating interest in community problems, and in changing attitudes which limit democracy." and, the proposal added, "If properly trained and supervised, they should be able to develop other leaders from among their fellow citizens."[9]

For various reasons, the project in its first year met with limited success. The Alabama community proved an unpromising selection because it was split by factionalism. An experimental effort to hasten the leadership development process by utilizing outside paid staff trained by Highlander also proved unpromising. The rural Tennessee communities were notably lacking in the kinds of crisis situations, the social ferment, which, beginning with the Bugwood Strike, had provided the School with a basis for initiating a program. In contrast, Johns Island, in the fall of 1954, had, from Highlander's point of view, two elements for developing a new program:

local leadership with which to begin and an emerging movement which was inspiring that leadership to take action.

The steps which followed in the next two years before the development of the Citizenship School Program were slow steps. "They had to be taken," Myles Horton pointed out, "by local people." And as a pre-condition, the island people needed, first, to be freed from their isolation and helped to achieve "the simple recognition that their problems were common problems which could only be resolved through common enterprise."[10] The educative process for almost a year involved frequent trips to the island by Myles and Zilphia Horton for informal field visits and meetings. Only then were the potential new leaders, stimulated by these interactions and encouraged by Esau Jenkins and Mrs. Clark, willing to leave their familiar island surroundings and venture into the unfamiliar world of integrated residential workshops in the mountains of Tennessee. During this period, a very conscious effort was made on the part of the Highlander staff to look to and defer to Esau Jenkins and Mrs. Clark in interpreting the School and its representatives to the island people, in arranging and planning visits, meetings and conferences to discuss local problems and in defining with local people the priority of problems to be faced.

The first visit in November 1954 was occasioned by an NAACP dinner in Charleston to which Highlander staff were invited by Esau Jenkins. A School record of the visit indicates, "Zilphia Horton represented the staff and was invited to the Jenkins home where she got acquainted with the family and neighbors. Sang at church and school."[11] From the point of view of island neighbors and others who saw the white woman or even heard about her visit, the process of moving away from isolation had begun. The mere fact that a white friend visited the Jenkins family and stayed in their home represented a glimpse into a new world (For Zilphia Horton, long time student of southern music, the opportunity to listen to the strange and powerful "shouting" style of music of the old spirituals, and the rich Gullah dialect spoken on the islands with its persisting African traits, also offered a glimpse into a new world.) Over the months, the visits included more structured meetings and learning activities. Thus, the Annual Report lists the following community leadership conferences and meetings held in the Sea Islands area: December 1954, a leadership conference for local political, school and church leaders on Johns Island and other parts of Charleston County, South Carolina; February 1955, a conference with Charleston County community leaders; March 1955, a so-called "Charleston County

Conference on Leadership Training" and by May 1955, individual and group conferences with community leaders and an "all day community meeting on Johns Island" with the panel members discussing: "Why should Negroes be organized?". "Who is responsible for less than 30% of colored people in South Carolina not [sic] being voting citizens?" and "Does buying power of the Negro, when wisely used, help change his condition?" Of the meeting, the Report notes, "There was a packed and attentive house."[12]

These meetings, participated in by resource persons from Charleston, from Highlander and from elsewhere in the South not only helped to bring many island people out of isolation and give them some sense of common problems and the possibility of common solutions but it affected, apparently, the thinking and the style of leadership assumed by Esau Jenkins as well as the educational role assumed by Septima Clark. Thus, Esau Jenkins wrote to Myles Horton in the spring of 1955

> My ideas of community leadership have changed in many ways since my stay at Highlander last year. I found that giving others something to do and help making better citizens in a community is very important . . . My old ways of doing was [sic] slow.[13]

In the same letter, he asked about the availability of scholarships for bringing "a man with leadership" and a high school girl or boy to the next Highlander workshop. And in the spring of 1955, Myles Horton reported to a representative of the Schwartzhaupt Foundation that Mrs. Clark had agreed to exchange her role as Charleston school teacher and civic leader for the role of Highlander staff[14] member for the coming southwide workshops on school integration and community leadership.

Other small but hopeful evidences of progress are to be found in the records of this preparation period before the Citizenship School Program was evolved. The Civic Club, one of the two Johns Island community organizations headed by Esau Jenkins, which had been dormant for some years, began to come to life. Myles Horton noted with pleasure in the minutes of the Civic Club monthly meeting for April 1955 that "Instead of a guest speaker there was an open discussion on Advantages of Registered Citizens." "It usually takes considerable time," he observed in a letter to the foundation, "to get people away from dependence on speakers."[15] During this period, too, the Civic Club decided to undertake a month-by-month campaign to register voters in hopes of doing what the club's president had attempted to do the previous year: elect a Negro to the school's governing board who would push for improvement of the neglected Negro schools on the island.

By June, Myles Horton could report that along with the Civic Club's voter registration campaign, "Some of the young people on the island are working on plans for a housing committee."[16] Highlander's role in such efforts was to help the group clarify its problems and goals and then to identify some of the resources available. In this case, a prominent architect friend of the School's, Horton noted, had agreed to "work out a housing plan adapted to the climate, materials and financial resources of the people of the Sea Island country." By June, too, Highlander through Esau Jenkins and Mrs. Clark, was meeting with people on neighboring Wadmalow Island who were stimulated by the developments on Johns Island. Out of one such meeting, plans were made for groups from the two islands to work together on registering voters for the next election.

Johns Islanders came to Residential Workshops

By the summer of 1955, both adult and young adult community representatives from Johns Island and Charleston attended two Community Leadership Conferences and a Public School Desegregation Workshop. "I used my car to transport three groups of six persons each to Highlander workshops,"[17] Mrs. Clark recalled. Transportation, of course, represented the culmination of the various efforts made to persuade islanders to come to the workshops. A lengthy interview by Mrs. Clark with one influential and well-to-do Negro farmer who had been fearful of jeopardizing his relationship with white people by supporting voter registration or other activities suggests the kind of careful diplomacy sometimes required. After expressing interest and admiration for his successful bus business, his truck farm and his home which "sets a pattern for comfortable living," Mrs. Clark suggested that he owed himself "a little vacation." When the farmer-leader protested that he could not afford it, she went on to describe the Highlander Folk School in Tennessee where "you can share your island experiences with many peoples [sic]" and where "for a week there is a scholarship offered to community leaders." With this personalized approach by a woman of Mrs. Clark's status, the prospective workshop participant, flattered and pleased, concluded by agreeing, "I do need a vacation."[18]

Another means which helped to encourage some potential leaders to attend Highlander workshops was the presentation of short films on previous workshops, showing integrated sessions participated in by Esau Jenkins, Mrs. Clark and others whom the group knew. The films were accompanied by their comments and observations about the experience and by opportunities for raising questions and exploring the idea further. As island participants began to return from workshops, excited by what they had experienced and learned, they, of course, became the most effective recruiters of new participants. And, inspired and stimulated by their days of intensive interaction with Negro and white community leaders from other parts of the South who were coping with some of the same or related school and community problems, the workshop graduates generally returned to the island with new ideas and an eagerness to put them into effect. Even before one such group of Sea Islanders had arrived home from a Highlander Community Leadership conference, Mrs. Clark reported that they held a "car meeting" and "each person was asked to do one thing this week."[19] Returning home to Charleston, she noted of the farm leader who had been reluctant to get involved

> My phone keeps ringing. Bellenger just called to say that he will cooperate with all our plans. We asked him to let the field hands know that the members of his family are registered voters and members of the Citizens Club. He said he would.[20]

And another of those who participated in the same leadership conference and in the "car meeting" on the return trip, a young Negro leader from Charleston, wrote to Myles Horton immediately after his return

> We are calling a large meeting at one of the schools with all the top farmers . . . to get them to see what we are trying to do . . . and why we must start with this credit union.

Looking ahead to the next proposed project, he added, "When it has been duly organized, then we can begin to do something about getting the clinic started . . . I am surrounding the island from all sides."[21]

By 1956, the Annual Report observed of the three-year residential and field program to develop more widespread and effective leadership and participation on Johns Island, "These leaders now have an awareness and an understanding of the problems of their community. They have learned to make decisions about their schools, roads, transportation, housing and

221

voting."[22] The School could also cite tangible results of this increased problem awareness and ability to decide on appropriate courses of action. Some 300 voters had been registered as a result of the Civic Club's campaign. No major housing program had been undertaken because island people still lacked the funds, but many had added to and improved their homes. Local people had been trained to interpret the need for inoculating children against diphtheria and, as a result, there had been no deaths from diphtheria reported for a year (in contrast to more than sixty deaths in the previous year). A consumer education program had also been initiated and plans were being discussed for a consumer cooperative.[23]

In addition to these community self-help projects, some of the island leaders who had attended several Highlander residential workshops in 1955 and in 1956 were assuming new roles as organizers of their own workshops. Myles Horton reported of this new development

> On Johns Island we had an excellent workshop this month run by the people we have developed there. The local leaders not only worked out the details and program of the workshop but lined up consultants from the area. The workshop topics were voting, housing and cooperatives.[24]

One major problem, adult illiteracy, was proving a stumbling block to other problem-solving efforts and particularly to the continuing voter registration efforts. Even among people who participated in the successful local workshop, it was noted, "About 10 percent . . . were unable to read the section of the South Carolina Constitution which is required for registration.[25]

First Citizenship School: A Literacy Program to Develop Registered Voters

Esau Jenkins, the Johns Island leader longest aware of the unsolved problem, had sought in his own bold and innovative way to deal with illiteracy. He was, in fact, responsible for the first literacy school of its kind to be conducted in the Sea Island area—or anywhere—an adult school on wheels! As he described it

> On Johns Island, in the year of 1948, I saw the condition of the people who had been working on the plantation for many years. And I knew that we were not able to do the things that would need to be done unless we could get people registered citizens. I operated a bus from Johns Island to Charleston

carrying people to their jobs. So I decided to get a group in the bus in the mornings and teach them how to read the part of the Constitution that we have to read before we are able to become registered citizens.[26]

As a persistent and strong-minded leader, Esau Jenkins managed through daily drill, reading aloud and having his passenger-students repeat after him, to inspire and assist a few to memorize whole sections of the Constitution well enough to obtain their voting certificates. As an educator, however, he largely failed. The fortunate few who registered were still unable to read. And most people were neither able to register nor to read, nor even, many of them, to write their names.

With the need becoming generally apparent and motivation growing among islanders to qualify as voters, the indomitable Mr. Jenkins approached the local Negro principal about offering night classes. The principal, however, was fearful of white reaction to classes for Negro adults who were trying to learn to read and write so that they could register to vote. It was at this point, in the fall of 1956, that Esau Jenkins turned to the Highlander Fold School for help in establishing the first Citizenship School, as it was called, on Johns Island.

The first Highlander-developed Citizenship School was held in the rear of a little cooperative store which members of the Johns Island Progressive Club, a recently revived community organization, had acquired, paying for it month by month. The first volunteer teacher was a Negro beautician and active NAACP member from Charleston, Mrs. Bernice Robinson, who, while attending a Highlander residential workshop with Esau Jenkins and Mrs. Clark, had learned of and become concerned about community problems on the nearby Sea Island. Although she insisted that she "couldn't teach because she never taught before," she agreed, at the urging of Septima Clark, with whom she had both family and movement ties, to "give some time and do whatever she could."[27]

The curriculum for this first Citizenship School came about almost entirely from its fourteen adult students. When asked by Mrs. Robinson, at the first meeting, what it was they wanted to learn, they readily responded: how to write their name, how to read the words of the South Carolina election laws . . . how to spell those words." And they wanted to know, too, "how to fill in blanks when they were ordering out of a catalog . . . how to fill in a money order . . ."[28] Along with responding to the needs as defined by her island students, needs related to becoming voting citizens and functioning more effectively in their day-to-day living situations, Bernice Robinson sought

223

to give them a larger view, a world view of citizenship. She herself had been inspired by this world view at a Highlander workshop on the United Nations. Now, as a Highlander teacher, she sought to share her new perspective. If this combination of local and world oriented goals and activities was not enough, Mrs. Robinson also agreed to work with a group of high school girls who wanted to learn to sew. The resulting program as it emerged is best described by the teacher herself

> The school which we planned for three months is in progress and the people have shown great interest. They are so anxious to learn. I have fourteen adults, four men and ten women, and there are thirteen high school girls enrolled to learn sewing. There are three adults that have had to start from scratch because they could not read or write. I start out with having them spell their names. About eight of them can read a little, but very poorly. So far, I have been using that part of the South Carolina Constitution that they must know in order to register. From that, I take words that they find hard to pronounce and drill them in spelling and pronunciation and also the meaning of the words so they will know what they are saying. We have to give them some arithmetic. The men are particularly interested in figures. I have never before in my life seen such anxious people. They really want to learn and are so proud of the little gains they have made so far. When I get to the club each night, half of them are already there and have their homework ready for me to see. I tacked up the Declaration of Human Rights on the wall and told them that I wanted each of them to be able to read and understand the entire thing before the end of the school.[29]

The adult population in this first Citizenship School grew during the School's two months of operation (January and February 1957) to thirty-seven. The materials used by the novice teacher included pieces of cardboard which she laboriously fashioned into name cards and money order forms and mimeographed sheets containing the South Carolina elections laws, requirements for Social Security, information about the school board and other kinds of basic information which, as Mrs. Clark expressed it, "they would have to know in order to start on their way to becoming first-class citizens."[30] The teaching methods, worked out with the help of Mrs. Clark, were, in part, methods which Mrs. Clark had learned in the 1930s from a white adult educator[31] and, in part, in the pragmatic Highlander tradition, they grew out of the interaction of the teacher who had never taught and her students who had never been to school.

Writing to an educational consultant with the Schwartzhaupt Foundation after a February visit to the Citizenship School, Myles Horton was excited by what he saw there, "I wish you could have seen the expressions on the faces of the people learning to read and write and spell, especially the older people." Describing the citizenship and sewing activities occurring simultaneously in the crowded classroom, he noted another group of learners as well

> Some thirty or forty more young men and boys and a sprinkling of older people were in the co-op store which is separated from the classroom by a partition. Many of them were listening to the entire class. I think all of them came into the room or stood near enough to hear when Bernice Robinson made a wonderful speech on citizenship and the county agent gave a talk.[32]

The story of the first Citizenship School is recorded on tapes and in the Highlander Folk School reports as well as in the teacher's notes and letters. Not only did a number of students manage to master the words, but as the educational supervisor, Mrs. Clark noted, "In two months' time, surprising to say, there were some who were ready to register."[33] In 1958 and 1959,the Citizenship School Program continued to grow.[34] A second and larger school was held on Johns Island for a three-month period in 1958. Out of these first two schools, a Highlander report indicates, "More than sixty persons passed the literacy test and became first-class citizens."[35]

Spread of the Program to Other Islands

Interest in the Citizenship School grew not only on Johns Island but on adjacent South Carolina Sea Islands, Wadmalow, Edisto, Daufuskie and St. Helena. On Johns Island, the enthusiastic new "first-class citizens" were convincing interpreters of the program to their neighbors. Elsewhere, the story of the Johns Island schools was told by Mrs. Clark, Highlander field staff member, who made visits to the islands, sometimes for several days or a week, to meet and talk with interested leaders and civic groups about their problems and the program as related to those problems.

Whether the island was a large one, such as St. Helena with a population of some 3,300 (3,000 of these Negroes) or a small one such as Daufuskie with a total population of 141 (133 of these Negroes), the pattern of involvement in the Citizenship School Program was essentially the same. A community group or groups would express an interest in having a school in their area. A leader or several leaders were invited to a workshop at the Highlander Folk School to learn more about the idea, as well as about other activities including registration and voting and community organization. They, in turn, returned home to organize a school under the guidance of and continuing supervision of the Highlander field staff which now included the first Citizenship School teacher, Mrs. Bernice Robinson.

Adult students on these islands were often day laborers from large plantations who worked long hours and came many miles to their unfamiliar new schools for citizenship. Field reports describe both the arduous process of instruction, beginning with many who had never learned to hold a pencil, and the sense of wonder and accomplishment on the part of volunteer teachers and students when "from their eyes you can see the gleam of light when they can write their names."[36]

According to the month-by-month records of these teachers, not only did large numbers of their students qualify as voters, but they formed voter organizations to urge their neighbors to qualify and met monthly, even when work on the plantation interrupted their classes, to discuss civic issues. These meetings, too, are recorded—in painstaking, pencil-written minutes, set down sometimes in the awkward hand and language of a new first-class citizen.[37] A Highlander Folk School Annual Report summarizes this expansion

1958-1959 saw four new Citizenship Schools opened in the Sea Islands and brought requests for three more in near-by communities.

The Report also describes the expanding curriculum with its immediate practical purpose continuing to be "to enable citizens to pass the South Carolina literacy test for voter registration," but also including "an all-around education in community development and better living."[38] Subjects in this broad "better living" category varied with the particular student group, but included, for example, cooperatives and information on tax supported services.

Music in the Citizenship School

With the coming of folk singer Guy Carawan to the Highlander staff in 1959, singing became an important part of the Citizenship School Program.[39] Singing, of course, had been a part of the lives of Sea Island people since slavery. Esau Jenkins recalled an old woman from his youth who had lived and worked most of her life on an island plantation. "The only thing that keep [sic] her going," he said, "was some day she would look up at the sun and sing 'Nobody Knows the Trouble I've Seen, Nobody Knows but Jesus.' And on other days she would sing, 'I Been in the Storm So Long.'"[40] But the younger people on Johns Island did not value the heritage and in the new Methodist church on the island with a mainland minister once a month the spirituals were set aside in favor of unspirited Protestant hymns. Carawan, who had read of the Sea Islands and their persisting folk culture in story and song and language, brought their songs into the Citizenship Schools. "One of the main purposes of the new singing program at the adult schools," be explained, "has been to help stimulate the continuance and development of this old spiritual singing tradition in the Sea Islands by giving it some recognition and a regular place in the program."[41] Thus, at the end of each of the three meetings per week of the Citizenship School classes, the session would end with singing—some new songs which Carawan taught to the group, but largely their own songs. "Each week," too, he indicated, "I've read something to them about the spirituals by various writers who hold them in high esteem . . . They were genuinely moved when I read them some parts of Alan Lomax's new book, *The Rainbow Sign*.[42] Guy Carawan, himself, was deeply moved by the spirituals which he heard and learned and took back to Highlander and to other groups within the civil rights movement.

Effects of the Program

As the most important single measure of the effects and effectiveness of the Sea Island Citizenship School Program, the Highlander Folk School asked its first volunteer teacher, Bernice Robinson, and subsequent teachers under her supervision to keep records on the number of their adult students who were able to register as voters, who became "first-class citizens." These records, kept by the inexperienced and over-worked volunteer teachers (along with their many other tasks as family, community and church members) indicate that of the thirty-eight persons enrolled in the Citizenship School on Edisto Island, December 1958-February 1959, ten students, ages twenty-one to seventy-six, became "successful registrants" by the close of the school; five planned to register the following April and nineteen were "previous registrants."[43] They indicate that on neighboring Wadmalow during the same period, twenty-six persons, ages twenty-seven to fifty-five, were enrolled in Citizenship School; that nine of these became "successful registrants" by the close of the school; that five planned to register in April and that ten were "previous registrants."[44] In general, this report on the four schools reveals that at least half of the students within the three-month period managed to read and write well enough to qualify as registered voters and that the others were preparing to register.

The numbers by themselves, however, fail to communicate the significance of the increase in voters on the several islands. They must be viewed in relation to the past. A Highlander report for 1959-1960, for example, indicates that there had been an estimated 300 per cent increase in the number of registered voters on Johns Island alone since the 1956 elections.[45] And this increase becomes even more significant in relation to the fact that Esau Jenkins and a little group from the Civic Club had worked for ten years prior to the program "to get some seventy-five or a hundred person [sic] registered."[46]

These figures need also to be viewed as a beginning, rather than the end of an action. Esau Jenkins, who launched and encouraged the growing voter registration activity in all of the islands and throughout Charleston County points out

> In 1954 in the county, there were 'round about 5,000 or 6,000 Negroes registered. In 1964, almost 14,000. So everybody is jubilant for the Highlander Folk School, who have [sic] helped them to see the light.[47]

Some notion of what the Citizenship School meant to its Sea Island students is communicated by them in laboriously-written letters addressed to their teachers or to Mrs. Clark and Myles Horton. A Johns Island woman, for example, who came, as did most of the Citizenship School students, as a beginner, sought to tell her teacher, Bernice Robinson, what she had gained

> I learn so much by going too it learn me how to read and pronounce my spelling and how to crochet tell I can make any thing I wont and most of all I learn how to read and I get my Registration Certificate now I can vote and it means so much to me.[48]

One of the Sea Island students with some prior schooling who came to the Edisto Citizenship School to increase his personal and community effectiveness wrote

> We learned much of what democracy means that we did not know before. We had some to register and many who are going to register. We learned what

many words meant and a better way of expressing ourself. We were inspired to help others toward first-class citizenship.[49]

A more difficult-to-measure but significant effect of the Sea Island Citizenship School Program was how participation in it affected those who helped to develop and carry out the new program. Mrs. Clark, as a teacher of children who were "not really citizens," Bernice Robinson as a beautician who had never taught and Esau Jenkins as a courageous but not always effective local leader had all assumed new and larger roles and, at the same time, roles which helped to develop others. In 1956, Mrs. Clark was asked to be Director of Summer Workshops at Highlander and in 1957, she was made Director of Education[50]—in charge of all residential workshops for civil rights and community leaders. Working closely with Myles Horton, now President of the School, the number and variety of workshops which she directed continued to grow until the School's closing in 1961.

Bernice Robinson who taught Citizenship School classes on Johns Island in 1957 and 1958 became, in 1959, the supervisor for seven new teachers on Johns Island and neighboring islands and in Charleston. The cardboard and mimeographed materials which she and Mrs. Clark had developed were now replaced by a "Citizenship School Booklet"[51] containing sections on voting and voter requirements, reading and writing exercises, simple arithmetic, check and order forms and information on various government programs. Along with assisting and supervising the new volunteer teachers (which required several hundred miles of travel each week while the schools were in session), she took part in a number of Highlander workshops and made community field trips to various parts of South Carolina to describe Highlander's program and invite the participation of new individuals and community groups, both in the Citizenship School Program and in resident workshops. She had developed, in two short years, from a full-time beautician with an interest in civil rights, to a Charleston area teacher-leader, to a South Carolina civil rights leader and the supervisor of Highlander s Citizenship School field program.

The world of Esau Jenkins, as has been indicated, had grown from Johns Island to the Sea Islands to Charleston County to the far-off mountains of Tennessee where, as a speaker and resource person for a number of Highlander workshops, he provided a leadership model for aspiring leaders in many communities of the South. In 1957, he became a member of Highlander's Executive Council and, having attended his first workshop in 1954, he was involved in helping to develop new programs, including a program for the Charleston area and beyond which he called "the Second Step Political Education School,"[52] to help newly registered voters become more effective participants in political affairs.

Expansion of the Citizenship School Program to Other Parts of the South: The Negro Voter Drive and Segregationist Opposition

The decision of the Highlander Folk School Executive Council in 1960 to extend the Citizenship School Program to new areas of the South came about, as in other periods, in response to the needs of an accelerating movement. The drive among Negroes to register and vote which had begun after World War II was a mounting one in the 1950s. The Civil Rights Acts of 1957 and 1960, dealing primarily with the right to vote, assisted the process. The Southern Christian Leadership Conference, the Negro civil rights organization founded in 1957 under the leadership of Dr. Martin Luther King, Jr., pledged itself specifically "to secure . . . unhampered use of the ballot, to achieve full citizenship rights."[53] In 1959, looking toward an election year, the NAACP and the SCLC announced a joint campaign to add one million Negroes to the voter roles of the South.[54] During this period, too, a number of local Negro voter organizations were formed such as the Chatham County Crusade for Voters in Southeast Georgia and the Haywood County Civic and Welfare League in West Tennessee which joined forces with the southwide movement for "full citizenship rights." Determined to block this movement, segregationist leaders evoked old voter qualification laws with new zeal as well as tightening voter laws in several Deep South states, warning, as one Louisiana spokesman expressed it, that "the Communists and the NAACP plan to register every colored person in the South . . . using their votes to set up a federal dictatorship."[55] In the midst of these southwide and local efforts and counter-efforts, a Highlander Report for 1959-1960 notes, "During the past year requests have come from centers in Georgia, Alabama and Tennessee for help with literacy and voter education, and the Citizenship School idea has begun to demonstrate its usefulness in parts of the South far distant from its birthplace."[56]

The Process of Expansion: Test Schools and Experimental Teacher Training Workshops

As an initial step in the planned expansion of its Citizenship School Program, Highlander sought, in the summer of 1960, to test the usefulness of the Program in two groups of rural and urban communities outside the Sea Islands. Working with and through former Highlander workshop participants, eight classes were organized in the Huntsville, Alabama, and Savannah, Georgia, areas. In both areas, two-thirds of the adult students were able to qualify as registered voters after attending the three-months evening classes.[57]

Having demonstrated to its satisfaction the transferability of the program, Highlander's task became one of developing a residential workshop for training groups of Citizenship School teachers to replace its individualized approach to supervision and training as evolved in the Sea Islands. In November 1960, and again in January 1961, the School held three-day experimental workshops utilizing the kinds of learning activities and the kind of format which it hoped to use in a series of larger, more detailed teacher training workshops in the coming year.

Those invited to participate in the experimental workshops were experienced volunteer teachers from the Sea Islands who, along with Bernice Robinson and Esau Jenkins, served as resource persons sharing their insights and experience with others; new teachers from Huntsville and Savannah for whom the workshop was an opportunity to add to their understanding; and prospective teachers and representatives of organizations desiring to assist the spread of the movement. These included an SCLC staff member, persons active in local voter organizations in Georgia and Alabama and a group of faculty and students from two Negro colleges in West Tennessee who planned to assist voter organizations there.

In keeping with Highlander's earlier programs, the trial workshop to train volunteer teachers and supervisors for Citizenship Schools began and ended with discussion of the broad, movement-related philosophy and goals of the program. In a discussion of the strong motivation among people in the Sea Islands to learn to read and write after a lifetime of illiteracy, Esau Jenkins explained

No one wants anything more than to be a first-class citizen. That is what makes you learn what you have to learn—if somebody will show you how.[58]

Of the larger goals of the program, a seamstress and volunteer teacher from Edisto Island stated that she expected her students to do more than acquire a voter registration certificate and learn "some practical thing" such as "how to make change" and "how to write letters and not to have to get somebody else to do it." Beyond this, she emphasized

> People need to feel that they are part of a community, and not only a community, but a county and a state and a world . . . When people feel they belong to something it makes them want to do the small things at home, too.[59]

Myles Horton, listening to the comments of Esau Jenkins and the various volunteer teachers, observed

> I think we're getting results from the schools, not only in terms of reading and writing but in terms of citizenship, simply because we assume in the first place that people could be citizens and begin treating them as if they were.[60]

He went on to explain, "It's not the method of teaching that makes the difference for even the best method of teaching can take you round and round if you don't have a goal. The difference," he indicated, "is that you have kept your eyes on the 'ought to be'—human dignity, brotherhood, democracy . . . a kind of world in which we need to live."

With this broad perspective on the goals and the role of the Citizenship School, the would-be teachers and representatives of voter organizations were introduced to the methods and procedures involved in organizing and teaching local schools. There were demonstration sessions, for example, in the teaching of reading using the methods which had proved effective in the Sea Islands and the kinds of materials such as state election laws which the adult students needed to master to qualify as voters. There were opportunities to discuss and question methods and to assume the teacher role.

In the evening, there were informal sessions featuring leaders of the new movement organizations such as the sharecropper voter organizations in Haywood and Fayette counties in Tennessee. There were films on politics and voting and group singing of freedom songs—the old spirituals of the Sea Islands and the new songs of the student sit-ins. These sessions were planned both to give local teacher-leaders a broader view of the southwide movement and, at the same time, to suggest activities which would enrich local Citizenship School programs. Thus, they were asked at the close of these sessions how movement speakers and films and songs might be used in their own classes.

The final session was devoted, like the initial one, to a discussion of broad goals, including "the world we would like to live in." A Charleston appliance salesman who had taught Citizenship School classes on one of the Sea Islands suggested that the program itself was part of that world

> The Citizenship School Program, it seems to me like, is a little sample of the way things can be in a good world, and it is teaching our people to make the world better and at the same time is teaching them how to live in it after they get it.[61]

Based on the experimental workshops, Highlander formulated a detailed day-by-day outline for a one-week teacher training workshop. Plans were also formulated for a three-day so-called "refresher workshop" designed to give volunteer teachers and supervisors the opportunity to return to Highlander after five or six weeks in their new roles to discuss local needs and problems and to make plans for the continuing program.

Highlander as a Training Center for Other Organizations

In preparing to offer the Citizenship School Program to local and Southwide organizations, Myles Horton issued a memorandum which stated in the broadest possible terms

> Highlander's educational resources are available for the use of any agency or organization which shares its views about the need for Citizenship Schools . . . . it is prepared to receive supervisors and teachers sent by any one of these agencies, and to hold workshops in which these people will be trained for organizing and conducting Citizenship Schools in their local communities.[62]

With this memorandum, Highlander embarked on a new kind of relationship with the maturing voter education and registration movement. Instead of relating directly to literacy and voter education needs of a limited group of communities, it was to serve as a training center to develop teachers and supervisors from a number of new Negro rights organizations which, in turn, were able to respond to those needs in many communities and parts of the South.

233

In an outline accompanying the memo, Highlander indicated the responsibilities which the participating organizations would be expected to assume. Among these, each was responsible for the recruiting of potential teachers and supervisors in the area where its activities were centered, for setting up and administering of classes following the teacher training workshops and for underwriting both the costs of training and of carrying on local Citizenship Schools.[63]

In February, March, April and June 1961, Highlander held a total of four Citizenship School teacher training workshops and four refresher workshops for volunteer teachers representing a number of organizations. The qualifications which the School established for those recruited as teacher trainees (other than their involvement in the movement and their desire to help their neighbors achieve first-class citizenship) were minimal: they should have "some high school education," the ability "to read well aloud" and "to write legibly on the blackboard" and certain basic information about community services and local voting and registration requirements.[64] Not surprisingly, therefore, those recruited varied widely in the kinds of training and experience which they brought to their new roles. Participants in the February workshop included a group of farmers and farm workers, a carpenter, a domestic worker and a salesman sent by the Crusade for Voters of Savannah, Georgia, and a beautician, retired teachers and a group of housewives sent by the Montgomery (Alabama) Improvement Association.[65] Participants in the March workshop included a group of ministers, a teacher, student and a hospital aide sent by the SCLC; a laborer, a mortician's helper, a barber, an unemployed dietician and two other persons listed simply as "unemployed" sent by the Southeast Georgia Crusade for Voters and several housewives sent by the Fayette County (Tennessee) Civic and Welfare League.[66]

Trainees also varied widely in age, education and general level of sophistication. A report on participants in the April workshop indicates that the Southeast Crusade for Voters sent twelve teacher-trainees, ages sixteen through thirty-five, all high school or college graduates who were "alert, knew a great deal about the political set-up in their cities and counties and asked many intelligent questions . . ."[67] The Fayette County Civic and Welfare League also sent a group of twelve trainees to the April workshop. In contrast, a report on these trainees, long deprived sharecroppers who had recently been evicted from the land as a result of their efforts to register and vote indicated, "This group knows nothing about the political set-up in their city and county. They saw the ballot for first time in November." The report concludes, looking ahead to their role in the program. "Although . . . they will need more training before they can qualify as teachers, they will provide support for Citizenship Schools and can recruit students for classes."[68]

The School's records on the results of its four teacher training workshops, February-June 1961, end, unfortunately, in June 1961. At that date, some of the trainees had not yet gotten their first classes underway and others were in the midst of the process. From available records, however, it seems clear that most of the eighty-eight participants—whether housewives, farmers, domestic workers, students or "unemployed," ages sixteen or seventy—did, in fact, become Citizenship School teachers. The June report on the program states, "These teachers have returned to over forty communities in the South and have organized evening classes where over fifteen hundred adults have been enrolled in the Citizenship School Program."[69] Of the 1500 adults, the same report notes that 713 had already become registered voters in Georgia, Alabama, South Carolina and Fayette County, Tennessee.

What is not available is the kind of follow-up information, as in the case of the Sea Islands program, which indicates the on-going activities of the new teacher-leaders and their students, their participation in voter organizations and community groups, their individual and collective efforts to bring about "the world we would like to live in."

Transfer of the Citizenship School Program to SCLC: "You Can't Padlock an Idea"

The real southwide impact and spread of Highlander's Citizenship School Program which had begun with fourteen students meeting in the back room of a little store on Johns Island was to occur after the parent institution was closed by the State of Tennessee in the fall of 1961.

Throughout the years 1959-1960, when Highlander was carrying out plans to expand the program, first, to other Sea Islands and then to other parts of the South, it was under almost constant attack from State and regional segregationist forces. (So, too, although the attacks were generally not as concerted or sustained, were institutions and organizations in a number of southern states which were accused of "pro-integration sentiment.")[70] The story of these attacks against Highlander—the use of a special committee of the Tennessee legislature (assisted and advised by the segregationist Attorney General of Arkansas) to investigate "subversive activities" at the Highlander Folk School; of a coterie of county and state law enforcement officials (led by the District Attorney General with instructions from the legislature) to carry out a "raid" on the School during a workshop for Negro church and community leaders; of televised court hearings and a jury trial (by jurors who admitted under questioning that it was "against their religion for whites and Negroes to sit together in the classroom") to find the School guilty of violating a turn-of-the-century law prohibiting integration of private schools—should be a study in itself.

What is relevant to the present study is the way in which Highlander managed, unintimidated, undeterred, to carry on and expand its movement related programs until 1961 when the attacks were finally successful. In the spring of 1959, following the Tennessee legislative committee investigation which, as the *Southern School News* reported succinctly "found no evidence of subversion,"[71] Myles Horton, as the *News* also reported, "invited the committee to attend an integration workshop at the school April 3-5 or May 17-19 so that they could see for themselves how the school operates."[72]

Again in the summer of 1959 when police and other officials "raided" the integrated school, arresting the sixty-one year old Director of Education, Mrs. Septima Clark (and several men who protested her arrest) for disorderly conduct, both students and staff managed a show of calm and even creativity in the crisis. ". . . the songs that the sixty or so people had learned at the workshop," song leader Guy Carawan recalled, "helped them through the frightening experience of sitting in the dark while the police surrounded them. They sang 'We Shall Overcome' and added for the first time the verse 'We Are Not Afraid.'"[73]

Moreover, as Mrs. Clark notes in her autobiography, soon after she and others were released from custody, Highlander held a workshop on "The Citizenship School Idea," participated in by a larger-than-usual group of movement leader-students, eager to prove that they were "not afraid."[74]

The legal harassments continued following the raid—and so did the workshops. In September, pending a hearing, the District Attorney General for Grundy County obtained a temporary injunction against the School as a "nuisance" which resulted in the padlocking of the main building. Addressing a workshop group gathered in makeshift quarters, Myles Horton confidently observed

You can padlock a building. But you can't padlock an idea. Highlander is an idea . . . You can't kill it and you can't close it in. This workshop is part of the idea. It will grow wherever people take it.[75]

Finally, after lengthy court proceedings beginning in November 1959, and ending in February 1960, the Circuit Court Judge of Grundy County handed down his decision to revoke the charter of the Highlander Folk School on the incontestable grounds that it had violated Tennessee segregation laws by "permitting integration in its school work" as well as on other legalistic and contested grounds.[76] The School's Executive Council, in reply, announced plans for an expanded program along with plans to appeal the decision to the Tennessee Supreme Court.[77]

In April 1961, the State Supreme Court upheld the decision of the lower court and did so in a manner which made review by the United States Supreme Court unlikely.[78] It was not until then that the School turned actively to the task of insuring the continuation of the Citizenship School Program whatever the fate of the parent institution.

In a real sense, Highlander had been engaged in this task from the beginning of the program. It had evolved, since 1957, an effective and inexpensive curriculum, firmly rooted in the movement, to enable illiterate Negro adults to read and write sufficiently well to qualify as voters and to begin to participate more fully in citizen affairs. It had developed over the years a nucleus of committed, field-trained volunteer teachers and supervisors representing a number of well-established voter organizations and a Highlander staff able to guide and administer the program at every level. And it had developed, most recently, a carefully conceived and tested model for a teacher training workshop, making it possible to multiply rapidly the number of teachers and schools.

Thus, when Highlander proposed that the Southern Christian Leadership Conference, as a southwide organization already helping to spread the Citizenship School Program, take it over as its own, the transfer was readily achieved. In July, arrangements were completed for Mrs. Clark to take a leave of absence from Highlander to work with the SCLC in developing a year-around program of teacher training workshops for its local affiliates across the South. At the same time, arrangements were completed to obtain a foundation grant to finance the program.

Under its new auspices and with increasingly generous foundation support, the Citizenship School Program grew rapidly in the next years. The first SCLC-sponsored teacher training workshop was held at a church-related,

Negro community center in McIntosh, Georgia, in July 1961.[79] From 1961 to 1965, some 1600 young and older volunteer teachers, able "to read well aloud" and "to write legibly on the blackboard," and eager, as they explained when interviewed, to "help my people," "to get them to understand what's happening in the movement," and "to become a key instrument in my community," attended SCLC workshops.[80] They, in turn, taught Citizenship School classes for more than 25,000 adult students and, together, as Mrs. Clark was able to report in 1965, these movement teacher-leaders and their students "were responsible for the enrollment of more than 50,000 registered voters!"[81]

This vastly expanded Citizenship School Program and the remarkable growth of voter registration activities across the South in the early sixties cannot be fully explained in terms of a zealous Southern Christian Leadership Conference and its affiliated organizations who took over a carefully developed Highlander program. The student sit-in demonstrations and the compelling new student movement which began in 1960 provided great inspiration and impetus for this and other southwide education and action programs. Highlander's role in relation to the student movement will be examined in the following chapter.

FOURTEEN

New Leadership and a New Agenda for the South: Workshops in Support of the Student Movement

The Sit-ins: "The New World Was on Its Way"

In February 1960, the same month when a judge in Grundy County, Tennessee, handed down his decision to revoke the charter of the Highlander Folk School, Negro college students in Greensboro, North Carolina, initiated the first spontaneous lunch counter sit-ins. The result was a new mass movement which spread across the South calling adults as well as students to action and a new and vital educational role for Highlander in its last year and a half of existence in its original location, under its original name. Of the beginning of the demonstrations at a Woolworth's lunch counter in Greensboro, *Southern School News* reported blandly

    February 1   Four freshmen students, Negroes, sat for an hour from 4:30 to 5:30 p.m. (closing time) without being served.

    February 2   The actual organized demonstrations began . . . when about 75 students appeared about 10:30 a.m. and remained until about 12:30 p.m. A&T college officials said they had no knowledge of the movement.

The drama gained in interest and intensity when on February 4 Negro college students were "joined by three white students from Women's College of the University of North Carolina" and on February 5 when "white students, Negro students and members of the Klan vied for seats . . . at the lunch counter,"[1] but it gave little hint of the developments soon to follow. Of these developments, Howard Zinn, an historian of the student movement writes

> In a matter of days the idea leaped to other cities in North Carolina. During the next two weeks, sit-ins spread to 15 cities in 5 southern states. Within the following year, over 50,000 people—most were Negroes, some were white—had participated in one kind of demonstration or another in a hundred cities, and over 3,600 demonstrators spent time in jail.[2]

The mass demonstrations and mass jailings had their effect: several hundred lunch counters were desegregated and, as a Highlander report observed, "The new world was on its way."[3]

Just two months after the sit-ins began, as an amazed adult generation of Negro southerners rallied behind the students and as their amazed (and shocked) white counterparts wondered how to stop them, the Highlander Folk School held a workshop for the young demonstrators, the "first occasion when a fairly wide cross-section of student leadership came together."[4]

College Workshops Before the Sit-ins

Yet with all its confidence in the grass roots vitality of the movement, in the capacity of local groups led by a Rosa Parks or an Esau Jenkins to find their own way of confronting the separate and unequal system, the School's leadership, in the very beginning, at least, was amazed, too, at the bold initiative assumed by the students. For six years prior to the sit-ins, Highlander had sponsored weekend workshops for Negro and white college students. For six years, beginning in 1954[5], the students had been invited to come together from their segregated campuses to discuss whatever problems concerned them. And, year after year, they chose to hold conventional academic lecture-discussion sessions on human relations, on interpersonal relations, on race relations. In 1959, the Sixth Annual Workshop, they evidenced an inclination to move from theory and analysis to dealing with actual problems when they selected as their topic, "Campus Leadership for Integration."

That inclination was reinforced by opening speaker Dr. Herman Long of the Race Relations Institute, Fisk University. Tracing the history of earlier generations of activist students, he asked the group, "Why have you been so silent?" He concluded by raising a series of questions calculated to rouse them: How can we stimulate college students to think of issues of today? What types of action can we address ourselves to? What is effective protest? What are the limits? But, a student report reveals, even this blunt approach failed. For the remainder of the weekend, discussions centered almost solely on campus questions. In their final session, students drew up a list of so-called action projects for 1960. These included: "A well-written newspaper for exchange," the promotion of "inter-collegiate activity" and a conference for representatives of eight private colleges on "The Role of Private Colleges in Criticizing the Social Order."[6]

First Workshop for Sit-in Leaders, April 1960

The Seventh Annual College Workshop held April 1-3, 1960, was unrelated to the workshops of the world before the sit-ins. Planned with and for student protest leaders on the action theme "The New Generation Fights for Equality," it marked a new relationship of Highlander to the students as it marked a new relationship of the students to their society. Mindful of this new relationship, Myles Horton explained to the independent young protest leaders as they convened

> As far as I know this is the first time since this protest started that a group of people from a variety of places has gotten together. Something may come of it that would help further the things you believe in. And I would just like to emphasize the fact that we are here to help you do what you decide to do, not to try to get you to join with us . . . because we don't have anything except a service to render.[7]

For the seventy-five students, two-thirds of these Negro, from fourteen southern colleges and universities, the workshop meant, first and foremost, an opportunity to meet, to come together from the forefront of early demonstrations in Nashville and Atlanta and Orangeburg, South Carolina. It meant an opportunity to know one another, to share experiences to get a larger sense of what their bold local efforts were accomplishing, to get the feeling of being as one sit-in leader expressed it, "one movement instead of many."

For Highlander, aware of the enormous social and educational potential of the new direct action movement which in a matter of weeks had dramatized to the South and the nation the immorality and irrationality of the segregated society, the workshop and those which followed in 1960 and 1961 represented an exciting opportunity to help the pragmatic young leaders to grow and develop, to look beyond a series of sit-ins to a continuing and broader movement.

The process of "feeling like one movement" began at the opening session when students discussed the spontaneous origin and spread of the sit-ins and reported on developments in their several areas. The historic reports are only briefly described in the workshop proceedings (For the activist students, the doing and the telling were important. The writing down was not.) They furnished, however, inspiring firsthand evidence of the gathering strength and momentum of their new movement. Sit-in leaders from Nashville, for example, where the demonstrations began just twelve days after Greensboro, could attest to growing support in their area not only among students from four Negro Institutions—Fisk University, Meharry Medical School, Tennessee A&I State University and American Baptist Seminary and from predominately white Vanderbilt University (all of which were represented at the workshop), but among a number of Negro and interracial church and community groups. Reports gave early evidence, too, of the unconquerable spirit of the new movement which was to take "We Shall Overcome" as it's theme song. Deep south workshop participants from Claflin College in Orangeburg, South Carolina, where a thousand students from two Negro colleges had joined together in a peaceful march to support the sit-ins, could announce that students there continued to march even after police used water hoses and tear gas and jailed more than 500.

The Movement Learns its Songs

Along with sharing experiences which were to become a part of their movement heritage, the young protesters began to sing "freedom songs," old and new, which contributed even more to their feeling of being a movement. At evening sessions and early and late and between sessions folk singer-song

242

leader Guy Carawan encouraged the students to share the songs which some were beginning to put together out of their experience and introduced them to many others which were part of an earlier heritage, of earlier struggles for freedom. "When the students came to Highlander," Carawan recalled, "they were singing mostly popular and religious songs, rock 'n' roll and calypso."[8] When they left they were singing songs collected in the Sea Islands, songs brought to Highlander by Negro union members, songs long rejected or ignored: "We Shall Overcome," "We Shall Not Be Moved," "Keep Your Eyes on the Prize," "I'm Gonna Sit at the Welcome Table," "This Little Light of Mine." "These songs," Carawan noted, looking back to the first workshop for sit-in leaders, "caught on immediately."[9] So quickly and completely, in fact, did the students take the songs as their songs, that the student movement, probably more than any other in the history of the South or the nation, was a "singing movement."

The Movement Looks at Itself

Encouraging the independent and spontaneous protest leaders to begin to think as one movement and to face some of the problems involved in building it was not so readily accomplished. Most of the students had little orientation or background for the new mass movement which they were initiating beyond an accumulated sense of injustice and impatience, some youthful memory of a bus boycott in Montgomery and Negro school children in Little Rock, and a protest method which they used because, as they explained to Helen Fuller of *The New Republic*, "It works."[10] In part the educative process involved arranging a learning environment in which the students would interact with "representatives of the wider community" whose points of view and perspectives on the movement differed from their own. Thus, as a Highlander report explained, several such representatives (including an activist Nashville minister, a Fisk University sociologist, an historian from the University of the South and a teacher from a progressive school in New York City) "were invited to state their views about the exclusive nature of the student demonstrations, and to require a clarifying of the students' eventual goal in the wider community."[11] (Also invited to raise questions and provide other views was a small number of students from outside the South—students from Kenya studying in Negro colleges and students from several northern colleges.)

243

The need for clarification began to be apparent, began to be voiced, in the opening session as reports on sit-in demonstrations in the several areas revealed that student leaders "differed considerably about the desirability of co-operation with the adult communities, Negro and white."[12] In subsequent sessions, one led by sociologist Herman Long (who had urged students the year before to become involved) and another led by Myles Horton, the students were confronted more pointedly with some of the unanswered questions of "the wider community." Long, after paying tribute to the unique student-inspired and student-led direct action movement, asserted that "liberal adults would like to help and could help if they had a little better idea of what the students were planning to do, and of what their basic philosophy is." He indicated as an example that the method of nonviolence needed to be clearly interpreted. He also indicated that the question of "whether or not students have broken laws, and the whole dilemma of law and morality" needed to be more carefully defined and understood "if the movement is to have permanent usefulness."[13]

In a rigorous follow-up session Horton, assuming the attitude of an "average liberal adult" in sympathy with the movement but wanting to be assured that it was acting entirely within the law, forced the students to define their positions and defend them. The lengthy exchanges which ensued revealed that "nearly every one of the students . . . was eager to act according to law"; that many or most were impatient with the legal processes in the South and believed in their right to defy an "unjust law" and that "they had not thought through clearly the implications of their own undertaking"[14]

With such encounters with Long, Horton and others making them increasingly aware of their lack of clarity, the new leaders divided into working committees to think through some of the problems and issues raised and to decide on next steps. Out of their intensive small group discussions on subjects defined simply as "Communications," "Philosophy," "Methods" and "Community Relations," they projected the broad outlines of a southern student movement which, in the years that followed, was to profoundly affect the South and the nation.

They arrived, first, at a brief non-ideological statement of their so-called "philosophy of the movement" which was to continue to be their essential philosophy.

> We believe in democracy. We are Americans seeking our rights. We want to do something. We are using non-violence as a method, but not necessarily as a total way of life. We believe it is practical.[15]

They suggested various kinds of new and continued action which, over the next five years, were to be important elements in their southern program. These included "better planned sit-in demonstrations as long as they are useful; participation in economic boycott when it is practical" and "picketing where it will be effective."[16] In addition, many in the group emphasized the need for "a religious basis for the protest" and recommended "prayer as a means and a method." "More participation in voting" was also urged. The committee explained, "this would give the Negro community more political power and especially in areas where the Negroes outnumber the white population."[17]

In their discussion of "Community Relations," the young leaders made it clear that they intended to be an independent movement. The workshop report indicated that "closer relations with the wider community were recommended [but] with the precaution that agencies and other movements, white or interracial, however sympathetic, should not be permitted to take control of the student movement."[18]

Finally, workshop participants proposed that "a southwide organization for promoting the student movement" be formed. In their discussion of the proposal, it was emphasized that the present sit-in leaders should meet together "as soon as possible" to establish the organization and that its function should be "not to direct activities but to coordinate them [and] discuss future activities for consideration by local bodies."[19]

From College Workshop to the Formation of SNCC

Just two weeks after the Highlander college workshop, at a meeting in Raleigh, North Carolina, convened by the Southern Christian Leadership Conference, sit-in leaders from fifty communities in twelve states formed the broad-purposed movement organization which they had proposed at Highlander, to be known as the Student Nonviolent Coordinating Committee.

At the founding conference, Guy Carawan was invited to lead singing and to introduce the old songs of freedom which he had taught to the smaller workshop group. Among the songs was "We Shall Overcome" which, he quoted later, "was immediately taken over as the unofficial theme song of the movement."[20] Looking back to the Raleigh meeting a white student from Virginia who was to become the first SNCC staff member, recalled the singing of "We Shall Overcome" and its powerful unifying effect. "There was no SNCC, no *ad hoc* committees, no funds," Jane Stembridge wrote, "just people who didn't know what to expect but who came and released the common vision of that song."[21]

Highlander's relation to the inspired but vague new organization and to the student movement which it hoped to coordinate continued until the School's closing in the fall of 1961. The songs sung at the first gathering of sit-in leaders and at the first SNCC conference were to be a sustaining force within the movement. They were sung by high-spirited young sit-in leaders to their jailers in Nashville. They would be sung by frightened but determined Freedom Riders as they waited all night, black and white together, for a bus to take them from Birmingham, Alabama, to Jackson Mississippi.

A significant part of SNCC's inner leadership group came from among the student demonstrators who attended the April 1960 college workshop. One of the workshop planners and participants, Marion Barry, Fisk University graduate student from Nashville, was elected first chairman. Another participant, John Lewis, an American Baptist Seminary student, also of Nashville, was to be third chairman. Still others such as James Bevel and Bernard Lafayette[22] of the Baptist Seminary served on the SNCC steering committee whose members assumed personal leadership in the jail-no-bail movement and later in the Freedom Rides, along with attempting to keep in communication with the free-wheeling centers of protest across the South.

Other Workshops for the Student Movement, 1960-1961

In response to the enormous demands placed on the young leadership and the enormous potential of their efforts for achieving a more democratic South, Highlander held three more workshops for and about the student movement between April 1960 and April 1961. These workshops provided an opportunity for students caught up in local crisis situations to gain a broader perspective on the rapidly growing movement and to discuss and deal with some of the problems affecting its development.

"The Place of the White College Student," November 1960

One of the problems with far-reaching implications was the role to be played by liberal white southerners in a movement which was Negro inspired and Negro-led. In response to this problem, Highlander held a workshop in November 1960, on "The Place of the White College Student in the Changing South," participated in by thirteen Negro movement leaders and forty-seven white students involved in or seeking to be involved in the movement. As in their first workshop, activities included the informal sharing of experiences and group singing of movement songs led by Guy Carawan and by student song leaders nurtured on the picket lines and in the jails. In this second workshop, however, student movement leaders who in April had barely considered the question beyond stating, "White students will be welcomed",[23] moved to a candid examination of the relationship of the white student to Negro leadership and the problem of whites gaining acceptance as movement leaders. "Even in the most progressive groups," Negro participants agreed, "the probationary period for the average white is a long one. Due to a lack of contact between the races the white is a stranger to most members of the group. In addition, they noted, caution must be exercised because of the number of whites who have become informers."[24]

The thoughtful final report of the workshop, as put together by several white participants from the University of the South, placed major emphasis on potential areas of cooperation between Negro and white students in the movement and on areas where white students might make unique contributions working independently. Beyond the report which received wide distribution among liberal white student groups over the South, the workshop experience itself, shared by Negro and white students from eighteen southern colleges and universities provided an opportunity for the kind of free and open interaction between young southern Negroes and whites which furthered the goal of an integrated movement in a period when that goal was espoused by most young leaders as well as by Highlander.

"New Frontiers," April 1961

The last of these Highlander workshops in April 1961, "New Frontiers for College Students" brought together ninety-three students and adults with a

247

wide variety of perspectives and points of view "to assess the meaning and direction of the students' struggle for democracy in the South.[25] At a time when leadership of the established (if not wholly organized) new movement tended to believe confidently in the rightness and inevitability of their cause, it included dispassionate social scientists and participants in earlier southern struggles for social justice as well as passionate believers in the current struggle of "radical love versus radical evil." At a time when the distance was widening between the activists (Negro and white) and those outside the movement, it included along with the majority of students who were deeply involved, a group who were sympathetic but not involved and a group of conservatives who (like their parents) felt more comfortable in the South before the movement, but who (unlike their parents) were willing to interact with their radical contemporaries. At a time when there was still little northern participation in the movement, it included a group of students from eastern and midwestern universities and colleges and a representative of the National Council of Churches college program who were seeking to actively relate to the southern student effort.

In their several days together, participants were addressed by a dedicated young Negro minister and Nashville sit-in leader, Rev. C. T. Vivian, who called upon the students to find ways of involving even conservative members of the community in their movement and of bringing southwide and nationwide "spiritual force" to bear on the Birminghams and the Rock Hills of the Deep South.[26] They were also addressed by Tuskegee research sociologist and Highlander Executive Council member Dr. Lewis Jones who, along with acknowledging the positive impact of the new movement called attention to the falling away of white liberals in the South and warned of the danger of the Negro middle-class falling away if the movement became too militant and of the possible bitter consequences of student disenchantment with their allies.[27]

Against this inspiring yet chastening background, students met in small groups to consider such subjects as "Keeping the movement alive and vital," "Role of the northern student," "Built-in problems of the involved student" and "Limitations of the movement." No written report was compiled of the ideas and decisions coming out of these discussion groups. It might be noted, however, that among the student leaders, Negro and white, who participated in the April 1961 workshop and sought to ponder new directions for the movement was a Spelman College sophomore and rising young SNCC leader from Atlanta and a group of activist students from Fisk University, Peabody

College and the American Baptist Seminary in Nashville who, one month later, were to undertake a courageous new direction for the movement, the Freedom Rides.[28]

It might also be noted that among the adult participants was a relatively unknown representative of the National Council of Churches, the Reverend Andrew Young, who, stimulated by the interaction with young and older movement leaders was to reappraise his own direction. Several months later, he returned South to serve, first, as administrator for the Highlander-developed Citizenship School Program for the Southern Christian leadership Conference and, later, as one of Dr. Martin Luther King's closest aides.[29]

The Challenge of the Student Movement: Highlander Reassesses Its Policy and Program

If Highlander had challenged the college sit-in leaders to project larger goals in the formative period before they were a movement, their movement was very soon challenging the School to re-examine its educational policies and program.

The Students as Adults

To begin with, the students who, from the first college workshop in 1954, had been treated as a separate, self-involved group which, it was hoped, could be encouraged to relate to problems beyond the campus, had suddenly come-of-age. In recognition of their coming-of-age, minutes of a Highlander Executive Council meeting in 1960 declared that, henceforth, "college students who have participated actively in sit-in demonstrations, thus assuming direct community responsibility, will be included as adults in . . . workshops."[30]

Not only were the students "included" but their movement very often provided the issues and problems, the subject-matter for the workshops. Thus, in May 1960, Marion Barry, John Lewis, and a dozen other student movement leaders were participants with some forty adult leaders of civil rights and community organizations in a workshop which focused on a problem raised, in large part, by their movement—"The role of the White Southerner in the Struggle for Social Justice." At the opening session, Myles

Horton explained to the group which included such well known pioneers of nonviolent direct action as Mrs. Rosa Parks and Reverend Fred Shuttlesworth, "We are just going to forget the fact that some of you people are still in college and some are out. We are here not as college students or community leaders of the more generally recognized types . . ." Instead, he emphasized, "we are here, all of us . . . to try to learn from each other."[31]

Thereafter, student and adult leaders came together for a variety of workshops. One of these, inspired by the singing student movement, was a "Sing for Freedom" workshop in August 1960. Led by Guy Carawan, it brought together some seventy-five student and adult singers and song leaders who discussed "techniques for group singing at mass meetings, organizational meetings, social gatherings and demonstrations. They also prepared a collection of freedom songs "spirituals, gospels songs and hymns, folk songs and contemporary topical songs," some written during the workshop which, like earlier Highlander collections for the labor movement, were mimeographed and shared with groups over the South.[32]

Workshops for New Organizations

At the same Executive Council meeting where students were accorded adult status, it was agreed that "Residential workshops at Highlander will seek cooperation with specific community organizations which have identified with student movements in meeting goals for integration."[33] Thus, although rosters of Highlander workshops for 1960 and 1961 continued to include participants from some of the older, more traditional organizations such as the NAACP or the local ministerial alliance, the School was relating its resources and services, more and more, to the newer movement-related organizations. This emphasis is most apparent in the case of workshops such as "New Alliances in the South" in February 1961, which specifically brought together student movement leaders and representatives of twenty or more of these organizations—the Council for Cooperative Action of Chattanooga, the Nashville Community Leadership Conference, the Alabama Christian Movement for Human Rights, the Chatham County (Alabama) Crusade for Voters—to determine ways of working together for integration and full citizenship. It can also be discerned in the growing participation of representatives of the new organizations in Highlander's continuing program of workshops on voter education and community leadership for integration.

Workshop for Beauticians, a New Leadership Group

Along with raising new questions and putting new demands on existing adult leadership, the student-led direct action movement inspired some in the community not traditionally viewed as leaders to assume new and active roles. Among the "new status people among Negroes," as Myles Horton observed at a staff planning meeting in the fall of 1960, were Negro beauticians. Citing some of their special attributes as independent business women, free of white community pressures and having wide contacts in the Negro community, he proposed that Highlander offer a workshop to strengthen and encourage their emergence. As a result, in January 1961, in its last months of developing programs for the student movement and organizations supporting the student movement, Highlander developed a unique three-day workshop for some fifty beauticians from Tennessee and Alabama on "New Leadership Responsibilities." In planning and carrying out the workshop, the School was able to involve several community-leader beauticians who had participated in earlier workshops on integration. They also served as interpreters of the proposed programs to their beauticians' organizations and provided contact with prospective participants, most of whom were unfamiliar with Highlander and with the residential workshop idea.

The process of educating the beautician-students to view themselves in more significant leadership roles and to make plans to assume those roles began even before the workshop. A letter to prospective students stated in part

> Highlander Folk School has been impressed with the leadership possibilities among beauticians. This is one of the professions which offers its members great freedom for leadership in community action. We also see it as offering opportunities especially suitable for professional women who . . . want to be active in the struggle for social justice in the South. We are, therefore, planning a workshop in which beauticians may discuss their opportunities and plan to use them.[34]

Early sessions of the workshop were planned to strengthen their image of themselves as a leadership group. The opening speaker, a Nashville beautician active in the Tennessee Beauticians Association and deeply involved in civil rights problems and issues in the State, provided a model for the new leadership as well as ideas for action. So, too, did the workshop coordinator—a former Highlander student and beautician-community leader from Chattanooga.

Myles Horton further reinforced that self-image. In preparation for group discussion on "What things can you do uniquely?" he suggested some of the reasons why beauticians were especially qualified to assume leadership in "the struggle for social justice." He spoke for example of their ability to relate to and influence people and of their beauty shops as community meeting places. Above all, he emphasized their independence. "We need the kind of leadership that is independent,"[35] he concluded.

By the time the workshop participants divided into small groups to discuss plans for action, their problem was not one of finding a role but of having too many roles. In response, for example, to a description by the opening speaker of the plight of the evicted sharecropper families in Fayette County, someone proposed that the beauticians might provide an emergency health center. Someone else suggested that beauty shops could raise funds for the center and for other movement projects. It was also suggested that, after hours, the shops could serve as voter education and literacy education centers.[36]

The atmosphere in which the several groups made their final reports was one of excitement, of exhilaration. It found expression, at the opening of the session, in the spontaneous singing of movement songs. The new leaders were not only ready to move. They had begun to move. Beyond submitting detailed plans, the group responsible for developing the health center had dispatched a workshop representative to the State beauticians' board meeting and had already received word that the health center proposal was accepted.

Correspondence with board members of the Volunteer Health Center for Fayette County and with other workshop participants documents some of the continuing tangible results of the brief educational experience. The results, however, like the results of other workshops of the period, can only be understood, can only be explained, in relation to the rising civil rights movement. It was the movement, awakening new hopes and new determination, which brought the fifty beauticians to Highlander and motivated their subsequent action. Without it, there would not have been a workshop.

The Educational Process that Could Not be Terminated

After April 1961, when the Supreme Court upheld the decision of the lower court that the Highlander Folk School should be permanently closed, the School developed no new programs. A few months later, in the fall of 1961, final action by the State of Tennessee against the School was completed. Its charter was revoked. Its property and assets were taken over by the State. Yet those who had achieved the termination of the civil rights movement-related institution did not understand that the educational process which it had initiated, related as it was to a social movement, could not, would not, be terminated. Thus, the college student leaders who met at Highlander in April 1960 to discuss the sit-in demonstrations became the SNCC leaders who met at Highlander in August 1961 to debate and define a new voter registration and direct action program which in the years 1961-1965 would affect the South and the nation as well as disenfranchised Negro voters.

From Highlander Folk School to Highlander Center

Nor, in fact, was the School itself terminated—except as a name, a place and a collection of buildings. On August 28, 1961, as the last Annual Report of the Highlander Folk School announced, a new institution the Highlander Research and Education Center of Knoxville was granted a charter by the State of Tennessee.[37] Based in a single rented building which served as a living place for staff and a meeting place for students, the new Highlander with the same founder, the same Executive Council and much of the same staff began again to relate its program to the southwide civil rights movement.

FIFTEEN

Conclusions

Any attempt to summarize the history of a complex period or institution is a tenuous undertaking. The undertaking is particularly tenuous when the history involves a movement-related adult school in interaction with four different groups of people seeking to achieve social betterment, social change, during a period of seemingly constant unrest. This concluding chapter, therefore, is rather an effort to review the institution-shaping social-educational ideas and goals and the common processes of program development during the history of the Highlander Folk School from 1932 to 1961. The chapter includes, finally, an assessment of those underlying ideas in relation to contemporary educational thought and of the institution itself in relation to adult education and recent social movements in the South.

The Founding Ideas and Goals

The Highlander Folk School and the educator primarily responsible for shaping it were peculiarly products of American social thought and experience. Myles Horton was a radical idealist in his dedication to political and social democracy, to the goal of a "new social order" and to education as one of the instruments for bringing it into being. In his analysis of conditions conducive to social learning and social change, he was a student of sociology, much influenced by the ideas of Lester F. Ward and Robert Park. And in his approach to adult education, he was an independent-minded, experience-educated pragmatist.

Out of his interactions with the limited and limiting southern environment in which he grew up, he came to an early awareness of some of the problems besetting the old order. His subsequent wider interactions, while a student at Union Theological Seminary, with an industrial North immobilized by Depression and with radical theologians, including Reinhold

Niebuhr and Norman Thomas, and radical educators, including John Dewey and George Counts, served to strengthen his dedication to the goal of democratic social change and to education as a means for achieving that change.

Through Professor Park at the University of Chicago he came to view involvement in a situation as vital to understanding. Through Park he also came to comprehend more fully the importance of social movements in the forming and re-forming processes of society. From the writings of Lester Ward, he derived the concept of conflict as a basis for initiating social change by presenting people with problems which demand solutions. His ideas on the pragmatic evolving of educational programs out of interaction with groups of people attempting to cope with problems had their beginning in a series of community meetings in a rural church near Ozone, Tennessee.

Beginning with the first fund-raising letter which proclaimed, "We are proposing to use education as one of the instruments for bringing about a new social order," Highlander remained steadfast in its espousal of radically democratic social-educational goals, whether stated in terms of working for "the expansion of political and economic democracy" through the building and strengthening of unions or seeking "to train the leaders who can secure full citizenship for all Negroes throughout the South." At the same time, the pragmatic approach to getting the institution underway which Myles Horton decided upon while in Denmark, searching unsuccessfully for an institutional model, was to characterize the development of the Highlander Folk School. What he would do, he concluded, was to "find the place, the people, the situation" and with his broad goals and notions of relating education to social movements to "simply start and let it grow." "It will," he predicted, "build its own structure and take its own form." Over the three decades which followed, the School's leadership continued to subscribe to this approach to institution and program-building.

The Common Process of Program Development

The present study has examined in some detail each of the pragmatically evolved major programs of the Highlander Folk School as they represent different and in some ways unique responses to the needs of groups of adults confronted with social problems, involved in movements or organizations striving for social change. And because the social context of each case was a changing one, each program has been examined as a changing as well as a unique response. Thus, the School's early program of organizing and education related to impoverished mountain workers and their families is traced from its beginnings as a response to a crisis situation in one community to its culmination as a response to growing unrest among underpaid and unrepresented workers throughout the surrounding county. Its workers' education program is examined over two decades from a response to a handful of worker-students seeking a role in a barely-stirring labor movement to a response in the form of southwide residential terms and extension services to the organization-defined needs of an established industrial union movement. Its Farmers Union program is described and analyzed from its conceptualization by Highlander's educational leadership as the basis for a farmer-labor people's movement to its limited development, organizationally and educationally, in response to the economic needs of small farmers in a three state area. Highlander's several programs related to the civil rights movement are examined from the first workshop on school desegregation in response to an anticipated Supreme Court decision to its many and varied workshops in response to the leadership needs of a southwide drive for "first-class citizenship" and a rapidly growing student movement.

Although each program represents a distinct and differing response to the educational needs of a given group at a given time, the data reveal important common elements with regard to the kinds of people who participated in the programs and the way in which the programs were developed. Highlander students, whatever their backgrounds, came from groups actively seeking solutions to their problems. In addition, although the kinds of students in field or extension programs were as inclusive as the groups served, most of those who participated in residential sessions were local leaders or potential leaders in the organizations and movements from which they were drawn.

Central to the findings of this study, analysis of the major programs indicates that in the case of the most effective programs—the community and county programs, the workers' education program and the several civil rights programs—the processes of program development were basically the same: (1) the way in which goals were defined; (2) the organization and movement-related kinds of learning activities and the way in which they were selected and organized; and (3) the procedures by which programs were evaluated. At every step, the student group, in interaction with the Highlander staff, played a determining role in the process. While the student group in the Farmers Union program was involved in much of the process, the definition of overall goals was a decision of the School's leadership.

Defining Immediate and Larger Goals

The initiation of each of Highlander's programs was preceded by a period of several months to several years of interaction with the potential students, generally in their community or movement settings. What was required was the kind of firsthand knowledge which Park advocated: a willingness on the part of the non-classroom-bound educators to go out to, to observe, to listen to and finally to understand the particular group of people and their problems. Required, too, as Ward's writings had suggested, were developments within the social situation which stimulated people to want to act, which provided them with a need or opportunity to deal with their problems. Until both of these conditions were met, Highlander learned from its early community education efforts, no effective program could get underway. Thus, although the founders spent several months coming to know their mountain neighbors before they attempted to begin a community program, their contrived early efforts to offer a series of evening classes which related to community interests and concerns were short-lived. It was not until some eight months after the School was founded that the conflict of a local strike by underpaid woodcutters provided the basis for developing a vital program related to the recognized needs of people.

But for the program to move beyond helping people to deal with local problems, there needed to be a larger social movement. The community and county programs, developed in response to the needs of the immediate relief-ridden area, never transcended those needs. In contrast, although Highlander's workers' education program was begun when the labor movement was barely stirring, it very soon moved beyond academically conceived courses and a response to needs of strikers in nearby Wilder and Harriman, Tennessee. As social unrest spread in the thirties, the radical idealist school had a basis for encouraging its students to enlarge their goals beyond winning a local strike, to view their efforts as part of a growing movement.

The development of Highlander's far-reaching Citizenship School Program, which began on Johns Island, South Carolina, with a series of efforts to help Negro leadership to deal with immediate problems required more than two years of interaction. At the end of that time after many field trips, conferences and workshops, the Citizenship School Program evolved in response to the growing desire of illiterate islanders to read and write in order to qualify as voters, to become "first-class citizens." From Johns Island, this slow-to-develop program was carried to aspiring, "first-class citizens" in movement-awakened communities across the South.

Selecting and Organizing Learning Activities

Beyond the process of interaction to define immediate and larger program goals, the carrying out of the several programs required considerable flexibility. Highlander's readiness to relate its educational resources to the needs of its students, to the demands and potential of the social situation rather than imposing a preconceived set of learning activities began soon after the School was founded. The mountain community of Summerfield represented a life-size laboratory for testing out the unorthodox ideas of founder Myles Horton and those who joined him in the experimental venture. Beginning with the Bugwood Strike, educational activities were carried on not primarily in classes but in strategy meetings of the strikers and in meetings of the Cumberland Mountain Workers League. In such meetings, Highlander teachers were both participating members and resource persons, raising questions, providing information, suggesting alternative courses of action. Later, when the community, led by the League members, decided to form new kinds of cooperative self-help organizations, Highlander undertook new kinds of learning activities as related to the planning and organizing sessions of the inexperienced cooperators.

With this kind of preparation, leaders developed in the community program were able to assume teacher-leader roles within Highlander's countywide program of organizing and education among relief workers and their families. And, again, the educational activities were carried on in a variety of contexts and "classrooms" from large-scale rallies featuring regional labor leader speakers to meetings of new local unions and their grievance committees to a residential "stay-in" of jobless workers and their families at the County WPA offices.

In its twenty year relationship to the southern labor movement, Highlander, through a varied program of extension activities, continued to relate its resources directly to the needs of new unions and their struggling local leaders. Thus, beginning in the early thirties at the request of local strike leaders, little groups of Highlander resident students and teachers visited besieged mining and mill towns in Georgia and Tennessee to plan demonstrations, present "educational speeches" and organize recreational activities. In 1937, in response to the vast needs of the CIO's first southwide organizing drive, Highlander set aside its residential program and devoted its efforts to an experimental summer school-in-the-field for newly organized Shirtworkers in Tennessee and to organizing and educating in the process of organizing for the Textile Workers in North and South Carolina. And when industry and industrial unions expanded rapidly during World War II, it worked with area union councils in New Orleans, Atlanta, Memphis and elsewhere to develop field institutes, classes and educational activities within union meetings for thousands of members of new locals and their officers. In carrying out these large-scale extension programs, as in its early community and county program, the School involved local leaders, working with the Highlander staff, as teachers for their fellow union members.

The Citizenship School Program illustrates, again, the way in which Highlander, in its extension programs, utilized "movement teachers" and movement-related learning activities and settings in response to adult student perceived needs (and staff perceived opportunities) within the social situation. With few exceptions, Citizenship School teachers had never taught before. Their qualifications, along with a desire to help their neighbors qualify as voters, included the ability "to read well aloud" and "to write legibly on the blackboard." Their classrooms were the back of a Negro-owned store, a church, or someone's "front room." The teacher and student-defined literacy curriculum included, along with basic reading and writing skills and information on state and local voting requirements, sessions on how to write a money order and fill out a mail order form, speakers from government agencies and from the movement, the singing of Freedom songs and discussions of the Bill of Rights and the International Declaration of Human Rights.

In its residential programs to develop leadership for the labor and civil rights movements, Highlander provided educational activities not only in response to immediate needs, but anticipated needs. Out of on-going interaction with each of the movements, it defined activities to help local leaders cope with the problems confronting them. At the same time, anticipating the growth of the southern industrial union movement in the early thirties and the southwide civil rights movement in the early fifties, it sought, utilizing the residential experience, to give participants a view of what their movement and society could become.

Thus, at each stage in the development of the labor movement, Highlander offered workers' education students the intensely practical kinds of learning activities which the situation required. In the early thirties, when the emerging movement had few experienced local leaders, the School provided a program which combined residential courses in Labor History and Economics, Labor Journalism and Public Speaking with an opportunity for aspiring movement leader-students to utilize their newly-acquired knowledge and skills, as they assisted with the School's organizing and educational program in the community and county and with its strike-supporting field services. Later, when the movement became a growing industrial union movement and those who came to residential terms were leaders of new locals seeking to deal with specific problems of union-building, they helped to reshape the program. Thereafter, it included more specialized courses and training sessions taught by union staff and officials, for example, Collective Bargaining, Labor Law and Duties of a Business Agent. It also included a course on Union Problems with the problems identified and dealt with by each new student group. By the forties, when the southern industrial union movement had become an established movement which interacted with the Highlander Folk School in established ways, the School staff and labor members of its Executive Council developed programs which, in large part, were organization-serving. The Annual Southern CIO School, proposed by CIO Council members, represents one such example. Regional officials assumed joint responsibility for planning and teaching, financing and recruiting for the one month School which featured a central course on CIO Policy and Organization.

At the same time, within the residential setting, the School provided worker-students with other kinds of activities, other kinds of experiences. From the earliest workers' education terms, as Myles Horton's "think notes" indicate, the residential community was viewed as a special sort of "educative environment." Here, workers drawn from struggling local union and strike situations could come to know other workers with common problems and some who had successfully confronted those problems. Out of their formal and informal interactions, they acquired new resources and a sense of their local efforts as part of a larger movement. Here, too, they came to know other kinds of "workers with hand and brain," representatives of the projected broadly-conceived movement. In attempting to give reality to that movement and to prepare worker-students for participation in it, Highlander sought to include a diverse group of resident students, racially as well as socio-economically, and a diverse group of visiting resource persons from organizations working for democratic social change in the South.

With a view to fostering movement spirit within these groups, the School made labor songs a significant part of the residential program. In daily after-supper sessions they learned old songs gathered by Zilphia Horton and other Highlander staff members on picket lines and brought to the School by earlier worker-students. They were also encouraged to write songs based on their own experiences, thus adding to the movement a heritage which they could carry back with them into local situations.

In order to suggest the kind of democratic society which was possible, the residential sessions were governed by a staff-student Workers' Council with each member having one vote. Together, staff and students participated in decisions affecting all aspects of their communal life from the allocation of household chores to changes in the educational program and together they implemented those decisions. In this way, Horton observed, the students could "gain an idea of the new social order in which workers have control."

Highlander's residential workshops for the civil rights movement represent the culmination of the interactive process of program development. In each case, workshops were planned to respond to movement-defined needs and, in each case, the School, making use of the residential setting, encouraged participants to look toward a broader movement, toward a South in which all Negroes would enjoy full citizenship. In its interrelated series of workshops on desegregation in the years from 1953 to 1957, Negro and white community leaders participated in the problem-centered sessions, returned to their local situations to put what they had learned into practice and returned again to Highlander to define new workshops based on interim developments and problems. In this way, desegregation workshops which focused specifically on local school problems and plans in 1953-1955 were basically redefined in 1956 after the action of a participant in the 1955 workshop, Rosa Parks, inspired the Montgomery Bus Boycott. Thereafter, staff and movement leader planners projected bold new desegregation goals and a new educational program to develop other leaders for local nonviolent direct action movements.

In the same way, college student sit-in leaders who helped to plan the southwide workshop for participants in the spontaneous protests in the Spring of 1960 returned to Highlander some months later to help develop and carry out workshops dealing with the problems of their new movement and to chart a new and broader course of action.

The integrated, cooperatively-administered, residential community setting which Highlander had provided for local union and Farmers Union leaders took on new meaning for Negro and white community leaders, Negro and white student leaders who came together specifically to cope with problems of desegregation in a separate and unequal southern society. To experience, as a woman from Alabama expressed it, "democratic living in practice" which "for the first time in my life was mine to observe" gave reality to their goals.

Evaluating the Activities and the Program

Just as it was the groups who participated in the several crisis and movement-related educational programs who defined and redefined the goals of the program, so it was they who played a determining role in evaluating them. They decided the goals and they decided whether the goals had been reached. And since their goals were generally defined in terms of actions to be taken and leadership functions to be performed this evaluation could readily be made.

The evaluation process was an on-going one which began during the resident terms or workshops where students were encouraged to criticize, to modify what was being offered to meet their needs. In the relatively structured workers' education and Farmers Union terms this evaluation was accomplished, in part, by the Workers Council or Steering Committee which, based on the criticisms and suggestions of the students worked with the teaching staff to add new courses or to make existing ones more useful, more relevant. It was also accomplished by the continuing, free interaction between students and Highlander teachers between students and visiting labor or Farmers Union speakers or resource persons. Thus, for example, workers' education specialists Kermit Eby and A. A. Liveright recalled the way in which visiting speakers were "educated" by union leader-students who insisted on simple, clear presentations which they, in turn, could carry back to their locals.

In the case of the problem-centered civil rights workshops, college student and community leaders played the decisive role, workshop by workshop, in defining and redefining the problems which they were facing and kinds of resources which they needed to achieve their changing local and southwide movement goals.

The critical, the ultimate, evaluation of the several residential programs occurred when the local labor, Farmers Union or civil rights workers returned home. Here the criterion was a tangible one: what did students do with what they learned? The workers' education terms were evaluated, first and foremost, in terms of the local leaders who were elected to new and more responsible offices or were selected for staff positions with their unions. Thus, a report assessing Highlander's workers' education program, 1932-1942, notes of the students in that period, "about ninety percent are international union officials, local union officials or organizers in the South." The workers' education terms were evaluated, too, in terms of the returning students who developed local classes, edited shop papers, produced labor plays or assumed new roles as labor representatives in community organizations. The Farmers Union Program-in-search-of-a-movement was evaluated, like the workers' education program, in terms of the leadership roles assumed by returning students, whether in organizing locals and cooperatives or in working with labor groups on issues and projects of common interest. Evaluated in these terms, the Farmer-Labor School held at Highlander in 1947 which was a pioneering educational effort, bringing together for the first time Southern Farmers Union and industrial union members was a failure: no on-going farmer-labor cooperation was achieved by participants. The civil rights workshops, beginning in 1953 were evaluated in terms of the community leaders who desegregated local schools or took other kinds of action—some with far-reaching results—to challenge racial patterns. The Citizenship School was evaluated both in terms of the volunteer teachers trained in Highlander workshops and the number of adult students prepared by those teachers to be voting citizens—some 1,500 in forty southern communities in 1960-1961. And the college workshops were evaluated in terms of the movement-building actions taken by student sit-in leaders following their deliberations at Highlander—the formation of the Student Nonviolent Coordinating Committee, the carrying of Freedom Songs learned in workshops to movement groups across the South and the initiation of new Deep South protest and voter registrations projects involving broad participation and support, among adults as well as students, North as well as South.

The Educational and Social Significance of the Highlander Folk School: The Significance of Its Founding Ideas

The significance of the social-educational ideas and goals of Myles Horton and other radical educators associated with the Highlander Folk School was not the ideas per se, nor the new social order goals which they espoused. The call for a new social order was widespread in the midst of the Great Depression when Highlander was founded. And as Merle Curti has observed in his study, *The Social Ideas of American Educators*, "the eighteenth century revolutionary tradition has come down continuously in the social theory of educators."[1] It was rather their insistence on applying these ideas which was significant, which set Highlander and its leadership apart. In an America characterized by "the same cleavage between fact and ideal in educational circles as in other groups,"[2] they determined to "live out" their ideas of a democratic society within the School and to utilize the resources of the School to strengthen and support groups striving to achieve political and economic democracy in the larger society.

Their basic method also set them apart instead of relating to individuals—the method chiefly relied upon by educators hoping to improve society through the schools—they related their programs to mass movements. John Dewey, who had long urged that education be an instrument for social change and that teachers assume social leadership, watched Highlander's bold application of his ideas with considerable interest and admiration, calling the School, first, "one of the most hopeful social-educational plans that I know of"[3] and, later, "one of the most important social-educational projects in America."[4]

Its Special Strengths and Limitations as a Movement-related Adult Education Institution

As a small, independent adult education institution, committed to developing its educational programs in interaction with the organizations and movements which it served, the School demonstrated extraordinary flexibility, a capacity to allow its structure and functions as well as its learning activities to evolve out of that interaction. Thus, in the course of a thirty year history, it served as a "community folk school," a residential workers' education school for the southern labor movement, the educational center for the Farmers Union in the South and the center for developing programs and leadership for the southwide civil rights movement. Although a study of growth patterns of adult education institutions by William Griffith[5] indicates that mature institutions may continue to interact with new groups, may continue to return to the so-called "plastic stage," none of the sample of institutions which he examines exhibit the degree of flexibility which Highlander characteristically exhibited. Moreover, there is every reason to believe, based on the programs developed by the Highlander Research and Education Center which has succeeded it, that the Highlander Folk School would have continued to interact with new groups had its existence not been terminated.

In appraising the achievements of the Highlander Folk School in the field of adult education, the kinds of groups which it was able to reach deserve special attention. Most of the School's students over the years, in terms of level of education, occupation and income, and a considerable segment in terms of age and race as well, represent groups which studies indicate are least inclined to participate in adult education.[6] Mountain worker participants in the community and county programs with few exceptions had a grammar school education or less, and most lived at a subsistence level. A high proportion of Negro and white industrial workers and small farmer participants in the residential workers education and Farmers Union programs had a grammar school education or its equivalent and, in a low income South, came from low income groups. Participants in Highlander's Citizenship School classes were primarily middle-aged or older Negroes, primarily laborers and service workers, who were unable to qualify as voters because they were unable to read or write. These participants in Highlander programs possessed another and critical characteristic not touched upon in the several clientele analysis studies: they were, as Ward's writings had suggested to Horton long before, motivated to learn by the social problems confronting them.

In reaching these groups, especially in reaching large numbers through its extension programs, Highlander utilized movement teachers and settings in free and innovative ways. The educational activities were offered, wherever possible, in the setting where what was learned could immediately be used and by an educational staff which included teacher-leaders selected from among the group's peers.

The School demonstrated a continuing capacity, as well, to adapt and utilize the residential setting and program in innovative and effective ways. Thus, it combined picket line activities with residential courses to give reality to early workers education terms. It involved leaders from the same communities and colleges in an on-going series of workshops related to the civil rights movement in order to have maximum impact. And in a segregated South, it utilized the integrated setting as an "educative environment," bringing together Negro and white southerners who interacted freely and informally as they dealt with the problems confronting them. In these ways Highlander provided well-tested answers to at least two of the commonly expressed criticisms of residential adult education: that it represents a withdrawal from reality and that it tends to be superficial.

Although the School's interactions with groups involved in social movements produced innovative programs and reached the kinds of adults least likely to participate in adult education, there were limitations and risks inherent in those interactions. In choosing to relate its resources to social movements, Highlander was limited in what it could do by the limitations imposed by the movements themselves in any given period or stage of development. Thus, in spite of almost twenty years of interaction with southern labor, developing many of its early leaders, supporting its strike and organizing activities and responding to its growing educational needs, the School was unable to influence the trend within the increasingly institutionalized postwar movement toward narrowly conceived, organization-serving educational goals and programs.

Nor could the School, no matter how socially desirable the projected movement or how carefully conceived and executed the organizing and educational program, stimulate or help create a movement where none existed. Thus, Highlander's efforts over a six year period to nurture the development of a new southern movement, beginning with the Farmers Union and organized labor, failed. The goals of most small farmers were not movement goals and most members of the labor movement, although they may have seen some advantage to joining forces with farmers on legislative issues, sought no closer, ongoing alliance.

Finally, the movement-related institution could not avoid being fatally attacked by those who opposed the kinds of basic social change which its programs sought to bring about. The Highlander Folk School proved remarkably able to cope with the attacks of anti-labor groups over the years, in large part because of labor's defense, but also because the School had a broader base of support among liberal educators, religious leaders and others committed to the defense of civil liberties and civil rights. Yet, in spite of this continued support, it was unable to defend itself against the more sophisticated, more sustained array of attacks by powerful segregationist forces in the State and region. These forces were ultimately successful, in the fall of 1961, in using the courts to close the hated school for helping to develop leadership of the southwide civil rights movement.

Its Role in Relation to the Southern Labor and Civil Rights Movement

Probably no other American adult education institution has been so directly, so totally involved in the major social movements of its time and region nor had so great an effect upon them. The Highlander Folk School made its educational programs an organic part of the southern labor and civil rights movements. Its workers' education staff were pioneer organizers as well as educators for the emerging labor movement. Most of Highlander's resident students in the thirties and early forties came out of the School's direct interaction with and services to the new movement. And this little group of worker-students provided needed local and regional leadership for the first CIO Southern Organizing Drive and the building of industrial unions which followed.

The School which had served as the educational meeting place for Negro and white union and Farmers Union students became the "movement meeting place," the "movement rallying place" for early groups of local civil rights leaders. Especially after the Montgomery Bus Boycott in 1955, increasing numbers of local movement leaders came together at Highlander, strengthened their resolve, fashioned their plans and went home to build, in a few short years, a southwide nonviolent direct action movement. And, in a few short months, the college students, whose sit-in demonstrations in February 1960 took the Negro as well as the white South by surprise, not only met and made plans at Highlander, but learned the songs of their singing movement and began to build their southwide organization and program which were to profoundly challenge political and social patterns.

So interrelated were the Highlander Folk School and the civil rights movement that its programs, like the effects of those programs, could not be terminated when the School itself was terminated. Its Citizenship School program was carried on and greatly expanded by a movement organization, the Southern Christian Leadership Conference. Nor could the radical social-educational ideas which had been the basis for the institution be terminated. With the basic requirements—"the place, the people, the situation"—readily fulfilled, Highlander's educational leadership was ready, in the fall of 1961, to start again and "let it grow."

Notes

PREFACE

1. *Social Action Collections at the State Historical Society of Wisconsin: A Guide*, Madison, State Historical Society of Wisconsin, 1983). The Highlander collection includes extensive archival material, microfilm and tape recordings. In addition, there are a number of collections which are Highlander-related, e.g. SNCC/Civil Rights workers Ella Baker, Julian Bond and others; papers of social activists Carl and Anne Braden and the Southern Conference Educational Fund; and papers of progressive unions and union leaders, including the Packinghouse Workers and its president, Ralph Helstein.

CHAPTER ONE

1. Although the Highlander Folk School was closed and its charter revoked by action of the Tennessee courts in the fall of 1961, shortly beforehand, a new institution, the Highlander Research and Education Center, with most of the same staff and Executive Council, obtained a charter and began operation.

2. In seeking funds for a proposed "Southern Mountains School" in early 1932, the founder of the Highlander Folk School projected the role which it would play in the training of labor leaders in southern industrial areas. This was five years before the newly-founded Congress of Industrial Organizations began its organizing drive in the South.

3. In identifying the kinds of questions to be raised, the framework for analysis of curriculum decision-making of Ralph Tyler and his associates (*Basic Principles of Curriculum and Instruction* [Chicago: University of Chicago Press, 1950]) has proved helpful.

4. *op. cit.*

5. Claudia Lewis in her volume, *Children of the Cumberland* (New York: Columbia University Press, 1940), describes the community nursery school

developed under her leadership as well as something of other local social-educational activities.

Septima Clark in her autobiography, *Echo in My Soul* (New York: E.P. Dutton & Co., 1962), gives a rather full account of her role in the development of Highlander's Citizenship School and other civil rights programs.

Guy Carawan, Highlander song leader, and his wife in their annotated collection of songs of the freedom movement, *We Shall Overcome!* (New York: Oak Publications, 1963) and in their recent volume, *Ain't you got a right to the tree of life?* (New York: Simon and Schuster, 1966), document with song and photograph as well as with words both Carawan's role and the role of Highlander programs in relation to the student movement and to the people of Johns Island, South Carolina.

6. Samuel Everett, ed., *The Community School*, Society for Curriculum Study (New York: D. Appleton-Century Co., 1938) contains references to the Highlander Folk School by the editor as well as a chapter, "The Community Folk School," by Myles Horton.

7. Volumes in the field of workers education which make reference to Highlander are: Theodore Brameld, ed., *Workers Education in the United States*, Fifth Yearbook of the John Dewey Society (New York: Harper and Brothers, 1941); Florence Schneider, *Patterns of Workers Education* (Washington, D.C.: American Council on Public Affairs, 1941); T. R. Adam, *The Workers' Road to Learning* (New York: Harper and Brothers, 1940) and A. A. Liveright, *Union Leadership Training* (New York: Harper and Brothers, 1951).

8. Two doctoral studies on residential adult education refer to the Highlander Folk School: Robert Schacht, "Residential Adult Education—An Analysis and Interpretation" (unpublished Ph.D. dissertation, University of Wisconsin, 1957) and Harold Judd Alford, "A History of Residential Adult Education" (unpublished Ph.D. dissertation, University of Chicago, 1966). In addition, Highlander is referred to in a long essay, *The Residential School in American Adult Education* by Royce Pitkin (Chicago: Center for the Study of Liberal Education for Adults, 1956).

9. Theodore Brameld, A. A. Liveright and Royce Pitkin were able to write from first-hand knowledge of the Highlander Folk School.

10. Hulan Glyn Thomas, "A History of the Highlander Folk School, 1932-1941" (unpublished Master's thesis, Vanderbilt University, 1964).

11. Journalist Bill Moyer's two-part interview, "The Adventures of a Radical Hillbilly, An Interview with Myles Horton" (PBS, June 5 and 11, 1981) is a notable example.

12. "You Got to Move," Lucy Massie Phoenix, Producer and Co-Director-Editor (New York: First Run Features, 1986). This award-winning film focuses on Highlander's Citizenship School and other civil rights programs and its more recent Appalachian programs as viewed by staff and participants as well as by Myles Horton.

CHAPTER TWO

1. This data was obtained informally and over a period of time as well as from specific interviews which are noted.

2. The purpose of the school is to be found in a letter of May 1932 to potential contributors to the "Southern Mountains School" and in numerous early reports of the Highlander Folk School.

3. Howard Odum, *Southern Regions of the United States* (Chapel Hill, N.C.: University of North Carolina Press, 1936), pp. 98-107.

4. Myles Horton, outline for an untitled talk at the Southern Summer School for Women Workers, c. 1933 (in the files of the School).

5. C. Vann Woodward, "The Historical Dimension," *The Burden of Southern History* (New York: Vintage Books, 1960), p. 28.

6. Dana-Ford Thomas, Interview with Myles Horton, March 9, 1959.

7. *Ibid.*

8. *Ibid.*

9. A. Horton, Interview with Myles Horton, November 1966.

10. In 1936, Mrs. Stockton ran unsuccessfully for the Governorship of Tennessee on a Socialist Party ticket.

11. D. Thomas, Interview.

12. *Ibid.*

13. Letter from Myles Horton to Mrs. J. Malcolm Forbes, Boston, Massachusetts, May 25, 1932.

14. D. Thomas, Interview.

15. *Ibid.*

16. Letter to Mrs. Forbes.

17. D. Thomas, Interview.

18. In notes Horton made while travelling in one such county, he observes: "Scott Countians were for the Union. Yes siree! When the State of Tennessee seceded, the patriotic old county squires duly met and duly drew up resolutions seceding from Tennessee. The vote was unanimous. They called their government 'The Independent State of Scott.'" (Untitled notes, June 28 1928.)

19. Letter from Myles Horton to P. J. Andreason, Brooklyn, New York, October 13, 1934.

20. A. Horton, Interview.

21. John C. Campbell, *The Southern Highlander and his Home* (New York: Russell Sage Foundation, 1921), p. 281.

22. A. Horton, Interview.

23. Merle Curti, "William James, Individualist," *The Social Ideas of American Educators* (3rd ed.; Patterson, New Jersey: Littlefield, Adams & Co., 1965), p. 454.

24. John Dewey, *Reconstruction in Philosophy* (New York: Holt, 1921), p. 156.

25. D. Thomas, Interview.

26. *Ibid.*

27. W. Rauschenbusch, *Christianity and the Social Crisis* (New York: Macmillan Co., 1912) pp.408-409.

28. ". . . not that he understood them particularly," Horton explained years later, "but somehow he encouraged me and he said that I was right to go ahead. (Thomas, Interview.)

29. Reinhold Niebuhr, "Build a New Party!" *The World Tomorrow*, XII (December 1929), 483.

30. Reinhold Niebuhr, "Property and the Ethical Life," *The World Tomorrow*, XIV (January 1931), 19.

31. Not coincidentally, the first fund-raising letter for the "Southern Mountains School" had as its address the editorial offices of *The World Tomorrow* and its signers included Niebuhr and Thomas.

32. Through this interest, he met Columbia University graduate student James Dombrowski who was doing a doctoral study, later a book, on *The Early Days of Christian Socialism in America* (New York: Columbia University Press, 1937). Dombrowski joined the Highlander staff in 1933. See p. 45.

33. A. Horton, Interview.

34. *Ibid.*

35. Robert Morss Lovett, "Progressives at Cleveland," *The New Republic*, LXXI (July 20, 1932), 258-259.

36. John Dewey, *Democracy and Education* (New York: Macmillan Co., 1907), p. 140.

37. *Ibid.*, p. 226.

38. George Counts, "Education—For What?" *The New Republic*, LXXI (May 25, 1932), 41.

39. Eduard Lindeman, *The Meaning of Adult Education* (New York: New Republic, Inc., 1926), p. 166.

40. A. Horton, Interview.

41. W. J. Cash, *The Mind of the South* (New York: Alfred A. Knopf, Inc., 1941), p. 345.

42. Tom Tippett, *When Southern Labor Stirs* (New York: Jonathan Cape and Harrison Smith, 1931), p. 125.

43. *Ibid.*, p. 294.

44. Named the Highlander Folk School when founded in 1932. Several years after its founding, Myles Horton wrote, "The School has participated actively in local strikes and members of its staff have been on the scene of every important strike since 1929. This experience resulted in the crystallizing of the main purpose of the School: to train rural and industrial leaders from the Southern rank and file itself." (Myles Horton, "A Tennessee Folk School," *The Inter-Collegian and Far Horizons* (May 1935), p. 197.

45. A. J. Muste, "My Experience in Labor and Radical Struggles of the Thirties," *As We Saw the Thirties*, ed. by Rita James Simon (Urbana: University of Illinois, 1967), p. 192.

46. A. Horton, Interview.

47. *Ibid.*

48. Lester F. Ward, *Dynamic Sociology* (New York: D. Appleton Company, 1883). It is interesting to note that C. Hartley Grattan in a rather recent collection of writings significant to adult education includes a selection from Ward: Lester F. Ward, "The Sociology of the Diffusion of Knowledge," *American Ideas About Adult Education*, ed. by C. Hartley Grattan (New York: Bureau of Publications, Teachers College, Columbia University, 1959), pp. 111-115.

49. Ralph H. Turner, "Introduction," *Robert E. Park on Social Control and Collective Behavior* (Chicago: Phoenix Books, University of Chicago Press 1967), p. xiii.

50. Letter from Myles Horton to Dr. Samuel Everett, Northwestern University, October 22, 1936.

51. A. Horton, Interview.

52. *Ibid.*

53. Lindeman, pp. xvi-xvii.

54. Campbell, pp. 297-298.

55. Holger Begtrup, Hans Lund and Peter Manniche, *Folk High Schools of Denmark and the Development of the Farming Community* (London. Oxford University, 1926), p. 83.

56. *Ibid.*, p. 92.

57. D. Thomas, Interview.

58. Letter from Fred Brownlee, American Missionary Association, to Myles Horton, University of Chicago, May 18, 1931.

59. Letter from Reinhold Niebuhr, Union Theological Seminary, to Myles Horton, University of Chicago, March 26, 1931.

60. Writing of the Danish economy shortly after he returned to the United States, he observed, "There is very little national wealth, but what there is, is more equally distributed." Of the effects of the depression, he wrote, Denmark has been "hard hit by the Depression," but, he added, "There have been no foreclosures or evictions. Schools have not been effected" [*sic*] and "any employed worker can take a five months course at the expense of the government and his union." (Myles Horton "Denmark" p. 4 [typed manuscript]).

61. Myles Horton, untitled notes (in the files of the School), c. December 1931.

62. *Ibid.*

63. *Ibid.*

64. *Ibid.*

65. Myles Horton, untitled notes for an article (in the files of the School), c. 1942.

CHAPTER THREE

1. Myles Horton, "The Highlander Folk School," c. 1933 (in the files of the School), p. 3.

2. Letter from Horton to Andreason.

3. Horton, "The Highlander Folk School," p. 3.

4. Myles Horton, untitled notes, c. 1931 (in the files of the School).

5. *Ibid.*

6. *Ibid.*

7. Myles Horton, "Christmas night, 1931, Copenhagen, Denmark" (in the files of the School).

8. *Ibid.*

9. D. Thomas, Interview.

10. For a fuller description of Dr. Johnson, her role in the community where the School was located and her relationship to the Highlander Folk School, see pp. 37-38.

11. Letter from Reinhold Niebuhr to potential contributors to the "Southern Mountains School," May 27, 1932. See Appendix I in the original of this dissertation for copy of letter.

12. While a growing number of educators in the thirties were talking about the community school idea, their notions of a community related curriculum had little in common with the program evolved by the Highlander Folk School. In a major volume on *The Community School*, editor-educator Samuel Everett concludes that most of the curricula described represent a transition "from an academic subject-matter type of orientation to a more functional type of program" (p. 448). He takes special note of the "divergent" point of view expressed by Myles Horton who identifies "educational and social concerns with the furtherance of the interest of the working class" (Everett, p. 453).

13. Don West was a graduate in theology from Vanderbilt University whose interest in education, like Horton's, had taken him to Denmark. He remained at the School some six months and then left to found his own workers' school in Georgia.

14. Myles Horton, "The Highlander Folk School" (in the files of the school, n.d.).

15. Odum, in describing the South's deficiencies, along with "marginal and submarginal lands and folks and its deficiencies in technological wealth," emphasized the "lack of sufficient numbers of matured man and women possessing experience, technical skill and interregional contacts" (Odum, p. 17).

16. National Emergency Council, *The Economic Conditions of the South*, Report to the President (Washington, D.C., July 25, 1938).

17. *Ibid.*, p. l.

18. Vera McCampbell, "Educational Survey of the Elementary Schools of Grundy County, Tennessee" (unpublished M.S. thesis, University of Tennessee, 1935), p. 107.

19. Myles Horton, "The Community Folk School," *The Community School*, p. 269.

20. Charles E. Allred *et al., Grundy County, Tennessee: Relief in a Coal Mining Community* (Tennessee Agricultural Experiment Station, University of Tennessee, April 1936), p. 6.

21. *Ibid.*, p. 22.

22. Robert Lowry and Hershal Macon, *Effect of Proposed National Forest Purchase on County Finances, Survey 7, Grundy County, Tennessee*, Tennessee Valley Authority, Social and Economic Division, Research Section (Knoxville, Tennessee: Tennessee Valley Authority, December 1936), p. 6.

23. Allred *et al.*, p. 4.

24. The individual studies tend each to be a catalogue of problems. A Department of Agriculture study, for example, states with regard to health problems, "Inadequate medical attention, poor diet, ignorance of hygiene, inadequacies of housing . . . contribute to high death rate and tend to undermine the economic efficiency of the population" (U.S. Department of Agriculture, *Economic and Social Problems and Conditions of the Southern Appalachians*, Miscellaneous Publications No. 205 [Washington, D.C.: U.S. Government Printing Office, 1935] p. 5).

25. M. McDonald, Notes on Family Visits, Fall and Winter, 1934-35. (Miss McDonald, a social worker by training, was one of a number of interested persons who volunteered their services to the School during the early years for shorter or longer periods of time.) (In the files of the School.)

Although the house-to-house visits to learn about living conditions, incomes, etc., of Summerfield families was not undertaken until the Fall of 1934 when a young woman with a social work background joined the Highlander staff for a brief period of time, the same essential conditions existed when the school was founded in 1932.

26. Myles Horton, untitled article, "Highlander Folk School," October 16, 1935 (in the files of the School).

27. McDonald.

28. Myles Horton "The Community Folk School," p. 270.

29. Of this tradition of individualism, John Campbell wrote in a major study of the Southern Highlander, "The temper of the Highlander is in fact the independent democratic temper of the frontiersman, caught between the ridges and hardened by isolation into an extreme individualism, while the frontier itself has passed on westward and vanished" (Campbell, p. 93).

30. Myles Horton, "The Community Folk School," p. 270.

31. *Ibid.*

32. Odum, p. 53.

33. Claudia Lewis in *Children of the Cumberland* gives a warm and sympathetic picture of family life in Summerfield, its strengths and its weaknesses. For information about Miss Lewis, a Highlander staff member and community nursery school teacher, see p. 58.

34. Humor as well as problems and poverty are recorded in community notes and staff reports of the period.

35. John C. Campbell discusses at some length the role of religion in the life of the mountaineer, his love of the scriptures, the stories, the hymns. He points out the rarity of the "infidel." Even the most "confessedly wicked," observes Campbell, "intends to achieve salvation some day" (Campbell, pp. 176-80).

36. McDonald.

37. Interview with May Justus, Summerfield community, August 15, 1963. Miss Justus, university-educated Tennessean, grew up in the Smokey Mountain area of East Tennessee where her parents and grandparents had also lived. She is the author of a number of children's books about the people of the region, their folk tales, music and customs.

38. Zilphia Horton, "Henry Thomas, Man of the People," c. 1945 (in the files of the School).

39. *Chattanooga Times*, August 14, 1892.

40. James Dombrowski, Interview with I. H. Cannon, First President of UMW Local, Tracy City, c. 1935 (in the files of the Highlander Folk School).

41. James Dombrowski, Interview with John Cleek, ex-miner and UMW member, c. 1935 (in the files of the Highlander Folk School).

42. Myles Horton, "The Community Folk School," p. 271.

43. *Ibid.*, p. 272.

44. Dr. Johnson not only turned over her home and property to Myles Horton for the Highlander Folk School, but took a keen interest in all phases of its educational activities until her death in 1956, at the age of ninety-two. The files of the School contain many letters from her, especially in the early years, which she described as "a test of your experiment" (letter to James Dombrowski, January 22, 1935). She not only served on the Board of Directors (a legal rather than an administrative body) in the early period, and gave advice on many matters, but attended a number of Highlander workshops as a student. In 1954, at the age of ninety, she wrote in regard to that experience, "What Highlander did for me was to accustom me to association with people of a class and race I had not known before, except as they served me"(letter to Myles Horton, c. April 1954).

45. One of the teachers was May Justus. The other was also a university educated East Tennessean, Vera McCampbell.

46. Myles Horton, "The Community Folk School," p. 270.

47. Interview with May Justus and Vera McCampbell, Summerfield Community, Tennessee, August 15, 1963.

48. Looking at the unsuccessful efforts of many devoted workers in the mountains—missionaries, philanthropists, educators—John C. Campbell, himself an educator of mountain people, warned against the pitfalls of "benevolent overlordship" and urged future workers in undertaking any plans for the betterment of mountaineers to "take the people themselves into account as contributors to their own welfare" (Campbell, pp. 299-300).

49. In writing about educational environments, Dewey warned, "Whether we permit chance environments to do the work, or whether we design environments for the purpose makes a great difference." He emphasized that "any environment is a chance environment . . . unless it has been deliberately regulated with reference to its educative effect" (Dewey, *Democracy and Education*, p. 22).

50. Myles Horton, "Folk School Idea," c. 1933 (in the files of the School). (Typed.)

51. These work aspects are specifically described in a report on the first year's activities: "All the work in the school is shared by teachers and students alike. All do some manual or housework everyday. There are no salaries. All are giving their time and services to the common cause. Life here is simple. Almost ascetic at times." Myles Horton, "The Highlander Folk School" (Monteagle, Tennessee, n.d.). (Mimeographed.) Although the School was located in Summerfield, its post office address was Monteagle, Tennessee, a town some two miles from Summerfield.

52. Myles Horton, "Folk School Idea."

53. Myles Horton, "The Highlander Folk School," (in the files of the School, n.d.). (Typed.)

54. *Ibid.*

55. "Community Night" c. November 1933 (in the files of the School).

In referring to the committee the staff report indicates "The school offered to advise and assist but made no effort to see that programs were arranged for. There were a number of lectures scattered throughout the year and two plays" (*ibid*).

56. A mimeographed flyer during this period announced a very special guest speaker and a very unorthodox subject for one of the Sunday evening religious meetings: "Reinhold Niebuhr will speak on 'Will the Depression end?'" (in the files of the School).

57. One of these music teachers was Rupert Hampton, graduate of Union Theological Seminary, who was a specialist in religious music and the organ, but came to know a good deal about mountain music while on the Highlander staff.

58. Early records indicate that two of the families whose children were in these classes, the Marlowes and the Eldridges, actually acquired some sort of pianos (McDonald).

59. The wrought iron craftsman who was also a puppeteer was Malcolm Chisholm who came to the School in 1933.

60. Myles Horton, "The Community Folk School," p. 272.

61. Myles Horton, "Experimental Education," c. 1933 (in the files of the School), p. 2.

62. *Ibid.*

63. *Ibid.*, p. 1.

64. An early report from the volunteer librarian reports that shelves had been made for 852 hooks, but indicating that there could he no system for pamphlets until the School "can afford to purchase pamphlet files." The report indicates that not only Summerfield, but a number of other neighboring communities were using the library. "It would have been helpful" the librarian ends, "if there had been a definite time when the librarian would be in the library for the benefit of helping people find books" ("Report of Highlander Folk School Library, August 15, 1933-August 15, 1934" [in the files of the School]).

65. By January 1933, Myles Horton and Don West could report to their friends, "Our four regular boarding students . . . have become an accepted part of the community and each is in charge of some phase of community activity." Along with Dorothy Thompson's activities and those of a student referred to as "Martin" who was holding meetings in behalf of a new social order, Myles Horton's sister, also a student, was working with a dramatics groups which, they reported, "will be producing plays to help with regular Saturday community evenings." The fourth student "our thirty-five year old student," they indicated "left school recently when he got a few days work on the road," but, they emphasized he took books and other material with him and "is urging on his fellow workers the necessity of a labor organization with a social vision " (Myles Horton and Don West "New Years Greeting from the Highlander Folk School" [in the files of the School]). (Mimeographed.)

66. The School files contain considerable correspondence on the meeting of the Fellowship of Southern Churchmen which James Dombrowski and others on the Highlander staff helped to plan.

67. According to a School report on the Summer School, "The consensus of opinion was that education for a new social order can best he effected by a large number of centers similar to the Highlander Folk School," ("Present Activities and plans of the Highlander Folk School," c. Summer 1933 [in the files of the School], p. 1). Along with holding the Southern Socialist Summer School at Highlander, staff members of the School assisted with the education program of the Socialist local which was formed in Summerfield in 1933 ("Report of Community and School Activities," c. November 1933-November 1934 [in the files of the School, p. 1).

68. Among the many visitors and speakers listed during one early year were: Lloyd Huntington, TVA, Wilson Dam, Alabama; Mrs. Naomi Mitchison, poet and writer, London, England; George Bidstrup, Barnholm Folk School, Denmark; Marguerite Butler, John C. Campbell Folk School, North Carolina; John Edelman, Amalgamated Hosiery Workers' Union, Philadelphia; Kate Thorncroft, writer, Sussex, England; Rev. Oscar Hawes, Unitarian Church, Brookline, Massachusetts; Leo Huberman, editor, *Monthly Labor Review*; Rev. and Mrs. Albert Barnett, Scarritt College, Nashville; Mr. and Mrs. Norman Thomas, New York City; W. E. Zeuch, Resettlement Administration, Washington, D.C.; Chorus of Tennessee State A & I College (Negro), Nashville and students and faculty from numerous other colleges and universities including New York University, University of Louisville, Swarthmore College, the International People's College of Denmark, College of the Ozarks and Berea College (Highlander Folk School, "Report of Activities for 1935" [in the files of the School]).

CHAPTER FOUR

1. By 1939, through its organizing and political education activities, the School related to most relief workers, miners and other members of organized labor in the community and county—some 1,000 in all (Myles Horton, "Mountain Men," c. 1939 [in the files of the School], p. 21).

2. The Charter was granted by the State of Tennessee on October 20, 1934.

3. Minutes of Staff Conference, Highlander Folk School, July 29-31, 1934.

4. For a summary of cash receipts and expenditures for the first fiscal year, see Appendix I in the original of this dissertation, p. 336-337.

5. For a list of early contributors, see Appendix I in the original of this dissertation, pp. 334-335.

6. For a copy of a sample of subsequent financial statements, 1941-1959, see Appendix I in the original of this dissertation, pp. 338-345.

7. The teaching staff worked without salaries until 1957.

8. Myles Horton, "About Finances," *Highlander Fling*, No. 1 (December 1933). (Mimeographed.)

9. In early 1935, Dr. Johnson wrote, "I have made these last years a sort of test of your experiment." In the same letter, she concluded, "Don't worry about the property [because] none of my family would contend any wish of mine and they know that I want it all for the good of the community" (letter from Dr. Lilian Johnson to Myles Horton, January 22, 1935).

10. The land in Allardt was a gift of Socialist farmer J. K. Stockton who had come to know Horton when he was teaching summer Bible school classes in the mountains as a college student.

11. Myles Horton, untitled manuscript, Highlander Folk School, Monteagle, Tennessee, c. 1933 (in the files of the School), p. 2.

12. *Ibid.*

13. Interview with Myles Horton, December 1, 1963.

14. Horton frequently used this phrase borrowed from Dewey in his early notes, meaning apparently education with a social purpose, in this case education directly related to the problems of the people of Summerfield.

15. A Highlander staff member calculated that a striker with a good-sized family, such as Henry Thomas, "was making about enough for each member of his family to spend about two and a half cents apiece per meal" (Dorothy Thompson, untitled manuscript, August 3, 1933 [in the files of the Highlander Folk School], p. 1).

16. "Statements made at Meeting of Cumberland Mountain Workers' League held November 30, 1933" (in the files of the School), p. 1.

17. Interview with Henry Thomas, Summerfield Community, August 15, 1963. A more detailed account of the strike is to be found in an unpublished manuscript by the educational director. It also included a description and background information on other community and county educational and organizing activities of the school during the years 1932-1939 (Myles Horton, "Mountain Men").

18. Dorothy Thompson, "Notes on Bug-wood Strike," July 5-19, 1933 (in the files of the School), p. 1.

19. *Ibid.*

20. *Ibid.*, p. 2.

21. *Ibid.*

22. "Constitution of the Cumberland Mountain Workers' League," unpublished document, n.d. (in the files of the School).

23. Letter from Will L. Brown, Secretary, Cumberland Mountain Workers' League, to President Franklin D. Roosevelt, May 3, 1934 (copy in the files of the School).

24. Zilla Hawes (ed.), *Committee on Correspondence: Bulletin No. 1* (August 1, 1933), p. 2. Apparently no *Bulletin No. 2* followed this first three-page, type-written edition. Since the editor, Zilla Hawes, an organizer-educator for the Highlander Folk School, was very much involved with steelworkers in the Knoxville, Tennessee, area, it may be that she, like her contributors, got too busy to continue it.

25. Letter from Roy Lane, President, Cumberland Mountain Workers' League, to Secretary of Labor Frances Perkins, November 14, 1933 (copy in the files of the School).

26. *Ibid.*

27. *Ibid.*

28. The article, "Woodcutters Take Wage Troubles to Washington" appeared in the *Chattanooga News*, November 22, 1933; "New Deal Slow in the Tennessee Hills," in the *Reading Labor Advocate*, November 24, 1933; "Tennessee Products Company Ousts Workers," *Bridgeport Herald*, December 10, 1933. There were articles in *The Milwaukee Leader* on November 18, 1933, and in *The Mid-West American*, November 2, 1933.

A Federated Press release for May 8, 1934, entitled "Tennessee Strikers Kids Shrivel Up, as Faith Dies in NRA," includes a history of the Cumberland Mountain Workers' League and reviews its efforts to get help in Washington (in the files of the School). (Mimeographed.)

29. Letter from W. L. Brown, Secretary, Cumberland Mountain Workers' League, May 3, 1934.

30. Myles Horton, unpublished and untitled article, c. November 1933 (in the files of the School).

31. Letter from W. L. Brown, Secretary, Cumberland Mountain Workers' League to President Roosevelt, May 3, 1934.

32. Interview with Henry Thomas, Summerfield Community, August 15, 1963.

33. Interview with Myles Horton, August 5, 1963.

34. Letter from Myles Horton, Highlander Folk School, to Dr. Lilian Johnson, December 26, 1933.

35. Florence E. Parker, "Consumers' Co-operation in the United States, 1920 to 1936," *Monthly Labor Review*, XLVII (August 1938), 223-39.

36. Dr. Johnson was vitally concerned with the School's educational efforts with regard to cooperatives and with sharing her experience and background. In her first letter after the community classes had begun, she wrote, "I do hope you can carry out your idea of the cooperative store. But do start it right, so many have failed because they have not followed the Rochdale principles" (letter from Dr. Lilian Johnson, Memphis, Tennessee, January 2, 1934). She tells of her own efforts in some detail in another letter (letter from Dr. Johnson to James Dombrowski, January 22, 1935) and in an article for the Farmers' Union Newspaper which the School published (Lilian Johnson, "History of Co-op," *The Tennessee Union Farmer*, November 1947, pp. 5-6).

37. "Application from the Cumberland Mountain Cooperative, located near Monteagle, Tennessee," to the Federal Relief Administration, manuscript, January 5, 1934 (copy in the files of the School).

38. Letter from Harvey P. Vaughn, Tennessee Valley Authority, January 12, 1934 (copy in the files of the School). In the same letter, Vaughn explained, "The people who are at the head of this school are native mountain people who have gone to Eastern educational institutions and have returned to work among the people whom they know best."

39. Cumberland Mountain Co-operative, "Questionnaires," n.d. (in the files of the School).

40. Even brief summaries where the cooperative is a short paragraph under "Recent Activities, Community" stress the broader purpose of the venture. "The purpose is to raise living standards and give actual experience in cooperative forms of living where mutual welfare of the entire community replaces the motive of

individual gain through competition" ("Highlander Folk School," c. Winter 1934-35 [in the files of the School], p. 1).

41. Letter from Brown to President Roosevelt, May 3, 1934.

42. "Report on the Highlander Folk Cooperative (cannery)," c. August 1934 (in the files of the School) p. 1.

43. *Ibid.*, p. 2.

44. *Ibid.*

45. The administrative head of the Highlander Folk School, James Dombrowski, worked painstakingly with the community cooperators in preparing the application. The statement endorsing the Highlander Folk Cooperative and expressing "sympathy and accord with the Cooperative Movement" also promised that the local officials "will advise the State Director of Self-Help regarding local conditions from time to time." (untitled document, November 23, 1934 [copy in the files of the School]).

46. An account of the withdrawal of funds and the reaction of the conservative press and business interests is contained in a documented narrative by Myles Horton ("Mountain Men," pp. 5-7).

In a long and bitter letter to the *Chattanooga News*, P. M. Horton, father of Myles Horton, who had come to the School in 1933 to be in charge of its farm and who, with his wife, was an active member of the several community cooperatives, wrote of the "many hours, days, yes, weeks" which the people of the community had spent "working to formulate a cooperative that would be best adapted to their needs." And after finally receiving the grant, "then came these false prophets from the East and other places . . . crying from the housetops saying the Highlander Folk School had applied for and received a grant of $7000" (letter from P. M. Horton, April 12, 1935).

47. "Edgerton Hits Fund for Reds," *Knoxville Journal*, March 31, 1935.

48. M. Horton, "Mountain Men," p. 5.

49. *Ibid.*, p. 6.

50. "Relief Grant to Radical School Stirs Citizenry," *Chicago Daily Tribune*, March 26, 1935.

51. Minutes of staff meeting, October 29, 1935, Highlander Folk School (in the files of the School).

52. Letter from Berthe Daniel, Highlander Folk School, to Dr. Toyahiko Kagawa, Nashville, Tennessee, January 7, 1936. Miss Daniel was, for a time, Highlander's librarian and teacher of Workers' Literature.

53. For a perceptive volume about the nursery school, the mountain children and their parents, see Lewis' *Children of the Cumberland*. Miss Lewis, who came to Highlander in 1938 from the Bank Street School in New York served as the first director of the Summerfield nursery school, 1938-1940.

54. Letter from W. E. Cheek, Secretary, Tennessee Federation of Labor, to Will Brown, President, Cumberland Mountain Workers' League, May 26, 1934.

CHAPTER FIVE

1. According to a report by the Tennessee Taxpayers Association, "The loose methods of handling the county's financial affairs together with rumors and official State reports of recurring shortages in some of the county offices . . . have caused an almost complete breakdown of the county government in general" (Tennessee Taxpayers Association, Inc., "The Finances and Management of Government of Grundy County, Tennessee" (Nashville, Tennessee, 1934).

2. The wages paid WPA workers in Grundy County represented the lowest wage rate in the Southeast where the highest wage paid was $75.00. Lowest wage rate in the North and West in 1935 was $40.00 and the highest was $94.00. According to an economist of the period, national relief authorities based the differential on "the lower level of living in the South," but government studies indicated that the cost of living was "not markedly different" (Broadus Mitchell, *Depression Decade* [New York: Rinehart & Co., Inc., 1941], p. 322).

3. Berthe Daniel, personal letter, August 23, 1936 (in the files of the School).

4. Lewie Vaughn "My Work in Grundy County," *We the Students*, Highlander Folk School, Winter Term, 1939, p. 69. (Mimeographed.)

5. These meetings, widely publicized in the county by means of handbills, were actually educational meetings to explain and discuss the need for unions. In order to assure widespread attendance, prominent union leaders were the featured speakers, including the District Organizers for the Mine Workers and the Common Laborers' Union, along with staff members from the Highlander Folk School.

6. The Highlander staff person, R. B. Tefferteller (who was also a specialist in square dancing and recreational activities with union groups) gave very specific instructions to the local WPA representative with whom he and the county field worker were working. "If you feel it would he unwise to meet at the court house, you must decide and inform the men otherwise . . . Be sure that you get word out to all the jobs through one or two good men as we mentioned during our short visit two weeks ago" (Letter from R. B. Tefferteller, Member Local 891, Monteagle, Tennessee, September 22, 1936).

7. Letter from W. D. Vaughn "carried by Lige Birdwell" to the President of the Palmer Local Union, July 4, 1936 (in the files of the School).

8. Berthe Daniel, personal letter.

9. Letter from Aubrey Williams, Assistant Administrator, Works Progress Administration, Washington, D.C., June 22, 1936. (Mimeographed.)

10. Minutes of the Joint Meeting of Executive Committees from the three Hod Carriers' and Common Laborers' Locals—Monteagle, Tracy City and Palmer, Tennessee, Miners' Hall, Tracy City, July 11, 1936 (in the files of the School).

11. Letter from the Hod Carriers' and Common Laborers' Union Locals, Grundy County, Tennessee, July 14, 1936 (copy in the files of the School).

12. Myles Horton, "Mountain Men," p. 10.

13. The WPA District Director wrote to the State Administrator during this period: "As District Director, I should like to state that the organization of Common Laborers, contrary to reports elsewhere, has, up to this writing, been a source of cooperation and unity in our program. Therefore, if it is possible in any

way to increase the wage scale for Tennessee or this district, I strongly urge that this be done. . . ."(*Ibid.*)

14. *Ibid.*, p. 12.

15. "WPA Workers Organize," *The Highlander Fling*, No. 9 (September 1936), p. 2.

16. Highlander Folk School, "Extension," *Report for 1936*, p. 3.

17. The music graduate was Zilphia Mae Johnson, later Mrs. Myles Horton. For more information about her and her role as a Highlander staff member, see p. 101, and pp. 117-121.

18. The member of the Clothing Workers' local was (Miss) Walter Brady. For more information about her, see pp. 101-102.

19. Community member students were: Henry Thomas, Mr. and Mrs. Ed Eldrige and William Marlowe.

20. "Report on Highlander Folk School for 1935" (in the files of the School).

21. "The School and Community," *Highlander Folk School Review* (Highlander Folk School, Winter Term, 1938), p. 28.

22. Of the informal interaction as it affected both resident students and community, it was emphasized: ". . . Classes, library and all social functions are always open to the people of the community. This spirit of neighborliness has meant much to both the welfare of the community and the progress of the school . . ." (*ibid.*)

23. The identification of resident students with workers in the community is apparent in the student newspaper and articles coming out of the resident sessions. As expressed by the students, "We feel that the problems of the community workers are ours, because our interests are so interlocked"(*ibid.*).

24. The activities described were participated in by community and resident students in the Summer Session, 1935 ("Report on Highlander Folk School for 1935").

25. Reports of the All-Southern Conference indicate that both students and faculty from Highlander served on committees of the Conference (Minutes of the All-Southern WPA and Relief Workers' Conference, March 22, 1936, Central Labor Hall, Chattanooga, Tennessee [in the files of the School]). (Mimeographed)

26. Myles Horton, "Mountain Men," p. 11.

27. *Ibid.*, p. 16.

28. *Ibid.*, p. 18.

29. See Chapter VII, pp. 102–111.

30. "A Newspaper for All Workers on WPA Projects in Grundy County, Tennessee," *The WPA Worker*, Vol. I, No. 1, Tuesday, August 2, 1938.

31. Myles Horton, "Mountain Men," p. 18.

32. Highlander Folk School Summary of Activities, January-October, 1938 (in the files of the School), p. 5.

33. Of the victory, the same writer observed: "Announcing a post primary rally 'at the cross tie pile' in Monteagle, the Workers' Alliance could head its multigraphed handbills: 'The Working People of Grundy County have Won a Vital Victory.' This is by no means a common occurrence; in fact there is probably no

other county in the Valley's hundred where such a thing could happen, yet." (Wilson Whitman, *God's Valley* [New York: Viking Press, 1939], p. 262.)

34. Lewie Vaughn, p. 68.

35. There are voluminous files on this bitter dispute between Col. Berry and local officials and unions, month by month, incident by incident—newspaper accounts, Highlander staff memos, complaints of union members, correspondence between government and union officials—which clearly document these anti-union actions of the State WPA Administrator.

36. Each issue of *We the People* contained lively, often humorous descriptions of meetings and activities under such headings as "A Day at the Relief Office." There were also progress reports on the stay-in, editorials on the strike goals and quotations from various spokesmen among the strikers on their grievances.

37. *We the People*, February 10, 1939.

38. Letter from James Dombrowski, Secretary, Highlander Folk School, February 10, 1939.

39. Lewie Vaughn, p. 68.

40. Letter from Dillard King, President, Workers' Alliance, Monteagle, Tennessee, March 1, 1939.

41. *Ibid.*

42. This class was taught by Mary Lawrence who came to Highlander in 1938 as a community worker and in subsequent years became a teacher in the county workers' education program and, later, the director of the School's southwide extension program. See Chapter IX.

43. *Work*, February 25, 1939.

44. Mary Lawrence, "Report on Community Program, September 1938-August 1939," Highlander Folk School (in the files of the School).

45. Minutes of the Grundy County Welfare Meeting, February 26, 1939 (in the files of the School).

46. *Ibid.*

47. In March 1940 a study of the county was undertaken by the APA (*Public Welfare and Related Problems in Grundy County, Tennessee* [Chicago: American Public Welfare Association, April 1940]). (Mimeographed.) The first-hand survey of "the county's economic and social assets, liabilities and possibilities" was heralded by the *Highlander Fling.* "This project," it stated, "is the kind of thing Highlander has been advocating as a step toward long-range planning to relieve the unhappy condition of Grundy County" ("Welfare Group Is Making Study of Grundy County," *Highlander Fling*, II [March 1940], 1). The *Chattanooga Times* also rejoiced at the announcement of the study of "Tennessee's greatest relief headache" to be carried out, they noted, in cooperation with State and Federal agencies. ("Experts to Study Grundy Problems," *The Chattanooga Times*, March 14, 1940.)

Yet when the Welfare Association study was completed, the County's future seemed, if possible, more bleak than before. At a meeting to examine the findings, the Survey Supervisor grimly predicted of the mountain area, "you can expect either poverty or a large amount of Federal or State aid is sometime to come." Although there was discussion at the same meeting of the need for re-forestation, the need to build up agriculture, the need to encourage people to raise more food and the possibility of developing new industries, the Survey Supervisor posed as an essential aspect of any solution: "migration as soon as there is pick-up in any other place in the country" (Minutes of Meeting of the Welfare Association study of Grundy County, September 9, 1940, Nashville, Tennessee [copy in the files of the School]).

48. There continued to be a cooperative study group. Quilting and pottery cooperatives were organized and there was a cooperative garden for families no longer on relief.

49. Myles Horton, "Mountain Men," p. 21.

50. Myles Horton, "The Community Folk School," p. 278.

51. The staff member was Elizabeth ("Zilla") Hawes. See Chapter VI.

CHAPTER SIX

1. Untitled material on the School's contribution to the CIO which was apparently used as an enclosure with fund-raising letters, n.d. (in the files of the School). (Mimeographed.)

2. For data on numbers of students in resident terms and extension classes, 1932-1947, see Appendix II in the original of this dissertation, pp. 347-349.

3. For names of labor members of the Executive Council in 1940 and for names of members of the Executive Council in various periods, see Appendix III in the original of this dissertation, pp. 357-360.

4. In 1944, approximately $8,400 was received from unions in board, tuition, field services and contributions out of a total income of $15,000 (Summary of Annual Report, p. 2.) In 1945, about $9,700 out of $19,000 was received from unions. For a financial statement for 1945, see Appendix I in the original of this dissertation, p. 339.

5. Untitled material on the School's contributions to the CIO.

6. Records of the resident students for the first five month term, November 1932 to April 1933, are incomplete and unclear. One account states, "Only three resident students stayed the full term. The total number of students living at the School was eight" (Myles Horton, "The Highlander Folk School," p. 5). Since the resident term opened with only one student, the first statement is clearly inaccurate.

7. Myles Horton, "Experimental Education," p. 2.

8. J. Charles Poe, "Socialist School Seeks Converts in Mountains," *The Chattanooga News* February 1 1933. An early letter about the School by visiting staff member John Thompson remarks on the same diversity within the resident group: "The intensive work is done with a small group of resident students who will become leaders in labor and rural work. In the group . . . there is no stereotype: some are college graduates, one finished only the sixth grade. One very intelligent boy thinks he is an atheist; one very zealous girl from the hills is tying up Socialism with her Fundamentalist religion and is going back to use the evangelistic method with her new ideas" (Letter from John Thompson to Professor Arthur Swift, Union Theological Seminary, February 6, 1933).

9. "Don West and Myles Horton Barred from County School Buildings by Orders of the Chairman," *The Cumberland Outlook*, December 15, 1932.

10. Miss Willie Lehr, unemployed nurse from nearby Gruetli, Tennessee, the author of this letter (*The Cumberland Outlook*, January 6, 1933) became a Highlander resident student in 1938.

11. Myles Horton, "The Highlander Folk School," p. 6.

12. "Tennessee Governor Refused Mediation But Will Not Hesitate to Send Troops to Wilder Field," *United Mine Workers Journal*, XLIII, No. 22 November 15, 1932), 11.

13. Letter from Myles Horton to the Editor, *Nashville Tennessean* (December 1, 1932).

14. The files of the School contain not only interview data gathered from miners and sworn affidavits of the inequitable distribution of Red Cross relief to strikers and non-strikers, but historical data on the history and financial status of the Fentress Coal and Coke Co.

15. Horton and West wrote a number of articles for the labor press describing conditions at Wilder and, later, the slaying of a local union leader. One of the resident students also published articles in the labor press.

16. An article in *The Progressive Miner* (c. March 1933), entitled "Tennessee Miners hear Norman Thomas Speak," described the March 5 meeting. "Thomas was brought to Tennessee at the request of Miles [sic] Horton, director of the Highlander Folk School, who first turned public attention to the Wilder strike last year."

17. Myles Horton, "The Highlander Folk School," p. 7.

18. *Ibid.*

19. "Capitalism Hit by Tiny School for Hill People," *The Chattanooga Times*, December 3, 1932.

20. "Socialist School Seeks Converts in Mountains," *The Chattanooga News*, February 1, 1933.

21. Letter from Myles Horton to P. J. Andreason.

22. A file of time schedules for residential sessions from 1932-1939 indicates the many efforts to change and improve the daily schedule which continued to be flexible and subject to modification by each new group of resident students in consultation with the teaching staff.

23. "The Highlander Folk School," c. Summer 1933, p. 2. (Mimeographed.)

24. Dorothy Thompson "Criticism of HFS," c. August 1934 (in the files of the School), p. 2.

25. For further information about Zilla Hawes and her activities as a labor organizer and Highlander staff member, see pp. 86, 89, 108-109.

26. Myles Horton "The Highlander Folk School," p. 7.

27. Myles Horton, untitled manuscript, c. 1942 (in the files of the School), p. 3.

28. "New Buildings at Highlander School," *The Chattanooga News* May 3, 1933.

29. "Socialists' School Set to Spread Party Creed," *The Chattanooga Times*, March 24, 1933.

30. Myles Horton, "Community Education," pp. 2-3.

31. The other staff member was James Dombrowski who had, as has been indicated, major administrative responsibilities.

32. "Report on Winter Session of Ten Weeks, March 14-May 25, 1934" *Highlander Folk School* (in the files of the School), p. 1.

33. *Ibid.*, p. 2.

34. *Ibid.*, p. 1. A small note in the Report on the session indicates that classes in public speaking were taken over by Myles Horton towards the end of the ten weeks when one of the teachers had to be away on a fund raising trip. One suspects that such educational experiences as the cross tie speeches were arranged during that period.

35. "Highlander Folk School Summer School Report and Summary of Other Educational Activities, September 1933-1934," p. 6. (Mimeographed.)

36. Evalyn Howard, "As a Student Sees It," *The Highlander Fling*, No.4 (May 1934), p. 2. (Mimeographed.)

37. The National Recovery Act became effective June 16, 1933.

38. Karl Lore, "Where Is Labor Organizing?" *The New Republic*, LXXIX (July 4, 1934), 200.

39. "Highlander Folk School Summer School Report and Summary of Other Educational Activities, September 1933-1934."

40. *Bread and Roses: The Story of the Shirtworkers 1933-1934* (New York: Amalgamated Clothing Workers of America, n.d.), p. 21. The young teacher-organizer later wrote her own history of the successful organizing of the Liebowitz Shirt Factory of Knoxville in the face of threats, firings, a company union and a lock-out. "At that hour, the Amalgamated Clothing Workers took root," she noted, "to grow until it embraces the 1800 clothing workers of Knoxville, the shirt and clothing makers of Nashville, Chattanooga, Atlanta and all the little runaway factories hidden in upland hollows." (Zilla Hawes, "The Amalgamated Comes South," n.d. [in the files of the School], p. 6.)

41. "Highlander Folk School Summer School Report and Summary of Other Educational Activities, September 1933-1934."

42. An editorial entitled "Textile Workers 'Betrayed' but not 'Fooled,'", concluded, "The strikers are wiser now. Many have come to look upon the NRA as a 'new deal' for the boss only." (*The Highlander Fling*, No. 2 [January 1934], p. 2.)

43. "Hosiery Mill Defies Board," *The Highlander Fling*, No. 2 (January 1934), p. 2.

44. Letter from J. Dombrowski to R. Niebuhr, Union Theological Seminary, New York, February 27, 1934.

45. Letter from Zilla Hawes to Local 90, Knoxville, Tennessee, December 11, 1933.

46. "Summer School," *The Highlander Fling*, No. 3 (May 1934) p. l.

47. "Summer Term Closes," *The Highlander Fling*, No. 4 (September 1934), pp. 1-2.

48. "Highlander Folk School Summer School Report and Summary of Other Educational Activities, September 1933-1934," p. l.

49. *Ibid.*, pp. 1-2.

50. *Fighting Eaglet*, No. l (June 1934) p. l.

51. *Ibid.*

52. "Highlander Folk School Summer School Report and Summary of Other Educational Activities, September 1933-1934," p. 4.

53. *Ibid.*, p. 2.

54. *Ibid.* It might be noted that a class in English Grammar was discontinued and, instead, "afternoon hours were spent in tutoring a number of the workers who found it difficult to do the necessary reading and writing" and "who had difficulty in understanding the regular classes."

55. *Fighting Eaglet*, No. 5 (July 1934), p. 1.

56. *Ibid.*, No. 1 (June 1934), p. 2.

57. "Highlander Folk School Summer School Report and Summary of Other Educational Activities, September 1933-1934," p. 3.

58. *Ibid.*

59. Rupert Hampton, "Public Speaking," *Ibid.*, p. 2.

60. Minutes of Staff Conference, July 29-31, 1934, Highlander Folk School.

CHAPTER SEVEN

1. Oliver Carlson, "Why Textiles Vote to Strike," *The New Republic*, (September 5, 1934), 95-96.

2. "The Textile Strike, Looking Forward and Backward," *Highlander Fling*, No. 5 (November 1934), pp. 3-4. (Mimeographed.)

3. These articles, sometimes not dated, were clipped from the *Chattanooga News*, *Chattanooga Labor World*, *Nashville Tennessean* and *Atlantic Journal* in January and February 1935.

4. James Dombrowski, "Report on Activities for 1935 and Winter Term of 1936," March 1936 (in the files of the School).

5. *Ibid.*

6. "Report on Extension Activity," Highlander Folk School, February 14–April 12, 1935 (in the files of the School).

7. Hilda Hulbert, "Excerpts from diary kept during Strike," February 1935.

8. "Report on Extension Activity."

9. As Horton explained years later, "The best results in work with students have been achieved by taking students from a situation where an extension program is being carried on and sending them back from a resident situation with additional enthusiasm and equipment." (Myles Horton, "The Highlander Folk School Extension Program," August 10, 1942 [in the files of the school]).

10. *Ibid.*

11. Highlander Folk School, "Winter Term Announcement, January 11–March 6, 1936." (Mimeographed.)

12. Highlander Folk School,"Program for 1936" (in the files of the School).

13. Highlander Folk School, untitled report, June 10, 1936. (Mimeographed.)

14. *Ibid.*

15. *Highlander Fling*, No. 9 (September 1936). (Mimeographed.)

16. *Labor Advocate* (Nashville), November 12, 1936.

17. Actually, an article by a participant indicates that picket line classes were held somewhat earlier that same year among members of a striking Amalgamated Clothing Workers' local in Norfolk, Virginia (Griselda Kuhlman, "A Picket Line Class," *Affiliated Schools Scrapbook*, I [June 1936], 18-19).

18. Highlander Folk School, "Field Work Programs 1933-1942" (in the files of the School), p. 2.

19. Letter from Edna Champion, Atlanta, to Zilla Hawes, April 5, 1936.

20. By 1946, an article in *The Nation* telling of Bradford's educational experience at Highlander, described him as "one of the men responsible for the remarkable growth in union membership which has taken place in the South in the past five years." (Alden Stevens, "Small-town America," *The Nation* [June 21, 1946], p. 784.)

21. Interview with Matt Lynch, Nashville, Tennessee, September 26, 1964.

22. An article many years later describes graphically Lynch's harried career as an early organizer for the Textile Workers and his more recent career as Secretary of the Tennessee Labor Council (Max York, "Labor's Tall Man on the Hill." *The Nashville Tennessean*, July 1, 1962.)

23. Myles Horton, "Textile Drive," n.d. (in the files of the School). It is clear from such items as a memorandum on "Projects under Consideration for Fall 1937" and rather specific plans for the summer term that Horton's decision was a sudden one. A *Highlander Fling* for Spring 1937 carried a front page article on the Fifth Annual Summer Term to be held May 10-July 3. Among the projects under consideration were an experimental extension program in mining villages, a workcamp for college students, a Labor-Cooperative Conference and the establishment of a community nursery school.

24. James Dombrowski, "Confidential Memorandum," Highlander Folk School, May 8, 1937 (in the files of the School).

25. Following the announcement of the TWOC drive, Horton recommended that the facilities of the School "be placed at the disposal of the . . . drive for weekend conferences and organizing meetings" and that he and Zilphia Horton be "at the disposal" of the organizing committee "for the duration of the textile drive, provided it does not last more than 1937." In terms of other staff members, he agreed that Dombrowski should "remain in charge of the School" and a new staff member, Ralph Tefferteller, "in charge of the community and county," but, he concluded, "If it can be worked out," they "should be sent out as regular organizers later." (Myles Horton, "Recommendations," n.d. (in the files of the School).

26. Highlander Folk School, "Field Classes for Labor Unions, an Experiment in Workers' Education," Monteagle, Tennessee, 1937, p. 1.

27. *Ibid.*, p. 6.

28. *Ibid.*, p. 5.

29. "Workers Education Rally, La Follette, Tennessee, and Vicinity, May 29-July 10, 1937" (in the files of the School).

30. Highlander Folk School, "Field Classes for Labor Unions," p. 2.

31. *Ibid.* p.3

32. *Ibid.* p 6.

33. *Ibid.*

34. *Ibid.*, p. 3. According to the report of the field library, there were ten books borrowed the first week and some fifty during the fourth week when circulation was at its highest.

35. "Spitting Contest Features Fair," *Advance*, August 1937.

36. "'The People of the Cumberlands,' a sound movie by Frontier Films," a Highlander report in 1938 announces, "had its premiere at the New School for Social Research on May 2nd . . . During the same week the film was shown at the White House and to friends of the School in Washington"(Highlander Folk School "Summary of Activities" January through October 1938, p. 9).

37. "La Follette Union Carries Out Successful Education Program," *Advance*, August 1937.

38. Highlander Folk School, "Field Classes for Labor Unions," p. 6.

39. Minutes of Highlander Staff Meeting, Asheville, North Carolina, September 12, 1937.

40. Letter from James Dombrowski to Myles Horton, Lumberton, North Carolina, September 24, 1937. The same letter urges Horton to "resign your organizing work" and "come back to help clear up the mess at the School." The "mess" was undefined.

41. James Dombrowski, "Confidential Memorandum."

42. Zilla Hawes, "Report for the Year 1937" (in the files of the School).

43. Fred Lassie, untitled manuscript based on a series of interviews with Myles Horton, 1950 (in the files of the School), pp. 18-19.

44. *Ibid.*, pp. 22-23.

45. *Ibid.*, p. 23.

46. TWOC, New York, N. Y., February 24, 1938.

47. "Mystery Veils Secret Probe of Folk School," *Chattanooga News*, February 6, 1937.

48. *Chattanooga Free Press*, February 7, 1937.

49. *Ibid.*

50. *Highlander Fling*, No. 10 (Spring 1937).

51. As James Dombrowski once expressed it in a letter to Dr. Lilian Johnson, "The same vested interests which obstruct and attempt to defeat our work also fight all progressive social movements . . . the measure of our effectiveness probably is to be found in the vigor of the opposition," c. 1935.

CHAPTER EIGHT

1. For an excellent analysis of the problems besetting the southern textile drive of the CIO, 1937-1941, see chapter ix, "Renascence of Textile Unionism", in Walter Galenson's *The CIO Challenge to the AFL, A History of the American Labor movement, 1935-1941* (Cambridge: Harvard University Press, 1961).

2. *CIO News*, March 26, 1938.

3. "CIO Attacks Filibuster on Lynching Bill," *CIO News*, January 29, 1938.

4. "Farmers, Workers Sign Pact," *Ibid.*, January 6, 1938.

5. "South Carolina League," *Ibid.*, February 19, 1938.

6. "Southern Churchmen Speak Out for Labor," *Ibid.*, January 6, 1938.

7. "Tennessee Labor School Completes Winter Term," *Ibid.*, March 5, 1938.

8. In a contemporary survey, Mark Starr, Education Director of the International Ladies Garment Workers Union, indicated that many trade unions during this period "have started and enlarged their educational activity and introduced new and varied patterns." (Mark Starr, "The Current Panorama," *Workers Education in the United States* [New York: Harper and Brothers, 1941], p. 102.)

9. Beginning in 1943, the Textile Workers Union of America had a full-time Southern Educational Director and in 1946, a full-time Director of Education for the State of Georgia. However, they had more union-sponsored educational programs in the South than many other unions. The only other year-around labor school in the South, Commonwealth College in Mena, Arkansas, which drew its students from throughout the country, was closed in 1940.

10. Three issues of the *Highlander Fling* during the winter resident term of January and February 1938 contained brief paragraphs about each of the worker-students and what they hoped to learn while at Highlander (*Highlander Fling*, Vol. I, Nos. 12-14 [January-February 1938]).

11. "Speakers featured at Resident Term," *The Highlander Fling*, Vol. II (September 1939).

12. *Highlander Folk School Review*, Monteagle, Tennessee, Winter Term, 1938. (Mimeographed.)

13. Highlander Folk School, *We the Students*, p. 9.

14. *Ibid.*, p. 8. Lists of "Union Problems" compiled term by term from 1938-1944 are contained in the files of the School and provide a kind of panoramic summary of new and persisting problems confronting southern unions during this period.

15. "Collective Bargaining " *Highlander Fling*, No. 11, December 1937.

16. William Fincke, "Creative Expression, A Symposium," *Journal of Adult Education*, VII (April 1935), 179-187.

17. "Highlander Folk School, A School for Workers in the South," 1939 Winter Term—January 9 to February 19, Summer Term—July 2 to August 13, Monteagle, Tennessee.

18. Brameld, pp. 98-101; 146-147; 162.

19. *Highlander Folk School Review*, p. 16.

20. *Ibid.*, p. 15.

21. Brameld, p. 146.

22. Highlander Folk School, *Five Plays About Labor* (Monteagle, Tennessee, August 1939), p. 1. (Mimeographed.)

23. "Lolly Pop Pappa," unlike the other plays, was written by Zilphia Horton, including the original music.

24. *Five Plays About Labor*, p. 1.

25. They were listed and described for example, in the Labor Education Service "Annotated List of Pamphlet Materials for Workers Classes" (New York: Affiliated Schools, 1938).

26. Letter from Fred Ramsey to the Highlander Folk School, c. February 1939.

27. Letter from Billye Bailey, ILGWU, Atlanta, to Myles Horton, September 23, 1939.

28. Letter from Jackie Kwallek, Lexington, Kentucky, to the Highlander Folk School, August 21, 1939.

29. This and other militant songs by Don West were included in Highlander song books for a decade or more.

30. The files of the Highlander Folk School contain words to a number of songs gathered on the picket lines, beginning with the Wilder strike. Some of these were printed in the student newspapers and some were included in the early mimeographed song books compiled by Zilphia Horton. Songs such as "The Union's Call" written by a Harriman striker and 1934 resident student, Hershel Phillips, to the tune of "The Red River Valley" were popular with strikers and students and appeared in various Highlander song books.

31. *We the Students*, p. 16.

32. Brameld, p. 147.

33. *We the Students*, pp. 20-21. Between resident terms, Zilphia as well as Myles Horton were much in demand at meetings of various southern unions. In a two week trip "through the Carolinas and Georgia," an issue of the *Fling* notes, "Myles spoke to local unions of the TWOC, Hosiery Workers and Workers Alliance" and at the same meetings, Zilphia sang and led groups in singing workers' songs." ("Hortons visit Unions," *Highlander Fling*, Vol. II, No. 1, January 1939.)

34. "Highlander Folk School Members Attend Textile Meet," *Highlander Fling*, Vol. II, No. 2, June 1939.

35. An article in the school paper notes that *Labor Songs* was published by a union press, *The Industrial Leader*, Winston-Salem, North Carolina, "on union water-marked paper." ("Zilphia Horton Edits Song Book for Union," *Highlander Fling*, Vol. II, No. 3, September 1939.)

36. Highlander Folk School, *Our Lives* (Monteagle, Tennessee, May, 1940), p. 1.

37. *Ibid.*, pp. 19-20.

38. *Ibid.*, pp. 25-27.

39. *I Know What It Means* (Monteagle, Tennessee, October 1940), pp. 12-13.

40. "Annotated List of Pamphlet Materials for Workers Classes."

41. Fincke, p. 186.

42. Lewie Vaughn, Highlander Folk School application form, Winter Term, 1939.

43. Dillard King, Highlander Folk School, application form, Winter Term, 1939.

44. Telegram from John Pate and Claud Willis, Lumberton, North Carolina, to Myles Horton, February 17, 1939.

45. Jimmie Woodward, Highlander Folk School application form, Summer Term,1939.

46. Miss Mason was a daughter of the aristocratic old South, descendant of the Randolphs of Virginia.

47. For the Mexican-American's view see Telesforo Oviedo, "Pecan Shelling in Texas, A Mexican Speaks," *We the Students*.

48. Brameld, p. 99.
49. *Highlander Folk School Voice*, Vol. I, No. 1 (January 23, 1939). (Mimeographed.)
50. Brameld, p. 99.
51. W. T. Couch, "Southerners Inspect the South," *New Republic*, XCVII (December 14, 1938), 168-169.
52. In 1940 and for some years thereafter, Mrs. Roosevelt contributed $100 to the Highlander Folk School annually for a scholarship to be given to a promising student from the southern labor movement. She also stood by the School on several occasions when it was under attack by anti-labor and segregationist groups and, in 1957, she visited the School on the occasion of its twenty-fifth anniversary.
53. In 1938, for example, there were three American Federation of Hosiery Workers' Institutes offered at labor schools—one in Pennsylvania at the Bryn Mawr Summer School and two in the South. In 1939, there were five institutes—two in Pennsylvania, two in the South and one at the University of Wisconsin School for Workers (Eleanor Coit and Mark Starr, "Workers' Education in the United States," *Monthly Labor Review*, XLIX (July 1939), 1-21.
54. "Dr. Graham will speak on February 5," *Highlander Fling*, Vol. II, No. 1 (January 1939).
55. "Education to Play Big Role," *Hosiery Worker*, Vol. XV (May 13, 1938).

CHAPTER NINE

1. L.R. Mason, "It's not the same old South!" *The CIO News*, IV (November 17, 1941), 14.
2. Alice Hansen, "Action and Study," *Workers' Education in the United States*, p. 118.
3. Mary Lawrence, *Education Unlimited* (Monteagle, Tennessee: Highlander Folk School, 1945), p. 9.
4. *Ibid.*, p. 4.
5. *Ibid.*
6. Mary Lawrence, "A Study of the Methods and Results of Workers' Education in the South," 1947 (in the files of the School), pp. 79-80.
7. *Ibid.*, p. 82.
8. Mason, p. 14.
9. It was former Highlander student and Executive Council member Matt Lynch who suggested, when he was helping to organize for the Federation of Hosiery Workers in New Orleans, that the Louisiana CIO Director might obtain help from the School in developing an educational program for its newly-organized locals. (Interview with Mary Lawrence Elkuss, Park Forest, Illinois, November 7, 1963.)
10. Minutes of the New Orleans Industrial Union Council Meeting, April 7, 1941, p. 2. (Mimeographed.)
11. Mason, p. 14.
12. Mary Lawrence describes the New Orleans extension program in "A Study of Methods and Results of Workers' Education in the South," pp. 80-89.

13. *Ibid.*, p. 93.

14. In seeking to help new officers, committeemen and stewards better understand the duties and procedures related to their several jobs, Mary Lawrence looked around in vain for a handbook which would meet their needs and then wrote her own. The handbook, *How to Build Your Union* (New Orleans, Louisiana: CIO Industrial Union Council, February 1942) continued to be used for a number of years as a guide and for orientation of new members.

15. Mary Lawrence, Report on New Orleans Extension Program, April 10-May 10, 1941 (in the files of the School), p. 1.

16. *Ibid.*

17. *Ibid.*

18. Mary Lawrence, "Evaluation of the New Orleans Extension Program," c. 1942 (in the files of the School), p. 3.

19. *Ibid.*

20. Lawrence, "Report on New Orleans Extension Program, April 10-May 10, 1941," pp. 1-2.

21. Lawrence, "A Study of Methods and Results of Workers' Education in the South," p. 84.

22. *Ibid.*

23. Four promising officers of New Orleans area locals were selected by Mary Lawrence to attend the Highlander Folk School Spring term in 1941. She wrote back to the School soon after they returned from the term, "They have already given a good account of themselves and I think they are going to be a tremendous help to me!" ("The New Orleans Program," *Highlander Fling*, III [July 1941], 2.)

24. *How to Build Your Union, An Officers, Committeemen and Stewards' Handbook.* This *Handbook* was circulated in mimeographed form before it was published and sold by the Council for fifteen cents per copy.

25. Mary Lawrence, "Fourth Session—New Orleans Educational Program," c. March 1942 (in the files of the School), p. 2.

26. Letter from Mary Lawrence to Robert Cruden, Publicity Director, United Rubber Workers of America, September 8, 1942.

27. Lawrence, "Evaluation of the New Orleans Extension Program," p. 1.

28. A 1941 Highlander report notes that of the seven students who attended resident terms during the year, "two have been employed for fulltime union work in New Orleans and one is assistant educational director" (Highlander Folk School, Ninth Annual Report [Monteagle, Tennessee: Highlander Folk School, 1941], p.17). An interview (some twenty years later) with the student who became assistant director indicated that as Sub-Regional Director of the Steelworkers he was still involved in labor education and was an important influence in politics and race relations in New Orleans (interview with Barney Morel, New Orleans, December 1962).

29. Lawrence, "A Study of the Methods and Results of Workers' Education in the South," p. 89.

30. "Highlander's Position in the Southern Labor Movement," 1942 (in the files of the School).

31. *Ibid.*

32. Schneider.
33. In examining the programs of Highlander and the Summer Schools at Bryn Mawr and in the South, she notes that the latter, although recognizing the function of collective bargaining, "do not train their students in its techniques to the same extent as the Highlander School." Nor do they emphasize as strongly, she observes, "the concept of the new social order" (*ibid.*, p. 59).
34. *Ibid.*, p. 29.
35. Adam, pp. 131-132.
36. Letter from John Dewey, Columbia University, to the Editor, *Nashville Banner*, October 12, 1940.

CHAPTER TEN

1. Highlander Folk School, Ninth Annual Report, p. 1.
2. With the staff depleted both by departures to the armed forces and to other organizations, Myles Horton, Zilphia Horton and Mary Lawrence, together with a variety of new and short-term teachers and college student assistants managed to carry on field programs such as the Atlanta Action for Victory Program, special resident sessions including a summer seminar to train students for jobs in union education, Junior Union Camps and War Workers Vacation Camps, a seminar on Labor Journalism, week-end institutes on "Labor's Part in Winning the War" and a short-lived, one-man Research Department which furnished former students and other union subscribers with summary information on rationing, production committees, War Labor Board actions and current developments in labor legislation.
3. "Statement of Purpose, Program and Policy," *Highlander Fling*, XIV, No. 1 (March 1942), 1.
4. Minutes of Executive Council Meeting, January 8-9, 1944, Highlander Folk School, Monteagle, Tennessee (in the files of the School).
5. George Soule, "Sidney Hillman," *The New Republic*, CXV, No. 3 (July 22, 1946), 67.
6. "Farmer and Worker," *American Federationist*, LI, No. 3 (March 1944), 27-30.
7. "Tennessee Labor United for Political Action," *Highlander Fling*, V, No. 4 (March 1944), 3.
8. Minutes of Staff Meeting, December 3, 1943, Highlander Folk School, Monteagle, Tennessee (in the files of the School).
9. Minutes of Executive Council Meeting, January 8-9, 1944.
10. "Plan for 1944," Highlander Folk School (in the files of the School).
11. Minutes of Executive Council Meeting, January 8-9, 1944.
12. Also participating were four college students, members of a seminar on workers' education.
13. Letter from Virginia Hart, Knoxville, Tennessee, June 5, 1944.
14. Evaluation of the CIO Term, May, 1945 (in the files of the School).
15. Highlander Folk School, Annual Report, 1944, p. 2.
16. Southern regional directors, through appeals to international unions, raised some $2,000 to underwrite this first CIO School.

17. Evaluation of the CIO Term, 1945 (in the files of the School), p. 1.

18. The first interracial term at Highlander was a United Auto Workers term in 1944. This, so far as the School was able to determine, was the first such interracial workers' term in the South.

19. Kermit Eby, "General Education for Economic Well-being," *Junior College Journal*, XVIII, No. 9 (May 1948), 511.

20. Evaluation of the CIO Term, 1945, p. 4.

21. Seven years later, the CIO made much of holding its first "integrated institute" in Alabama ("Bias Tossed Out as Workers from 7 States Attend Alabama CIO School," *The CIO News*, June 9, 1952.)

22. Evaluation of CIO Term, 1945, p. 3.

23. Minutes of Executive Council, January 20-21, 1945.

24. W.D. Moore, *60 Million Jobs*, Southern CIO School, 1945, p. 6.

25. Emile M. Zoller, "Highlander Does a Swell Job," *International Oil Worker* (July 1945).

26. Highlander Folk School, Report of 1945 Activities, p. 2. (Mimeographed.)

27. Report of Education and Publicity Committee, adopted by Sixth Annual Convention, Tennessee State Industrial Union Council, Nashville, Tennessee, n.d. (in the files of the School).

28. Minutes of the Executive Council, April 1946, Highlander Folk School, p. 2.

29. Staff minutes note, "Myles will write Dalriple and Van Bittner about term, inviting them down and tieing it in with Southern organizing drive" (Minutes of Staff Meeting, March 31, 1946, Highlander Folk School [in the files of the School]).

30. Thomas Ludwig, an Arkansas-born graduate of the University of California, joined the Highlander staff in January 1946.

31. The Union Publicity Workshop was taught by Joseph Gaer, Publications Director of the CIO-PAC.

32. A series of Antioch College students came to Highlander during the war for their three-month work periods. One of these was Aleine Austin who, as a result of her Highlander experience, undertook to write a popular history of the American labor movement, *The Labor Story* (New York: Longmans, Green and Co., 1949), widely used in workers' education classes.

33. Mary Lawrence, "Follow up of Southern CIO School at Highlander Folk School," 1946, p. 149.

34. "Southern CIO Term," *Highlander Fling*, VI, No. 2 (July 1946), 1.

35. "500,000 Organizing Goal Set by Textile," *CIO News*, April 29, 1946.

36. Philip Taft, *Organized Labor in American History* (New York: Harper & Row Publishers, 1964), p. 589.

37. Minutes of Executive Council Meeting, April 1946.

38. Minutes of Staff Meeting, July 29, 1946.

39. Woodward, *The Burden of Southern History*, p. 177.

40. George Googe, "Southern Drive Is Launched," *American Federationist*, LIII. No. 6 (June 1946), 6.

41. A.G. Mezerik, "The CIO Southern Organizing Drive," *The Nation*, CLXIV January 11, 1947), 38-40.

42. Minutes of Executive Council, April 1946, pp. 2-3.

43. Highlander Folk School, Program for 1946. (Mimeographed.)

44. The only four week CIO Summer School was held at Highlander. Other Schools were held at the University of Indiana, Danebod Folk School in Minnesota, the University of Wyoming, Pendle Hill in Pennsylvania, Hampton Institute in Virginia, Montebello Vacation Camp near St. Louis and Hudson Shore Labor School, New York.

45. *Local 1025 Round-up*, Southern CIO Term, Vol. I, No. 1 (July 5, 1947).

46. Letter from George Guernsey, Research and Education Department, CIO, Washington, D.C., June 11, 1947.

47. "Student Evaluation of Class Taught by Anthony Smith," CIO Term, 1947 (in the files of the School).

48. Zilphia Horton, untitled manuscript, 1947 (in the files of the School). The original title of the song was "We Will Overcome." It was later changed and sung by the civil rights movement as "We Shall Overcome." See pp. 236, 243, 245-246.

49. Mary Iemmoia, *We're on the Freedom Trail* (Monteagle, Tennessee: Highlander Folk School, 1947), p. 1. (Mimeographed.)

50. Clay Ledford, *Ibid.*, p. 3.

51. Bob Price, *Ibid.* p. 9.

52. Liveright, pp. 50-51.

53. *Ibid.*, p. 156.

54. Minutes of Staff Meeting, n.d. (August 1947), Highlander Folk School, Monteagle, Tennessee (in the files of the School).

55. *Ibid.*

56. Minutes of Executive Council Meeting, January 14-15, 1948, Highlander Folk School, Monteagle, Tennessee (in the files of the School).

57. Carol Ware, in a 1946 study for the American Labor Education Service, reported the following university and college-sponsored labor education programs in the South: residential institutes offered at the University of North Carolina and the University of Virginia, beginning in 1945; labor education classes included in the evening extension program of Hampton Institute and the University of Virginia; a course in Union Problems available through People's College of Atlanta University and labor education programs proposed, but not yet offered by the University of Alabama, Extension Division and Marshall College, Huntington, West Virginia (*Labor Education in Universities* [New York: ALES], pp. 95-102).

58. Letter from W. H. Crawford, United Steelworkers of America, Atlanta, December 22, 1947. This decision, in effect, in the South of the forties meant that the programs would be offered on a segregated basis since the colleges were segregated.

59. Minutes of Executive Council Meeting, January 14-15, 1948, p. 1.

60. *Ibid.*

61. Highlander Folk School, Annual Report (Monteagle, Tennessee, 1948), p. 2. (Mimeographed.)

62. Minutes of Executive Council Meeting, January 14-15, 1948, p. 4.

299

63. In 1950, two other independent labor education institutions in the South, the Southern School for Workers, established in 1926 as the Southern School for Women Workers, and the Georgia Workers' Education Service found it necessary to close. With their closing, an Annual Report observed, Highlander was now "the only workers' education center in the South" (Highlander Folk School, Eighteenth Annual Report, p. 2). Actually, it was in large part because it had changed from solely a workers' education center that it managed to survive. 64. Soule, p. 67.

65. Robert Bendiner, "Surgery in the CIO," *The Nation*, CLXIX (November 12, 1949), 458-59.

66. "The Purge in the CIO," *New Republic*, Vol. 121, Number 20 (November 14, 1949) p. 5.

67. Bittner's reaction was the subject of a lengthy Highlander staff meeting in the latter part of October 1947.

68. The former CIO organizer explained his thinking in a letter to the Director of the CIO Organizing Committee for Tennessee, "As you already know, I am not making lightly this move from the CIO Organizing Committee to Highlander Folk School. The considerations that prompted that move arose from my earnest conviction that I could render my best service to the labor movement, to the farm movement and to the South." (Letter from Louis Krainock, Highlander Folk School, April 6, 1948, to Paul Christopher.)

69. Letter from Myles Horton, December 16, 1948.

70. *Ibid.*, MM and SW is the Mine, Mill and Smelter Workers.

71. Letter from Stanley Ruttenberg, Director, Research and Education Department, CIO, Washington, D.C., to Myles Horton, July 5, 1949. See Appendix III in the original of this dissertation, pp. 364-65 for copy of letter.

72. Minutes of the Executive Meeting, January 22-23, 1949, Highlander Folk School (in the files of the School). See Appendix III in the original of this dissertation, p. 366, for copy of letter.

73. Letter from Stanley Ruttenherg, July 5, 1949.

74. Myles Horton, memorandum to Highlander Executive Council, September 1949. (Mimeographed.) For a copy of memorandum and correspondence with Ruttenberg, see Appendix III in the original of this dissertation, pp. 361-65.

75. *Ibid.*

76. "Highlander Folk School Statement of Purpose, Program and Policy," April 5, 1950. (Mimeographed.) See Appendix III in the original of this dissertation, p. 366, for copy of statement.

CHAPTER ELEVEN

1. See financial reports for 1945 and 1947 in Appendix I in the original of this dissertation, pp. 339-342.

2. Tom Ludwig was the Field Representative for Tennessee.

3. Tom Ludwig, "Farmers Union Membership," January 1970.

4. Compiled from rosters of the several terms.

5. The Film Center with a staff of two persisted until 1954. It was discontinued because it failed to find a sufficient basis of support.

6. For a list of Executive Council members in 1947 see Appendix III in the original of this dissertation.

7. The library was named for a young workers' education staff member who was killed in the war. The buildings were designed by an architect friend of the School and built, in large part, by volunteer workcamp and community labor.

8. Minutes of Executive Council Meeting, November 27-30, 1949, Highlander Folk School, Monteagle, Tennessee (In the files of the School).

9. Minutes of Executive Council Meeting, January 8-9, 1944.

10. Woodward treats this subject in his essay, "The Populist Heritage and the Intellectual," *The Burden of Southern History*, pp. 141-166.

11. Historian Theodore Saloutos (as well as Woodward and others) make mention of the courageous early position of southern Populists with regard to Negroes. "The Populists," he wrote, "sought the Negro vote and urged the Negro to join the party on the premise that the forces of monopoly did not respect race, color or creed." ("The Professors and the Populists," *Agricultural History*, XL, No. 4 (October 1966), 250.

12. For an excellent study of the early Farmers Union movement, see Theodore Saloutos' chapter "The Farmers Union, 1902-1913," *Farmer Movements in the South* (Berkeley: University of California Press, 1965) pp. 184-213.

13. John A. Crampton, *The National Farmers Union, Ideology of a Pressure Group* (Lincoln: University of Nebraska Press, 1965), p. 7.

14. *Ibid.*, p. 232.

15. W.P. Tucker, "The Farmers' Union, The Social Thought of a Current Agrarian Movement," *The Southwestern Social Science Quarterly*, XXVII, No. 1 (June 1946), 48-49.

16. These Farmers Union educational aims were among those listed in an anniversary issue of the *National Union Farmer* (March 1952).

17. *Highlander Fling*, V, No. 5 (July 1944), 1.

18. Z. Horton, "Henry Thomas, Man of the People."

19. *Highlander Fling*, V, No. 5 (July 1944), 12.

20. "Annual Report, 1944," *Highlander Fling*, Vol. V, No. 7 (February 1945).

21. *Highlander Fling*, Vol. V, No. 4 (March 1944).

22. Highlander Folk School, Annual Report, 1944, p. 5.

23. Letter from Myles Horton to Aubrey Williams, National Farmers Union, Washington, D.C., March 2, 1945.

24. Letter from Myles Horton to Aubrey Williams, National Farmers Union, Washington, D.C., April 9, 1945. Horton enclosed a protest poem which Crabtree had written to the anti-labor union, anti-Farmers Union editor of *The Nashville Banner* who had published a poem of his own warning farmers against "the Communists," in the form of the Highlander Folk School and the Farmers Union ("From the Shoulder," *The Nashville Banner*, March 21, 1945). Crabtree in his reply, "From the Shoulder—Up," wrote in part:
"Well, let's see for OURSELVES,
Who are the Communists?

They are the organized laborers
In every branch of industry;
They are the AAA;
They are the FSA;
They are the TVA."
25. Letter from Myles Horton to Aubrey Williams, June 7, 1945.

26. "Tennessee Farmers Are Organizing," National Farmers Union, Tennessee Organizing Committee, Decherd, Tennessee, c. August 1945.

27. Summary of 1945 Program, Highlander Folk School, Monteagle, Tennessee, p. 1. (Mimeographed.)

28. For an overall description of Farmers Union education during this period, see Mrs. Jerome Evanson, "The Educational Program of the Farmers Union," *Education for Rural America*, ed. Floyd W. Reeves (Chicago: University of Chicago Press, 1945), pp. 200-207.

29. *Tennessee Union Farmer*, Vol. I, No. 2 (October 10, 1945).

30. The contribution represented one-fourth of the total amount which the Highlander Folk School had hoped, based on a budget proposal to the Joint Labor Legislative Committee, would be contributed by the several labor organizations on that committee which also included the CIO, the Teamsters and the Brotherhood of Locomotive Firemen and Enginemen (Minutes, Tennessee Joint Labor Committee, Nashville, Tennessee, April 16, 1945).

31. Throughout most of 1945 and the beginning of 1946 (when a full-time field representative-newspaper editor, Tom Ludwig, was hired) Highlander staff member Ermon Fay Johnson, sister of Zilphia Horton, functioned as a part-time Educational Director for the Tennessee Farmers Union. The position was discontinued for lack of funds.

32. Letter from Myles Horton to J. S. King, Secretary-Treasurer, East Tennessee Dairy Cooperative, Greenville, Tennessee, November 29, 1945.

33. Letter from Myles Horton to J. S. King, Greenville, Tennessee, December 27, 1945.

34. Letter from Myles Horton to H. N. Hatley, President, East Tennessee Dairy Cooperative, July 30, 1946.

35. "Educating toward democratic unity through small farm organizations," Highlander Folk School, n.d. (Mimeographed.)

36. *Tennessee Union Farmer*, Vol. I (October 10, 1945).

37. Letter from James Patton, National Farmers Union, Denver, Colorado, to Myles Horton, November 30, 1946.

38. Letter from Fred Wale, Julius Rosenwald Fund, Chicago, Illinois, to Myles Horton, December 3, 1946.

39. "Highlander goes to farmers . . . Farmers come to Highlander," *Highlander Fling*, VI, No. 4 (March 1947), 2.

40. The Tennessee Farmers Union Term is described in articles appearing in the *Tennessee Union Farmer*, II (March 1947), 1, 5-6.

41. *Ibid.*

42. *Ibid.*

43. Minutes of Staff Meeting, February 25, 1947, Highlander Folk School, Monteagle, Tennessee (in the files of the School).

44. "Another School Set for July," *Tennessee Union Farmer* (March 1947), p. 6.

45. Minutes of Executive Council Meeting, June 21-22, 1947, Highlander Folk School, Monteagle, Tennessee (in the files of the School).

46. *Ibid.*

47. *Tennessee Union Farmer*, II, No. 9 (September 1947), 2.

48. *Farmers Union Workshop News* (Monteagle, Tennessee), Vol. I (July 31, 1947).

49. *Ibid.*

50. *Ibid.*

51. *Ibid.*

52. *Ibid.*

53. *Tennessee Union Farmer*, II, No. 9 (September 1947), 3.

54. *Farmers Union Workshop News*, Vol. I (July 31, 1947).

55. Labor papers which featured stories included *The CIO News* (September 22, 1947); *The Hosiery Worker* (September 1947); *The Shipyard Worker* (September 22, 1947) and *The Tri-State News* (September 30, 1947).

56. Executive Council Minutes, June 21-22, 1947.

57. Minutes of Staff Meeting, August 19, 1947, Highlander Folk School, Monteagle, Tennessee (in the files of the School).

58. Announcement, Farmer-Labor School, September 14-27, 1947. (Mimeographed.)

59. Several friends and former staff members also participated, including Dr. Lilian Johnson, eighty year old donor of the original building and acreage who had been interested in cooperatives during much of her life.

60. Minutes of Staff Meeting, August 19, 1947.

61. "Unions Talk Unity, Plan Joint Action at Highlander Term," *Tennessee Union Farmer*, II, No. 11 (November 1947), 5.

62. Letter from Myles Horton to Elaine Van Brink, May 31, 1949.

63. Armand Ruderman, "Rural Awakening in the Near South," *The Nation* (August 28, 1948), pp. 234-35.

64. Report of Program—1948, Highlander Folk School, Monteagle Tennessee, p. 1. (Mimeographed.)

65. Report on Farmers School, October 17-22, 1948, Highlander Folk School, Monteagle, Tennessee, p. 1.

66. "Community Leadership Schools Draw Good Attendance in Tennessee, Alabama Areas," *Union Farmer* III (June 1948), 1, 3.

67. Gladys Talbott Edwards, "Farmers Union Grows in the South," *National Union Farmer* (June 1948).

68. *Highlander Fling*, Vol. VI, No. 5 (June 1948).

69. Saloutos, *Farmer Movements in the South*, p. 192.

70. U.S. Department of Labor, *Labor Unionism in American Agriculture* (Washington, D.C: U.S. Government Printing Office, 1945), p. 291.

71. "Alabama Delegates Determine What Farmers Union Stands For," *Union Farmer*, IV, No. 1 (January 1949), 6.

72. Lee Fryer, "Operating Guide for the Southern Area, National Farmers Union," March 1, 1949. (Mimeographed.)

73. Report on the South, National Farmers Union, n.d., p. 19. (Mimeographed.)

74. A Southern Farmers Union School was scheduled for 1951 and later canceled.

75. C. Winston, "Report on Altoona Project," February 24, 1950 (in the files of the School).

76. Myles Horton was present at the 1951 National Farmers Union Board Meeting when the decision was announced. (Interview with Myles Horton, Knoxville, Tennessee, January 29, 1964.)

77. Letter from James Patton, President, National Farmers Union, Denver, Colorado, to Aubrey Williams, Editor, *Southern Farmer*, Montgomery, Alabama, March 27, 1951.

78. Several articles by Mezerik on the CIO in the South are cited elsewhere in this study. He is author of *The Revolt of the South and West* (New York: Duell, Sloan and Pearce, 1946) and at one point was asked by the Farmers Union to write its history for which, apparently, he completed the research before the project was laid aside.

79. Letter from A. G. Mezerik to Aimee I. Horton, April 26, 1968.

80. Interview with Tom Ludwig, Knoxville, Tennessee, December 2, 1967.

81. Interview with Louis Krainock, San Francisco, January 24, 1964.

82. Interview with Myles Horton, Knoxville, Tennessee, December 3, 1967.

83. Increasingly, beginning about 1948, articles about Highlander, whether in labor papers, farm or church publications, national circulation newspapers or Negro newspapers and publications, feature the School's role in race relations in the South.

84. The Farmers Union leader who served as director for Highlander's workshops on school desegregation in the summer of 1953 was Paul Bennett.

CHAPTER TWELVE

1. Highlander Folk School, Twenty-first Annual Report, October 1, 1952-September 30, 1953, p. 11.

2. This amount in itself represented an impressive show of support since the School was limited to non-tax exempt contributions from individuals.

3. The income in 1958 was over $114,000 (Highlander Folk School, Twenty-sixth Annual Report, October 1, 1957-September 30, 1958, p. 4); in 1959 over $110,000 (Highlander Folk School, Twenty-seventh Annual Report, October 1, 1958-September 30, 1959, p. 4); and, in 1960 over $122,000 (Highlander Folk School, Twenty-eighth Annual Report, October 1, 1959-September 30, 1960, p. 4).

4. The office administrator was Mikii Fowlkes Marlowe.

5. Myles Horton's administrative assistant, who had previously worked with Highlander Council member A. A. Liveright at the Center for the Study of Liberal Education for Adults, was Anne Lockwood.

6. For a list of members of the Executive Council in this period, see Appendix III in the original of this dissertation, p. 360.

7. Twenty-first Annual Report, p. 4.

8. Twenty-ninth Annual Report, p. 4. For data on enrollments in residential and extension programs, 1953-1961, see Appendix II in the original of this dissertation, pp. 352-55.

9. Horton, "Christmas Night, 1931."

10. Letter from William M. Seaman, Knoxville College, Knoxville, Tenn., December 11, 1933.

11. Memorandum, October, 1934, Highlander Folk School, Monteagle, Tenn. (Mimeographed.)

12. The earliest Negro student groups to visit the School came from Fisk University and the Tennessee A and I College in Nashville. A letter from the School's Secretary to a northern contributor tells of one such visit: "Yesterday we were pleased to have some fifty negro [sic] students from the negro college in Nashville. One of the students, the son of the President, said that he was planning to start a similar school for negroes in West Tennessee so I reckon we are making some slight impression on this section of the South."

13. Memorandum, October 1934, Highlander Folk School, Monteagle, Tennessee. (Mimeographed.)

14. Writing after an early visit to say that he was forwarding one of his books, Dr. Johnson commented that he would "rather present it to the Highlander Folk School than to any other library I can think of . . ." (Letter from Charles S. Johnson, Director, Department of Social Sciences, Fisk University, January 10, 1935.)

15. "Races and Social Objectives Meet in Great Conference," *Christian Century* (May 15, 1935), p. 677.

16. Zilphia Horton, "Community Reaction to Negroes at Highlander" (Monteagle, Tennessee, c. 1946), p. 2.

17. *Ibid.*

18. *Ibid.* p. 3.

19. These included a one-month CIO School in May 1945 and one-week terms for the United Auto Workers and the United Rubber Workers in June and July, 1944.

20. Z. Horton, "Community Reaction to Negroes at Highlander," p. 4.

21. Special Staff Meeting, c. June 1947, Highlander Folk School (in the files of the School).

22. Zilphia Horton, "Bob Jones Speaks His Mind" (Monteagle, Tennessee: Highlander Folk School, c. June 1947), p. 2.

23. Letter from Lucy Randolph Mason, CIO, Atlanta, June 17, 1942.

24. Miss Mason's book contains a number of references to the School's leadership, philosophy and program and its role in bringing Negroes and whites,

farmers and workers together in the South (L. R. Mason, *To Win These Rights; A Personal Story of the CIO in the South* [New York: Harper, 1952]).

25. Minutes of Executive Council Meeting, January 14-15, 1948.

26. This one-year program for the United Packinghouse Workers of America which experimented with ways of developing widespread local leadership, using a small national staff to train that leadership, deserves itself to be studied. Kermit Eby makes mention of the program and Horton's educational thinking with regard to it in an article ("'Drip' Theory in Labor Unions," *Antioch Review*, XIII [March 1953], 95-102).

27. Charles S. Johnson, "A Southern Negro's View of the South," *The Journal of Negro Education*, XXVI (Winter 1957), 4-5.

28. Report of Special Highlander Executive Council Meeting, April 27-28, 1953, Highlander Folk School, Monteagle, Tennessee (In the files of the School). For copy of Report of April 1953 Executive Council Meeting, see Appendix II in the original of this dissertation, pp. 367-71.

29. *Ibid.*

30. A note at the end of the Minutes indicates, "Alfred Mynders, editor of the *Chattanooga Times*, predicts the court decision on segregation in the public schools will come early in June."

31. *Ibid.*

32. Highlander Folk School, Twenty-first Annual Report.

33. Irene Osborne and Richard K. Bennett, "Eliminating Educational Segregation in the Nation's Capital," *The Annals of the American Academy of Political and Social Science*, CCCIV (March 1956), 98-109.

34. Highlander Folk School, Twenty-first Annual Report, p. 4.

35. Introductory Notes on the Workshop, July 12-18, 1953, Highlander Folk School, Monteagle, Tennessee, p. 2. (Mimeographed.)

36. Highlander Folk School, Twenty-third Annual Report, October 1, 1953-September 30, 1954, p. 1.

37. Harold Fleming, "The South Will Go Along," *The New Republic*, CXXX (May 31, 1954), 7.

38. Charles Johnson, "A Southern Negro's View of the South," p. 8.

39. Highlander Folk School, Twenty-second Annual Report, October 1, 1953-September 30, 1954, p. 1.

40. *Ibid.*

41. The following people agreed to serve on the Advisory Committee: Mrs. Septima Clark, Dr. Charles Gomillion, Mrs. Rebecca Gershon, Henry Harap, Miss Irene Osborne, Miss Anna Kelly, Mr. and Mrs. Will Thomas, William Van Til and Mrs. H. H. Wilcox.

42. See Chapter XII of this study.

43. Minutes of the Executive Council Meeting, March 26-27, 1955, Highlander Folk School, Monteagle, Tennessee (in the files of the School). (Mimeographed.)

44. *Ibid.*

45. Highlander Folk School, "The South Prepares to Carry Out the Supreme Court Decision Outlawing Segregation in Public Schools, July 24-August 6, 1955."

46. Highlander Folk School, Twenty-third Annual Report, pp. 2-3.

47. "Report by Rosa Parks on the Montgomery, Alabama, Passive Resistance Protest," March 1956 (in the files of the School). (Mimeographed.)

48. Letter from Irene Osborne, August 9, 1955 to Dr. Franklin D. Patterson, Phelps-Stokes Fund (in the files of the School).

49. Highlander Folk School, "Synopsis of Program, Workshop on Desegregation, July 24-August 6, 1955" (in the files of the School). (Mimeographed.)

50. The films included were: "De-segregation in the Public Schools" (Edward R. Murrow); "Picture in Your Mind"; "Songs of Friendship"; "One People: The House I Live In"; "Heritage"; "Born Equal"; "Of Human Rights"; "Boundary Lines"; "Man—One Family"; "Brotherhood of Man."

51. One "Questionnaire on Leadership Training" was prepared and administered by the Highlander staff in 1955; the other "Follow-up Questionnaire" which attempted to get at what participants felt was most important to them about the workshop experience was administered by the present investigator in 1966.

52. Pitkin.

53. *Ibid.*, p. 34.

54. Letter from Woodrow Cooper, Tuskegee, Alabama, May 28, 1955, to Myles Horton.

55. Response by George Bellenger, Johns Island, South Carolina, to Highlander Folk School Questionnaire, August 1, 1955.

56. Pitkin, pp. 34-35.

57. Letter from Bernice Robinson, Charleston, South Carolina, July 19, 1955, to Myles Horton.

58. For more information on this first teacher in the Citizenship School Program, Bernice Robinson, see Chapter XIII, pp. 223-225, 229.

59. Interview with Mr. and Mrs. Kenneth Kennedy, Knoxville, Tennessee, May 24, 1966.

60. Reply by Mrs. Rosa Parks to Follow-up Questionnaire on Workshop on Desegregation, May 20, 1966.

61. Pitkin, p. 35.

62. Interview with Mr. and Mrs. Kennedy.

63. Interview with Mrs. Ernestine Felder, Charleston, South Carolina, c. August 1964.

64. Letter from Mrs. Beulah C. Johnson to Mr. F. D. Patterson, Phelps-Stokes Fund, July 27, 1955.

65. Letter from Esau Jenkins, Johns Island, South Carolina, April 28, 1955, to Myles Horton.

66. Jack Painter, Report on the Knoxville Joint Committee, August 22, 1955.

67. Francis Manis, Field Reports, Tennessee Council on Human Relations, 1955.

68. Will Thomas, Reply to Highlander Folk School Questionnaire on Leadership Training, April 1955.

69. See Chapter XIII of this study.

70. Letter from Mrs. Clifford Durr, Montgomery, Alabama, January 30, 1956.

71. Harold Fleming, "Resistance Movements and Racial Desegregation." *The Annals of the American Academy of Political and Social Science*, CCCIV (March 1956), 44.

72. Planning Conference on Public School Integration, March 3-4, 1956, Highlander Folk School, Monteagle, Tennessee. (Mimeographed.)

73. Highlander Folk School Workshop on School Integration, August 1956, transcript of Tape 7 (Nashville, Tennessee: Tennessee State Library and Archives), p. 121.

74. Ibid., p. 118.

75. Highlander Folk School, Highlander Reports, Twenty-fourth Annual Report, September 1, 1955-October 30, 1956, p. 1.

76. Septima Clark, *Champions of Democracy* (Monteagle, Tennessee: Highlander Folk School, c. 1956), p. 4.

77. "Witness Ejected at Hearing" *The New York Times*, CII (March 21, 1954), 1.

78. "Ejected Witness Denies He Is a Red," *The New York Times*, CII (March 23, 1954), 12.

79. "Highlander Folk School, Communist Training School, Monteagle, Tennessee" (Atlanta, Georgia: Georgia Commission on Education, 1957).

80. M. L. King, Jr., "The Look to the Future," address delivered at the Highlander Folk School Twenty-fifth Anniversary, September 2, 1957. Along with wide circulation of the broadside, a picture from it of Dr. King and Myles Horton with the "Communist Training School" heading was blown up and placed on billboards in various parts of the South.

81. Highlander Reports, Twenty-fifth Annual Report, October 1, 1956-September 30, 1957, p. 4.

82. Among the adult educators who came to the School's defense with statements which paid tribute to its role in American adult education were: Professor Edmund de S. Brunner, Columbia University; Professor Theodore Brameld, Boston University; and Malcolm Knowles, Executive Director, Adult Education Association of the U.S.A.

83. Twenty-fifth Annual Report, p. 3.

84. By 1956, the School's income had increased threefold from the decade before to some $69,000. Of that amount, almost three-fourths or about $43,000 was from funds and foundations. This money, of course, would no longer have been forthcoming if the school had lost its tax exempt status.

CHAPTER THIRTEEN

1. Clark, *Echo in My Soul*, p. 51.

2. Carawan, *Ain't you got a right to the tree of life?*, p. 140.

3. *Ibid.*

4. Letter from Myles Horton to Leo Gerngross, April 30, 1956.

5. Clark, *Champions of Democracy*, p. 1.

6. Carawan, *Ain't you got a right to the tree of life?* p. 168.

7. Transcript of United Nations Workshop, August 2-8, 1954, Highlander Folk School (Nashville, Tennessee: State Library and Archives), p. 156.

8. *Ibid.*, pp. 157-158.

9."Three Year Project for Training of Local Leadership in Southern Communities," Highlander Folk School, Monteagle, Tennessee, March 1953 (in the files of the School), p. 1.

10. Letter from Myles Horton to Leo Gerngross, April 30, 1956.

11. "Index of Developments on Johns Island," September 1954-July 1955 (in the files of the School), p. 1.

12. Highlander Folk School, Twenty-third Annual Report, p. 3.

13. Letter from Esau Jenkins, Johns Island, South Carolina, to Myles Horton, April 23, 1955.

14. Letter from Myles Horton to Carl Tjerandsen, March 28, 1955.

15. Letter from Myles Horton to Carl Tjerandsen, June 20, 1955.

16. Ibid.

17. Clark, Echo in my Soul, p. 120.

18. Septima Clark, Interview with George Bellinger, Johns Island, South Carolina, June 23, 1955 (in the files of the School).

19. Septima Clark, Follow-up Report on Community Leadership Conference, July 3-6, 1955 (in the files of the School).

20. Septima Clark, Follow-up Report, Charleston, South Carolina, July 14, 1955 (in the files of the School).

21. Letter from Jesse Middleton, Charleston, South Carolina, July 13, 1955.

22. Highlander Reports, Twenty-fourth Annual Report, p. 3.

23. Letter from Myles Horton to Leo Gerngross, April 30, 1956.

24. Letter from Myles Horton to Carl Tjerandsen, March 1, 1956.

25. Ibid.

26. Carawan, Ain't you got a right to the tree of life?, p. 167.

27. Tape recorded interview with Mrs. Septima Clark on how the Citizenship Program began, January 7, 1960 (in the files of the School).

28. Ibid.

29. Letter from Bernice Robinson to Septima Clark, January 20, 1957.

30. Clark, Echo in My Soul, p. 150.

31. The white educator was Miss Wil Lou Gray who was State Supervisor for adult schools in South Carolina.

32. Letter from Myles Horton to Carl Tjerandsen, February 16, 1957.

33. Tape recorded interview with Mrs. Clark.

34. In this same period there were workshops, for example, for Negro and white college students on "Building Leadership for Integration of College Campuses" and for Negro and white adult leaders on "Community Service. and Integration" and on "Leadership for Integrated Housing" (Highlander Reports, Twenty-fifth Annual Report, p. 2).

35. Ibid.

36. Tape recorded interview with Mrs. Clark.

37. The files of the Highlander Folk School contain month-by-month reports of the volunteer teachers on the several islands as well as minutes of civic meetings.

38. Highlander Reports, Twenty-fifth Annual Report, p. 3.

39. Zilphia Horton, who had made Highlander a "singing school" for more than twenty years, died in 1956. With her death, the full and creative use of music as an integral part of the educational program was missing.

40. Carawan, *Ain't you got a right to the tree of life?*, p. 10.

41. Guy Carawan, "Spiritual Singing in the South Carolina Sea Islands," c. 1959, p. 4. (Mimeographed.)

42. *Ibid.*

43. Factual Report of Adult Schools, December 1, 1958-February 26, 1959 (in the files of the School).

44. *Ibid.*

45. Highlander Reports, Twenty-eighth Annual Report, p. 4.

46. Carawan, *Ain't you got a right to the tree of life?*, p. 168.

47. *Ibid.*

48. Letter from Mrs. Janie Owens, Johns Island, South Carolina, to Miss Bernice Robinson, March 5, 1959.

49. Letter from Solomon Brown, Edisto Island, South Carolina, to Mr. Myles Horton and Mrs. Clark, March 5, 1959.

50. The cover of Highlander Reports, Twenty-fifth Annual Report, bears a picture of Mrs. Clark, new Director of Education.

51. "My Citizenship School Booklet" (Monteagle Tennessee. Highlander Folk School, 1960), p. 18. (Mimeographed.)

52. Carawan, *Ain't you got a right to the tree of life?*, p. 169.

53. *The SCLC Story* (Atlanta, Georgia: the SCLC, 1964), p. 14.

54. Henry Lee Moon "The Negro Vote," *The Nation*, CXCI (September 17, 1960), 155.

55. "Literacy—Louisiana Style," *The New Republic*, CXL (March 9, 1959), 9.

56. Highlander Reports, Twenty-eighth Annual Report, p. 3.

57."Tabulation of Citizenship Classes," October 1960-June 1961. (Mimeographed.)

58. Transcript of a tape recording, Workshop for Training Leaders for Citizenship Schools, January 19-21, 1961, p. 2.

59. *Ibid.*, p. 4.

60. *Ibid.*, p. 5.

61. *Ibid.*, p. 8.

62. Myles Horton, Memorandum on the Citizenship School Training Program, Highlander Folk School, December 1960. (Mimeographed.)

63. The workshop costs, based on Highlander's field experience, were $8.00 per day for room, board and tuition. The cost per Citizenship School class was estimated to be $35.00 for classes of twenty meeting twice per week (Highlander Folk School, Citizenship School Training Program, Monteagle, Tennessee, November 1960, p. 7).

64. "Selection of Teachers for Citizenship Schools," November 1960.

65. Septima Clark, Report on Training Leaders for Citizenship Schools Workshop, February 13-18, 1961.

66. Septima Clark, Report on Training Leaders for Citizenship Schools Workshop, March 13-18, 1961.

67. Septima Clark, Report on Training Leaders for Citizenship Schools Workshop, April 10-15, 1961.

68. *Ibid.*

69. Highlander Folk School, Memorandum on the Citizenship School Program, June 26, 1961, p. 2. (Mimeographed.)

70. In the same period, committees of the state legislatures of Arkansas, Georgia, Florida, Louisiana, Virginia and Mississippi initiated harassing and suppressive investigations of various institutions and organizations, including the NAACP, church councils and state colleges. Of these investigative committees, *New South* noted in a survey article that they "consistently attempted to equate desegregation with Communism." (M. Manderson, "Segregationists' Aim—A Solid South—Or Else," *New South* XV [April 1961], 6.)

71. "Tennessee Legislative Action," *Southern School News*, V (April 1960), 9.

72. *Ibid.*

73. Guy Carawan, untitled notes on his work in the South, summer 1959-winter 1965, 1965 (in the files of the School), p. 3.

74. Clark, *Echo in My Soul*, p. 206.

75. "Hold Workshop Despite Padlock," *Chicago Defender*, October 10, 1959.

76. Of the first grounds, Circuit Court Judge Chattin noted that the School admitted that it had violated the law. "The Court is of the opinion that segregation laws of the State as applied to private schools are constitutional and valid," he stated. Relatively objective sources such as *Southern School News* and *The New York Times* featured this charge and made only passing reference to the other two. *The News* announced, "Judge Chattin, in addition to the integration issue, based his ruling on charges that Highlander sold beer and other merchandise without a license and that its president, Myles Horton, operated the school for personal gain . . ." ("Tennessee Legal Action," *Southern School News*, Vol. VI [March 1960]).

77. The Council indicated, in a widely noted statement that it "would continue and expand the program regardless of the outcome of the litigation to dissolve its charter" and that it would take its appeal "all the way to the Supreme Court if necessary" ("Folk School Tells of Expansion Plan," *The New York Times*, Vol. CIX [February 25, 1960]).

78. The Tennessee Supreme Court in its April 1961 decision ("Highlander *et al.* v. State *ex rel.* Sloan," *Reports of Cases Argued and Determined in the Supreme Court of Tennessee*, CCVIII [Nashville, Tennessee, Rich Printing Co., 1961], 242) chose not to rule on the only aspect of the lower court's decision, namely, that of the School's violation of a 1902 Tennessee statute making it unlawful for private schools to be integrated, which raised a potential constitutional issue.

79. Participants in the first SCLC workshop came from Louisiana, Georgia and South Carolina and included retired and unemployed persons, housewives, farmers, a union member, an undertaker's helper, a dressmaker, a building contractor and a minister. (Aimee I. Horton, "A Workshop for Volunteer Teachers in the Citizen-Education Program of the Southern Christian Leadership Conference, 1965," *An Analysis of Selected Programs for the Training of Civil Rights and Community Leaders in the South* [Nashville, Tennessee: Fisk University, 1966], p. 102).

80. Interviews with participants in an August 1965 SCLC workshop for Citizenship School teachers indicated both continued diversity of background and continued high motivation. (*Ibid.*, pp. 112-115.)

81. Septima Clark, Report of the Highlander Center Board of Directors, Nashville, Tennessee, May 14, 1965.

CHAPTER FOURTEEN

1. "College Students Lead Lunch Counter Demonstrations," *Southern School News*, Vol. VI (March 1960).

2. Howard Zinn, *SNCC, The New Abolitionists* (Boston: Beacon Press, 1964), p. 16.

3. Highlander Reports, Twenty-eighth Annual Report, p. 2.

4. *Ibid.*

5. The first "College Week-end Workshop on Human Relations" was held October 29-31, 1954. Noted only briefly in the school's Annual Report, its purpose was "to discuss problems challenging students in facing up to the effect of world problems and pressures on their own lives" (Highlander Folk School, Twenty-third Annual Report, p. 1).

6. Highlander Folk School, Report of 1959 College Workshop. (Mimeographed.)

7. Myles Horton excerpt from tape of the Seventh Annual College Workshop, April 1, 1960 (in the files of the School).

8. Carawan, untitled notes, p. 3.

9. *Ibid.* In analyzing why the songs were so immediately accepted after years of being ignored or rejected, Carawan suggests in an introduction to a collection of these songs, "It has taken the hardships and crises of student demonstrations, along with the need to bolster the morale and courage of those participating to give the old songs new meaning." (*We Shall Overcome*, p. 8.)

10. Helen Fuller, "We Are All So Very Happy," *The New Republic*, CXLII (April 25, 1960), 13.

11. Highlander Reports, Twenty-eighth Annual Report, p. 2.

12. "The New Generation Fights for Equality," Report of the Seventh Annual Highlander Folk School College Workshop, April 1-3, 1960, p. 2.

13. *Ibid.*, p.3

14. *Ibid.*, p. 4.

15. Report of discussion group on "Philosophy" (in the files of the School). Howard Zinn, writing of the student movement four years later emphasized, "The young people have not become followers of any dogma, have not pledged themselves to any rigid ideological system. Unswerving as they are in moving toward certain basic goals, they wheel freely in thinking about society and how it needs to be changed." (Zinn, pp. 6-7.)

16. Report of discussion group on "Methods" (in the files of the School).

17. *Ibid.*

18. Report of discussion group on "Community Relations" (in the files of the School).

19. Report of the discussion group on "Communications" (in the files of the School).

20. Carawan, Untitled notes, p. 4.

21. Zinn, p. 33.

22. These names are signed in a book which served as a roster for the several student and other civil rights workshops. Unfortunately the roster is incomplete since some participants, including, for example, Julian Bond, neglected to sign it.

23. "The New Generation Fights for Equality," p. 7.

24. *Consideration by Southern White Students of their Roles in the Struggle for Democracy in the South* (Highlander Folk School, March 1961), p. 5.

25. Highlander Reports, Twenty-ninth Annual Report, p. 2.

26. Tape recording of "New Frontiers" Workshop (in the files of the School).

27. In a volume written in 1961, Lewis Jones noted the danger attendant upon the students holding to "the great human values uncompromisingly. A problem raised by this kind of conception," he wrote with disquieting social insight, "is the possibility of joining the divisive black nationalist movements of the United States which would be a rejection of all the arduous struggle for integration with the results of further tension and conflict" (Lewis Jones, *Cold Rebellion* [London: McGibbon & Kee, 1962], p. 176).

28. The Atlanta student was Ruby Doris Smith. The Nashville students were: James Zwerg and Susan Herman, Fisk University; Susan Wilbur and Salyann McCollum, Peabody College, and William Barbee, American Baptist Seminary.

29. In the spring of 1961, there was discussion in staff meetings about inviting Andrew Young to join the Highlander staff. However, in view of the School's uncertain future, it was recommended, instead, that he serve as administrator of the Citizenship School Program which was to be taken over by the SCLC.

30. Minutes of Executive Council Meeting, July 21-22, 1960, Highlander Folk School (in the files of the School), p. 2.

31. Transcript of tape recording of workshop on "The Place of the White Southerner," May 28-29, 1960.

32. This songbook was distributed by workshop members and by Guy Carawan when he led singing at movement gatherings such as the SCLC annual conference and the southwide SNCC conference.

33. Minutes of Executive Council, July 21-22, 1960, p. 2.

34. Letter from Septima Clark, Highlander Folk School, December 1960.

35. Tape recording of "New Leadership Responsibilities" workshop, January 1961 (in the files of the School).

36. *Ibid.*

37. Highlander Reports, Twenty-ninth Annual Report, p. 1.

CHAPTER FIFTEEN

1. Merle Curti, *The Social Ideas of American Educators* (2nd ed. rev.; Patterson, New Jersey: Littlefield, Adams & Co., 1965), p. 590.

2. *Ibid.*

3. Letter from John Dewey, September 27, 1933.

4. Letter from John Dewey, October 12, 1940.

5. William S. Griffith, "A Growth Model of Institutions of Adult Education" (unpublished Ph.D. dissertation, Department of Education, University of Chicago, 1963).

6. Recent studies are cited by Alan B. Knox in "Clientele Analysis," *Review of Educational Research*, XXX, No. 3 (June 1965), 231-233. Earlier studies are cited by Edmund de S. Brunner in "Participants and Participation in Adult Education," *An Overview of Adult Education Research* (Chicago: Adult Education Association of the U.S.A., 1959), pp. 89-118.

Selected Bibliography

BOOKS

Adam, T. R. *The Workers' Road to Learning*: New York. Harper and Brothers, 1941.

Ain't you got a right to the tree of life? Recorded by Guy and Candie Carawan. New York: Simon and Schuster, 1966.

Brameld, Theodore, ed. *Workers' Education in the United States*. Fifth Year-book of the John Dewey Society. New York: Harper and Brothers, 1941.

Campbell, John C. *The Southern Highlander and His Home*. New York: Russell Sage Foundation, 1921.

Cash, W. J. *The Mind of the South*. New York: Alfred A Knopf, Inc. 1941.

Clark, Septima. *Echo in My Soul*. New York: E. P. Dutton & Co., 1962.

Crampton, John A. *The National Farmers Union, Ideology of a Pressure Group*. Lincoln: University of Nebraska Press, 1965.

Curti, Merle. *The Social Ideas of American Educators*. American Historical Association, Commission on the Social Studies. 3rd ed. Patterson, New Jersey: Littlefield, Adams & Co., 1965.

Dewey, John. *Democracy and Education*. New York: Macmillan Co., 1907.

Galenson, Walter. *The CIO Challenge to the AFL, A History of the American Labor Movement 1935-1941*. Cambridge: Harvard University Press, 1960.

Hegtrup, Holger; Lund, Hans; and Manniche, Peter. *Folk High Schools of Denmark and the Development of the Farming Community*. London: Oxford University, 1926..

Horton, Myles. "The Community Folk School." *The Community School*. Edited by Samuel Everett. New York: D. Appleton-Century Co., 1938.

Jones, Lewis W. *Cold Rebellion*. London: MacGibbon & Kee, 1962.

King, Martin Luther, Jr. *Stride Toward Freedom, The Montgomery Story*. New York: Harper & Brothers, 1958.

Knowles, Malcolm. *The Adult Education Movement in the United States*. New York: Holt, Rinehart and Winston, Inc., 1962.

Lewis, Claudia. *Children of the Cumberland*. New York: Columbia University Press, 1946.

Lindeman, Eduard. *The Meaning of Adult Education*. New York: New Republic, Inc., 1926.

Liveright, A. A. *Union Leadership Training*. New York: Harper and Brothers, 1951.

London, Jack. "Program Development in Adult Education." *Handbook of Adult Education*. Edited by Malcolm Knowles. Chicago: Adult Education Association of the U.S.A., 1960.

Mason, Lucy Randolph. *To Win These Rights: A Personal Story of the CIO in the South*. New York: Harper and Brothers, 1952.

Meyer, Adolph E. *The Development of Education in the Twentieth Century*. 2d ed. New York: Prentice-Hall, 1939.

Mitchell, Broadus. *Depression Decade*. New York: Rinehart & Co., Inc., 1941.

Myrdal, Gunnar. *An American Dilemma*. New York: Harper & Brothers, 1944.

Odum, Howard. *Southern Regions of the United States*. Chapel Hill, North Carolina: University of North Carolina Press, 1936.

Park, Robert E. *On Social Control and Collective Behavior*. Selected Papers. Edited by Ralph B. Turner. Chicago: Phoenix Books, University of Chicago Press, 1967.

Reddick, L.D. "The History of the SCLC." *The SCLC Story*. Atlanta: Southern Christian Leadership Conference, 1964.

Reeves, Floyd W., ed. *Education for Rural America*. Chicago: University of Chicago Press, 1945.

Saloutos, Theodore. *Farmer Movements in the South*. Berkeley: University of California Press, 1965.

Schneider, Florence. *Patterns of Workers' Education*. Washington, D.C.: American Council on Public Affairs, 1941.

Simon, Rita James, ed. *As We Saw the Thirties*. Urbana: University of Illinois, 1967.

Taft, Philip. *Organized Labor in American History*. New York: Harper & Row Publishers, 1964.

Tippett, Tom. *When Southern Labor Stirs*. New York: Jonathan Cape and Harrison Smith, 1931.

Tyler, Ralph W. *Basic Principles of Curriculum and Instruction*. Chicago: University of Chicago Press, 1950.

Ward, Lester F. *Dynamic Sociology*. New York. D. Appleton Company, 1883.
—"The Sociology of the Diffusion of Knowledge." *American Ideas About Adult Education*. Edited by C. Hartley Grattan. New York: Bureau of Publications, Teachers College, Columbia University, 1959.
We Shall Overcome! Compiled by Guy and Candie Carawan. New York: Oak Publications, 1963.
Whitman, Wilson. *God's Valley*. New York: Viking Press, 1939.
Woodward, C. Vann. *The Burden of Southern History*. New York: Vintage Books, 1960.
Zinn, Howard. *SNCC, The New Abolitionists*. Boston: Beacon Press, 1964.

ARTICLES

Bendiner, Robert. "Surgery in the CIO." *The Nation*, November 12, 1949, pp. 458-59.
Braden, Anne. "The Southern Freedom Movement in Perspective." *Monthly Review*, July-August, 1965.
Carlson, Oliver. "Why Textiles Vote to Strike." *The New Republic*, September 5, 1934, pp. 95-96.
CIO News, January 6-March 26, 1938.
Clark, Septima. "Success of SCLC Citizenship School Seen in 50,000 New Registered Voters." *SCLC Newsletter*, September 1963.
Cobb, Alice. "Residential Workshops: The Case For Them." *Adult Leadership*, March 1961, pp. 278-81.
Coit, Eleanor, and Starr, Mark. "Workers' Education in the United States." *Monthly Labor Review*, July 1939, pp. 1-21.
Couch, W. T. "Southerners Inspect the South." *The New Republic*, December 14, 1938, pp. 168-69.
Counts, George. "Education–For What?" *The New Republic*, May 25, 1932, pp. 38-41.
Eby, Kermit. "'Drip' Theory in Labor Unions." *Antioch Review*, March 1953, pp. 95-102.
—"General Education for Economic Well-being." *Junior College Journal*, March 1948, pp. 504-11.
Fleming, Harold. "The South Will Go Along." *The New Republic*, May 31, 1954. pp. 6-7 .

Fuller, Helen. "We are all so very happy." *The New Republic*, April 25, 1960, pp. 13-16.

—"A Good School Under Fire." *The New Republic*, December 9, 1940, p. 776.

Hochman, Julius. "High Tide at Atlantic City." *The Nation*, November 6, 1935, pp. 539-40.

Horton, Myles. "Two New Labor Colleges in the South." *Progressive Education*, April-May 1934, pp. 302-3.

—"The Highlander Folk School." *The Social Frontier*, January 1936, pp. 117-18.

— "It's a Miracle–I Still Don't Believe It." *Phi Delta Kappa*, May 1966, pp. 490-497.

Johnson, Charles S. "A Southern Negro's View of the South." *Journal of Negro Education*, Winter 1957, pp. 4-9.

Mason, Lucy Randolph. "It's not the same old South." *CIO News*, November 17, 1941.

Mezerik, A. G. "The CIO Southern Organizing Drive." *The Nation*, July 11, 1947, pp. 38-40.

—"Experiment in the South." *The Nation*, November 27, 1954, p. 465.

National Union Farmer, March 1952.

Niebuhr, Reinhold. "Build a New Party!" *The World Tomorrow*, December 1929, p. 493.

—"Property and the Ethical Life." *The World Tomorrow*, January 1931, p. 19.

Osborne, Irene, and Bennett, Richard K. "Eliminating Educational Segregation in the Nation's Capital." *The Annals of the American Academy of Political and Social Science*, March 1956, pp. 98-109.

Pitkin, Royce. *The Residential School in American Adult Education*. Notes and Essays. Chicago: Center for the Study of Liberal Education for Adults, 1956.

Ruderman, Armand. "Rural Awakening in the Near South." *The Nation*, August 28, 1948, pp. 234-35.

Schwertman, John. *I Want Many Lodestars*. Notes and Essays, No. 21. Chicago: Center for the Study of Liberal Education for Adults, September 1958.

Soule, George. "Sidney Hillman " *The New Republic*, July 22, 1946, pp. 66-68.

Stevens, Alden. "Small-Town America." *The Nation*, June 29, 1946, p. 784.

Tennessee Union Farmer, 1945-1948.

Thomas, H. Glyn. "Highlander Folk School: The Depression Years." *Tennessee Historical Quarterly*, December 1964, pp. 358-371.

"A Unique Labor School." *The American Teacher*, November-December 1936, p. 27.

Wakefield, Dan. "The Siege at Highlander." *The Nation*, November 7, 1959, p. 323.

"Wartime Developments in Workers' Education." *Monthly Labor Review*, August 1945, pp. 301-318.

MANUSCRIPT COLLECTIONS

1. Highlander Center Research Library, Knoxville, Tennessee

Citizenship School Program. Student Letter File.

Cumberland Mountain Cooperative File.

Cumberland Mountain Workers League File.

Federated Press Release File, 1932-1939.

Highlander Folk Cooperative File.

Highlander Folk School Correspondence Files, 1932-1961.

Highlander Folk School Staff Reports, Notes and Memoranda Files, 1932-1961.

Highlander Folk School Twenty-fifth Anniversary File.

Hod Carriers, Building and Common Laborers Union File.

George Mitchell Letter File.

Investigations and Attacks on the Highlander Folk School, 1932-1961, Newspaper Clipping File.

Labor's Political Conference of Grundy County File.

Labor Press Clipping File on the Highlander Folk School, 1933-1953.

Dr. Lilian Johnson Letter File.

National Farmers Union Correspondence File.

Personal Files and Records of Myles Horton, 1924-1961.

Reinhold Niebuhr Letter File.

Responses of Students in Highlander Folk School Workshops, 1955, to "Questionnaire on Leadership Training" File.

Southern Civil Rights Movement Newspaper Clipping File, 1954-1961.

Southern Strikes Newspaper Clipping File, 1932-1939.

Tennessee Farmers Union Correspondence File.

Workers' Alliance File.

Workers' Education Student Files, Highlander Folk School, 1932-1939.

2. *Tennessee State Library and Archives, Nashville*

Highlander Folk School Audio Collection.

Zilphia Horton Folk Music Collection.

Highlander Folk School Manuscript Records Collection.

HIGHLANDER FOLK SCHOOL STAFF, STUDENT AND OTHER MATERIAL

Carawan, Guy. Untitled notes on his work in the South, 1959-1965, Highlander Folk School, 1965.

Clark, Septima. *Champions of Democracy*. Monteagle, Tennessee, Highlander Folk School, 1956.

Dewey, John. Letter to Highlander Folk School, September 27, 1933.

—Letter to the Editor. *Nashville Banner*, October 12, 1940.

Highlander Fling, December 1933-March 1947.

Highlander Folk School. *Annual Reports*, 1933-1961.

—*Consideration by White Students of their Roles in the Struggle for Democracy in the South*. Monteagle, Tennessee, March 1961.

—"Educating toward democratic unity through small farm organizations." Monteagle, Tennessee, n.d. (Mimeographed.)

—*Farmers Union Workshop News*. Monteagle, Tennessee, July 31, 1947. (Mimeographed.)

—*Five Plays About Labor*. Monteagle, Tennessee, August 1939. (Mimeographed.)

—*A Guide to Community Action for Public School Integration*. Monteagle, Tennessee, October 1955.

—"Field Classes for Labor Unions, An Experiment in Workers' Education." Monteagle, Tennessee, 1937. (Mimeographed.)

—*Highlander Folk School Review*. Monteagle, Tennessee, Winter Term, 1938. (Mimeographed.)

—*I Know What It Means*. Monteagle, Tennessee, Fall Term, 1940. (Mimeographed.)

— *Let's Sing*. Monteagle, Tennessee, 1937. (Mimeographed.)

—*Let Southern Labor Speak*. Monteagle, Tennessee, Winter Term, 1938. (Mimeographed.)

—Minutes of Executive Council Meetings, 1940-1961.

—Minutes of Staff Meetings, 1933-1961.

—*My Citizenship School Booklet*. Monteagle, Tennessee, 1960. (Mimeographed.)

—*Our Lives*. Monteagle, Tennessee, May 1940. (Mimeographed.)

—*60 Million Jobs*. Monteagle, Tennessee, Summer 1945. (Mimeographed.)

—*Songs of the Field and Factory*. Monteagle, Tennessee, 1940. (Mimeographed.)

—"Training Leaders for Citizenship Schools." Monteagle, Tennessee, n.d. (Mimeographed.)

—*We the Students*. Monteagle, Tennessee, Winter Term, 1939. (Mimeographed.)

—*We're on the Freedom Trail*. Monteagle, Tennessee, Summer, 1947. (Mimeographed.)

—*Workers Songs*. Monteagle, Tennessee, 1935. (Mimeographed.)

Horton, Zilphia, ed. *Labor Songs*. Winston-Salem, North Carolina: The Industrial Leader, 1939.

King, Martin Luther, Jr. "The Look to the Future." Address delivered at the Highlander Folk School Twenty-fifth Anniversary, September 2, 1957.

Lawrence, Mary. *Education Unlimited*. Monteagle, Tennessee: Highlander Folk School, 1945.

—*How to Build Your Union*. New Orleans, Louisiana: CIO Industrial Union Council, February 1942.

We the People. (Highlander Folk School), February 1939.

The WPA Worker. (Highlander Folk School), August 1938.

UNPUBLISHED MATERIALS

Carawan, Guy. "Spiritual Singing in the South Carolina Sea Islands." Monteagle, Tennessee, c. 1959. (Mimeographed.)

Horton, Aimee I. "Analysis of Selected Programs for the Training of Civil Rights and Community Leaders in the South." Cooperative Research Project (S-291), U.S. Office of Education, Department of Health, Education and Welfare, 1966.

Horton, Myles. "Mountain Men." Unpublished manuscript, Highlander Folk School, c. 1939.

Lawrence, Mary. "A Study of the Methods and Results of Workers Education in the South." Unpublished Rosenwald Foundation Study, 1947.

Thomas, Hulan Glyn. "A History of the Highlander Folk School, 1932-1941." Unpublished M.A. thesis, Vanderbilt University, 1964.

INTERVIEWS

Clark, Mrs. Septima. Dorchester Center, McIntosh, Georgia, November 9, 1965.

Elkuss, Mary Lawrence. Park Forest, Illinois, November 7, 1963.

Felder, Mrs. Ernestine. Charleston, South Carolina, August 1964.

Horton, Myles. Interviewed by Dana-Ford Thomas. Highlander Folk School, Monteagle, Tennessee, March 9, 1959.

—Series of interviews, Knoxville, Tennessee, August 5, 1963-December 3, 1967.

Justus, May. Summerfield community, Grundy County, Tennessee, August 15, 1963.

Kennedy, Anne. Knoxville, Tennessee, May 20, 1966.

Kennedy, Kenneth. Knoxville, Tennessee, May 20, 1966.

Kornhauser, William. University of California, Berkeley, September 1964.

Ludwig, Tom. Knoxville, Tennessee, December 2, 1967.

Lynch, Matt. Nashville, Tennessee, September 26, 1964.

Krainock, Louis. San Francisco, January 24, 1964.

McCampbell, Vera. Summerfield Community, Grundy County, Tennessee, August 15, 1963.

Robinson, Bernice. Dorchester Center, McIntosh, Georgia, November 8, 1965.

Thomas, Henry. Summerfield Community, Grundy County, Tennessee, August 15, 1963.

MISCELLANEOUS

Allred, Charles, *et al. Grundy County, Tennessee: Relief in a Coal Mining Community.* Knoxville, Tennessee, Tennessee Agricultural Experiment Station, University of Tennessee, April 1936.

"Highlander *et al.* v. State *ex. rel.* Sloan." *Reports of Cases Argued and Determined in the Supreme Court of Tennessee.* Vol. CCVIII (1961).

Labor Education Service. "Annotated List of Pamphlet Materials for Workers Classes." New York: Affiliated Schools, 1938.

National Emergency Council. *The Economic Conditions of the South.* Report to the President. Washington, D.C.: U.S. Government Printing Office, July 25, 1938.

"The People of the Cumberlands." New York: Frontier Films, 1938.

U.S. Department of Agriculture. *Economic and Social Problems and Conditions of the Southern Appalachians.* Miscellaneous Publications No. 205. Washington, D.C.: U.S. Government Printing Office, 1935.

U.S. Department of Labor. *Labor Unionism in American Agriculture.* Washington, D.C.: U.S. Government Printing Office, 1945.

Index

Adam, T.R.
  Highlander discussed in his book *Workers' Road to Learning*, 138
Adams, Frank, ix
Addams, Jane
  influence on Myles Horton, 24-25
  on Highlander in early period, 39-41
Advance (national paper of the Amalgamated Clothing Workers), 106
Alabama Christian Movement for Human Rights
  sends representatives to workshops, 250
Alabama Farmers Union, 186-187
Alcoa, Tennessee
  Highlander extension work there (1940), 131
Alexander, W.W.
  member of Highlander Advisory Committee, 46
Alford, Harold Judd, 272n8
Amalgamated Clothing Workers, 100
  Zilla Hawes organizes for, 86
American Association of University Women, xiii
American Baptist Seminary
  support for sit-in movement there, 242
American Civil Liberties Union, 201
American Economic Life (Tugwell)
  outside reading in course, 86-87
American Federation of Hosiery Workers, 92, 97, 99, 100
  annual institute at Highlander, 126
  and 1946 Highlander term, 153
  Highlander organizes three local study groups, 98
American Federation of Teachers, 72
  and Highlander staff members, 123
  participate in Labor's Political Conference of Grundy County, 68
  representative on Highlander Executive Council, 198
Atlanta Industrial Union Council
  and Highlander extension program, 137
Austin, Aleine, 150

Bakery Workers
  participate in Labor's Political Conference of Grundy County, 68
Bank Street School, 58
Barbee, William
  participant in college workshop, 313n28
Barry, Marion
  participant in college workshop, 246, 249
Basic Policies for Presentation to Local School Boards
  Highlander publication, 207, 210
Bennett, Paul, 304n84
  director of Highlander workshops, 201
Berry, Harry S., 286n35
  Tennessee State Works Progress Administration head, 65
Bevel, James
  participant in college workshop, 246
Bittner, Van (Director of CIO Southern Organizing Drive)
  fight with Highlander, 159-160
Blackman, L.A.
  Highlander participant, 212
Bradford, J.D.
  Highlander student and teacher, 101
Brady, Walter, 285n18
  student at Highlander, 101
Brameld, Theodore, 308n82
Brannon, Charles (Secretary of Agriculture), 187
Brazeal, B.R.
  consultant to Highlander, 203
  member of Highlander's Executive Council, 198
Bread and Roses:The Story of the Rise of the Shirtworkers, 1933-1934, 89
Brookside Cotton Mill
  strike against, 89
Brookwood Labor College, 75
  Myles Horton's visit there, 21-22
Brotherhood of Railroad Trainmen
  contribution to Farmers Union, 174
Brotherhood of Sleeping Car Porters
  and proposed march on Washington, 199

"Bugwood" Strike, 46-52
Brunner, Edmund, de S., 308n82

Caldwell, Erskine
  involvement with film *People of the
    Cumberlands*, 106/107
Callaghan, Edward, 126-127
Campbell, John C.
  on folk schools, 25
  quoted, 277n29, 277n35, 278n48
Carawan, Guy, 272n5, 312n9
  leads "Sing for Freedom" workshop, 250
  leads singing at college workshops, 247
  leads singing at first SNCC meeting, 246
  singing as part of citizenship program,
    226-227
  and singing at college workshops,
    242-243
  and singing of *We Shall Overcome*, 236
Chatham County (Alabama) Crusade for
    Voters
  sends representatives to workshops, 250
Chaucer, Geoffrey
  Myles Horton's reading of, 13-14
The Chicago Tribune
  condemns Highlander Folk Cooperative
    grant, 55-56
Chisholm, Malcolm, 279n59
  member of first Highlander Board of
    Directors, 45
Christianity and the Social Crisis
    (Rauschenbusch)
  read by Myles Horton, 19
Christian Socialists
  Myles Horton's study of, 19-20
CIO, 73, 77, 78
  Highlander's close work with, 79-80
  Southern CIO Schools at Highlander, See
    Chapter 10
  Textile Workers Organizing Committee
    (TWOC) campaign (1937), 102-112
  Southern Organizing Drive (1946)
    Highlander's lack of participation,
      151-152
Citizenship School Booklet (Highlander), 229
Clafin College
  and sit-in movement, 242
Clark, Septima, , ix, 194, 272n5
  and Citizenship School Program, 215-225
  encourages Esau Jenkins to attend
    Highlander, 204-205

  her arrest, 236
  her career as Highlander staff member
    described, 229
  her Highlander participation, 203
  joins Highlander staff, 219
  quoted, 221
  works with SCLC on Citizenship School
    Program, 237-238
Coach, W.T., 125
Cohn, Alex, 103
Committee on Economic and Racial Justice,
  125
Congress of Industrial Organizations (*See
  CIO*)
Council for Cooperative Action of
    Chattanooga
  sends representatives to workshops, 250
Counts, George S.
  influence on Myles Horton, 21, 255/256
  on Highlander Advisory Committee, 23,
    46
Crabtree, Homer, 173
Crawford, W.H.
  his resignation from Highlander's
    Executive Council, 157-158
Cristopher, Paul (CIO Regional Director),
  197
Cumberland Mountain Cooperative
  submits proposal to Federal Emergency
    Relief Administration, 53
Cumberland Mountain Workers League,
  258-259
  and "Bugwood" strike, 48-52
  history of, 282n28
  letter to Frances Perkins, 49/50
  letter to President Roosevelt, 50-51
  sends delegation to Washington, 50-51
Cumberland University
  Myles Horton's experiences there, 13-14
Curti, Merle
  his book *The Social Ideas of American
    Educators*, 265

Daniel, Berthe, 283n52
  describes early union meetings, 62
Daniel Franz
  on failure of United Textile Workers' 1934
    general strike, 96
Danish Folk Schools
  Myles Horton's study of, 25-26, 29-30
Daves, J. Herman

TITLES IN THE SERIES

Martin Luther King, Jr.

and the

Civil Rights Movement

DAVID J. GARROW, EDITOR